E
807
.A25
1973

Roosevelt, Franklin
Delano, Pres.
U.S. 1882-1945.

The sunny side of
FDR

DATE		
JAN 4 '84		
NOV 1 7 1987		
JUL 2 6 1990		
MAR 5 '91		
DEC 03 '91		
MAY 06 1996		

© THE BAKER & TAYLOR CO.

THE
SUNNY
SIDE
OF FDR

FDR at Jackson Day Dinner
Washington, D.C., January 7, 1939

Courtesy of the Franklin D. Roosevelt Library, Hyde Park, N.Y.

THE SUNNY SIDE OF FDR

Compiled and edited by

M. S. VENKATARAMANI
Dean and Professor of American Studies
School of International Studies
Jawaharlal Nehru University, New Delhi

OHIO UNIVERSITY PRESS

CONTENTS

I

"DAMNED GOOD FUN"

He was among the most beloved of America's presidents and was recognized in his own lifetime as worthy of being classed among the greatest of them. He entered the White House at a time when the United States was in the throes of the most serious economic crisis in its history. His dynamic, imaginative, and confident leadership gave hope to a troubled people and set them on the road to recovery. At a time when in many other parts of the world the aftermath of war and the grinding misery of the Great Depression spawned totalitarian regimes of varying degrees of degeneration, his leadership kept the spirit of democracy and representative government flowering in the United States and made the American soil resistant to the growth of an incipient fascism.

As the darkening clouds of war gathered, millions in many lands looked to him as the hope of the world. As the principal leader of the great coalition against the Axis Powers, he attained a position of power and influence perhaps unparalleled in modern history. Of course he faltered at times and he made mistakes. But the record of achievements of this great American, Franklin Delano Roosevelt, is impressive, judged by any test.

Among the stalwarts of blood and iron, of ambition and resolution, who strode the world arena during those troubled times, Roosevelt was a man with a difference. He knew how to laugh—at others and at himself. He loved pranks and practical jokes. And he could tell stories! True, his good friend, Winston Churchill, was clever and witty, but the British Prime Minister's posture was aloof, superior, and often arrogant. In addition to his aches and fevers, the Prime Minister suffered from the mind-limiting virus of toryism and the debasing disease of imperialism. The men who had to work with him closely during the war years admired his indomitable spirit but were sorely tried by his tantrums. FDR was a very different kind of a man. He was earthy and very human and he could laugh much more easily than the tories, totalitarians, dogmatists, and puritans of his time.

Roosevelt was a man who radiated cheerfulness. "He had an infectious sense of humor," recalls his old friend, Judge Samuel Rosenman. "His sense of humor was always evident," says Bernard Baruch.[1] "I have a cheerful disposition; that is the only thing that is left," FDR once quipped.[2] But that was the ingredient that set him apart from most other makers and shakers of human affairs. What an experience must it have been for those who had an opportunity to come into close personal contact with one whose gaiety was so contagious! "I don't suppose there has ever been a President of the United States who bound the members of his Administration to him with such bonds of affection and loyalty," wrote the poet Archibald MacLeish. Playwright Robert Sherwood did not exaggerate when, in a letter to FDR, he gratefully acknowledged "the incomparable privilege and honor (and damned good fun) that I've had in your service."[3]

Damned good fun! That was the truth—as long as the Roosevelt sun shone on the person concerned. During the hectic years of depression and war, "that Man in the White House" could not merely laugh at his critics and at himself but also make those around him share the fun. Listen to what Justice William O. Douglas says, as he recalls those years:

> Once more I was in his study at Hyde Park listening to his yarns. I could hear his hearty laughter coming from the Oval Room of the White House. I saw him once again mimicking a giant of the fairy tales who had the appetite of a cannibal or a pompous lady who had a capacity for dullness. I was at a poker table with him, learning about his superstitions. I was back in the Oval Room of a Sunday afternoon, being "sentenced to a lifeterm in the marble temple up on the Capitol Hill." . . . I was back at Shangri-La with him, listening to his talk of Stalin, Teheran, and the Rus-

[1] Samuel I. Rosenman, *Working with Roosevelt* (New York, 1952), p. 24; Bernard M. Baruch, *Baruch: The Public Years* (New York, 1960), p. 354. On Baruch's 73rd birthday FDR sent him one of his usual humorous messages. "Keep at it," he wired. "Some day you will grow up." *Ibid.*

[2] Press conference, 26 January 1937, "The Press Conferences of Franklin D. Roosevelt," 22 volumes, Franklin D. Roosevelt Library, Hyde Park, New York. The Library will hereafter be indicated as FDRL.

[3] Archibald MacLeish to Franklin D. Roosevelt, 5 December 1944; Robert Sherwood to Roosevelt, 1 February 1942, FDRL.

sian scrub-women who wore Russian army uniforms under their skirts and carried revolvers on their hips. . . . There was laughter and banter, serious talk and long discussions.[4]

It was not only to exalted personages as judges of the Supreme Court that Roosevelt presented the sunny side of his personality. Humbler people who came into contact with him felt his warmth and geniality. To the people of Warm Springs, for instance, FDR was "just a big jolly brother."[5] He could eagerly listen to a story narrated by a White House usher while riding the elevator and promptly recount it, with his own inimitable embellishments, to Winston Churchill. It was a story about the sailor who walked into an auction shop and began bidding on a parrot:

> The sailor bid $5, was raised, bid $10, was raised again, and finally got the parrot for $35.
> "Thirty-five dollars is a lot to pay for a bird," said the sailor as he emptied his pocket. "Can the bird talk?"
> "Can the bird talk!" exclaimed the auctioneer. "Why, that parrot was bidding against you!"[6]

He had a smile that could tame a grizzly bear. It was a formidable asset and he employed it on all he came into contact with. Kingsley Martin of the *New Statesman and Nation* thought at first that FDR's smile had become stereotyped but soon found himself being captivated by it. Wrote Ira R. T. Smith, who had run the White House mail room under many Presidents:

> He was jovial, chatty, and informal and this struck me as an almost professional attitude of good fellowship. He could turn on his dazzling smile as if somebody had pressed a button and sent a brilliant beam from a lighthouse out across the sea—shining on whatever ship happened to be there.[7]

David Lilienthal, Chairman of the Tennessee Valley Authority, wrote in a similar vein in his diary on 18 December 1940, after attending his first "big affair" at the White House:

[4] Foreword to Grace Tully, *F.D.R. My Boss* (New York, 1949), p. vii.

[5] Jane Ickes, ed., *The Secret Diaries of Harold L. Ickes* (3 vols., New York, 1953–54), I, p. 127. Diary entry, 29 November 1933.

[6] Quoted in Raymond Clapper, *Watching the World* (New York, 1944), p. 92.

[7] Kingsley Martin, *Editor* (London, 1968), p. 227; Ira R. T. Smith, *Dear Mr. President* . . . (New York, 1949), p. 156. Smith added that he did not think that FDR's friendliness was insincere—it was "just a charming, almost irresistible knack that he used, perhaps, subconsciously."

> The President shook hands with this mob. . . . Every person gets a feeling that he has just been sitting there waiting for him to come along. Nevertheless, his cordiality, even when you know how large a supply of it he has on tap, is a heart-warming business.[8]

Editor William Allen White, the Sage of Emporia, who loved Roosevelt dearly, teased him about his ever-present grin. White once found a photograph that showed FDR decked out in a seersucker suit and looking quite stern. He promptly requested the President to autograph the unusual photograph for him. "I am not enamoured of your smile," White wrote. "I like you better when you bark than when you wag your tail and this is a barking picture." FDR's inscription on the photograph conveyed affectionate regards "from the sucker to the seer"![9]

Even those who believed that they disliked FDR found it no easy task to resist his "charm" in a face-to-face meeting. What could they do when confronted by his gay laughter and his homely tales? Huey Long of Louisiana, the "Kingfish," described the problem in ornithological terms. According to him, Roosevelt was a scrootch owl—unlike Herbert Hoover, who was a hoot owl. A hoot owl would knock a hen off the roost and seize her as she toppled down. "But a scrootch owl slips into the roost and scrootches up to the hen and talks softly to her. And the hen falls in love with him, and the first thing you know, *there ain't no hen*."[10]

II

From his earliest days in the White House, Roosevelt projected the impression among most Americans that he was a man of laughter and of a sunny disposition. So great an authority as Will Rogers told the American people after a visit to the White House in May, 1933, that he had never been in a home since 1929 "where it really looked like there was joy and happiness and good spirits like that one. . . . When I came in I said to Mrs. Roosevelt, 'Where is the President?' She said, 'Wherever you hear the laugh.' So I went in there, and there he was." Will went on to say:

> I don't mean that he is unmindful of all those out of work. But, by golly, he is not sitting down moping over it. He has a grin on his face. This man absolutely believes that he is going to help those people. It is not conceit, it is absolute confidence. . . . He knows things are going to be all right. Humor and laughs. My goodness, I dident [*sic*] get anywhere with my little jokes.[11]

    [8] David E. Lilienthal, *The Journals of David E. Lilienthal: The TVA Years 1939–1945* (New York, 1964), p. 240.

    [9] Roosevelt to William Allen White, 4 March 1938, FDRL.

    [10] Quoted in Arthur M. Schlesinger, Jr., *The Politics of Upheaval* (Boston, 1960), p. 56.

    [11] Donald Day, *Will Rogers: A Biography* (New York, 1962), p. 308.

The Presidency has always been, as Teddy Roosevelt put it, "a bully pulpit," but because some of the sacerdotal aspects of the pulpit cling to it, an incumbent has to be wary of displaying any skill that he may have in political humor. The British Parliamentary system provides a far more congenial atmosphere for such displays. The British politician must make his mark in the rough and tumble of Parliamentary debate. It is not enough if the Prime Minister can deliver a learned speech packed with facts and figures. He must have the capacity to unnerve his opponents and inspire the faithful by his interruptions, interventions, repartees, and rejoinders. An agile mind, a quick tongue, a gift for phrasing, a capacity for civilized but devastating invective—qualities like these, sharpened in years of practice in the arena of the House of Commons, propelled men like Benjamin Disraeli, Winston Churchill, Aneurin Bevan, and Harold Wilson into political prominence.

Roosevelt did not have any such training. Nor did he have an opportunity to build up a reputation as a wit and raconteur in Congress as did such men as Alben Barkley of Kentucky, Sam Ervin of North Carolina, and Brooks Hays of Arkansas.[12] Clement Attlee once told an interviewer that "there is more wit in our Parliament than in your Congress because you tend to make orations for the *Congressional Record*, very often written in advance and delivered from the written page, whereas we face each other across the House and make real debating speeches, subject to interruption."[13] In Congress a member's importance depends a great deal on his "seniority" and his committee assignments. The chairman of an important committee is a power to reckon with, whatever his limitations in eloquence and wit. The relative laxity in party discipline means that members belonging to both the major parties may be found on opposing sides on most issues. Since the antagonist of today on a given issue may be the ally of tomorrow on another vote, members tend to engage much less in interruptions and sallies than they do in the British Parliament. The more leisurely pace of proceedings in Congress and the longer time available for speakers do enable a Barkley or a Hays to win recognition as a humorist and raconteur.

The President confronts a different type of situation. Unlike the British Prime Minister, the President does not have to lead his men in daily confrontations in the legislature. In his appearances before Congress he is given a respectful hearing and is seldom interrupted or heckled. Even in public appearances during election campaigns the American President is not subjected to the kind of badgering that the Prime Minister often encounters. A President thus runs the risk of lapsing into pomposity and platitudes. The mystique enveloping the

---

[12] Alben Barkley, *That Reminds Me* (New York, 1954) ; Brooks Hays, *Hotbed of Tranquility* (New York, 1968).

[13] Quoted in Leon Harris, *The Fine Art of Political Wit* (London, 1965), p. 203.

Presidency inhibits an incumbent from any display of public jollity. "Never make people laugh," a veteran Senator once admonished James Garfield. "If you would succeed in life, you must be solemn as an ass. All great monuments are built over solemn asses." [14]

American politicians aspiring to the Presidency or actually holding the office have, with very few exceptions—Abraham Lincoln for one, generally paid respectful heed to such an admonition. Adlai Stevenson, who paid a price for neglecting this commandment in 1952 and 1956, said that the advice that Presidential aspirants continually received was "to err on the side of conventionality and banality rather than wit and humor. You get your nose rubbed into this solemnity and this serious-ness of our time and it begins to have its effect on you, it buries your natural spontaneity of personality." [15]

It is not surprising that as a result of various constraints and pressures Presidential orations are often dull and insipid. Few of Roosevelt's speeches, however, were damp squibs. His beaming smile and engaging personality usually ensured a friendly and receptive audience for him. His voice was magnificent and his delivery superb. Even when his lis-teners heard him only over the radio, they could not easily resist his "necking" kind of voice. He was by no means an orator in the grand tradition, but he was very persuasive. He could talk to his people "in a vein of old-fashioned country philosophy" and he could carry conviction.

Roosevelt's public addresses were carefully chiselled efforts—the work of many hands, but bearing his unmistakable stamp. They projected in remarkable fashion his vigor, confidence, and optimism. In his prepared speeches he made but sparing use of stories and witticisms. Well aware of the political pitfalls that jokes involving race, religion, and sex might lead to, he steered clear of them. He rarely engaged in invective and, when the occasion warranted, he employed humor to make fun of his critics. With a few simple and well-chosen words he could raise doubts in people's minds concerning the accuracy of press and Congressional portrayals of him as a dangerous threat to basic American freedoms and could make them regard him as "just one of us, plain folks." In a speech at Chapel Hill, North Carolina, on 5 December 1938 the President said:

> You . . . who see me for the first time have read your news-papers and heard on the air that I am, at the very least, an ogre—a consorter with Communists, a destroyer of the rich, a breaker of our ancient traditions. Some of you think of me perhaps as the inventor of the economic royalist, of the wicked utilities, of the money changers of the Temple. You have heard for six years that I was about to plunge the Nation into war; that you and your little brothers would be sent to the bloody fields of battle in

[14] *Ibid.*, p. xii.
[15] *Ibid.*, pp. 169–70.

Europe; that I was driving the Nation into bankruptcy; and that I breakfasted every morning on a dish of "grilled millionaire."

Actually I am an exceedingly mild mannered person—a practitioner of peace, both domestic and foreign, a believer in the capitalistic system, and for my breakfast a devotee of scrambled eggs.[16]

Roosevelt could slip with effortless ease into a story while speaking to a group extemporaneously and informally. At a meeting in Hyde Park, New York, for instance, he told the chairman that he needed to have a subject to talk about, and the latter, in his introductory remarks, referred to an ocean voyage that the President had recently taken. Describing it as a fishing trip, Roosevelt said:

> You do not always need a hook to catch a fish. I got a 110-pound sailfish without a hook. . . . Way down at a place called Cocos Island, about five hundred miles west of the Panama Canal, we were out fishing, trolling for sailfish. One of them took my line which was out about two hundred feet beyond the boat with a hook and feather on the end. He jumped in the air and, apparently, while he was on the end, another sailfish came along and got his beak all snarled up in the line. The fish that got caught on the hook got away, but the fish that got caught on his nose was hauled in.
>
> As a matter of fact, there had been so much discussion on previous trips, about the size and weight and length and species of fish, that this year I took a full-fledged scientist with me from the Smithsonian Institution in Washington, Dr. Waldo Schmitt, who was such a success that we decided to change the Smithsonian to "Schmittsonian."
>
> When we started from San Diego out on the West Coast, we ran down the Coast to Lower California which, as you know, belongs to Mexico. In talking to Dr. Schmitt that first day, I said: "Is there any particular thing or animal that you would like to find?" He said: "Oh, yes, I am writing a monograph. I have been on it two years, and the one thing I am searching for in these waters of Mexico and the islands of the Pacific—I want to find a burrowing shrimp."
>
> "Well," I said, "Dr. Schmitt, why leave Washington? Washington is overrun with them. I know that after five years."[17]

A man who could talk like that did not need to employ invective

---

[16] Samuel I. Rosenman, *The Public Papers and Addresses of Franklin D. Roosevelt, 1938* (13 vols., New York, 1938–50), p. 615. This source will be described hereafter as *Public Papers and Addresses*.

[17] Informal remarks at a meeting of the Roosevelt Home Club, Hyde Park, 27 August 1938, *ibid.*, pp. 502–03.

against his opponents. He drew greater response from his audience by confiding to them laughingly that his next book would have a chapter in it about bedtime stories—political bedtime stories. "It will be a very amusing chapter. I am going to fill it with whispering ghosts and stalking bogey-men, and I am going to end the chapter by telling how the American men and women on the third of November, 1936, refused to be frightened by fairy tales. You people do not look to me the least bit frightened." [18]

On another occasion FDR asked the people to judge for themselves whether there was any truth in the allegations of his opponents that his policies were "new-fangled" and would lead to "dire results." Sure, all of them realized that there was nothing new in those prophecies of gloom. Perhaps they too would enjoy a little poem that he had read in the paper somewhere entitled "Going to the Dogs":

> My grandpa notes the world's worn cogs,
> And says we're going to the dogs;
> His granddad in his house of logs,
> Swore things were going to the dogs;
> His dad, among the Flemish bogs,
> Vowed things were going to the dogs;
> The caveman in his queer skin togs,
> Said things were going to the dogs;
> But this is what I wish to state—
> The dogs have had an awful wait. [19]

Roosevelt's speech before the Teamsters during the 1944 campaign, in which he made an amusing reference to Republican charges concerning his dog Fala, is often described as an excellent example of the use of humor in the arena of political contest. [20] At the Jackson Day dinner on 8 January 1940 he told a story of a type familiar to his close friends and associates. The champ was in good form as he mocked his Republican critics. Said Roosevelt:

> There are, of course, some people—in addition to the political viewers-with-alarm—who always look on the dark side of life. There are some who complain that things are not as they were once, and who firmly believe that everybody who disagrees with them is a moron or a crook. They belong, it seems to me, to the type of unfortunate individual—and almost every family has one of

[18] Campaign address at Wichita, Kansas, 13 October 1936, *Public Papers and Addresses, 1936*, pp. 456–57.

[19] Radio address to the Young Democratic Clubs of America, 24 August 1935, *Public Papers and Addresses, 1935*, p. 342.

[20] Address at a dinner of the International Brotherhood of Teamsters, 23 September 1944, *Public Papers and Addresses, 1944*, p. 290.

them—the unfortunate individual of whom it is said "he is enjoying bad health."

Sometimes when I listen and listen to people like that I can
better understand old Uncle Jed.

"Uncle Jed," said Ezra, one day, "Ben't you gittin' a leetle
hard of hearin'?"

"Yes," said Uncle Jed. "I'm afraid I'm gittin' a mite deef."

Whereupon Ezra made Uncle Jed go down to Boston, to see an
ear doctor.

Uncle Jed came back. And Ezra asked what happened. "Well,"
said Uncle Jed, "that doctor asked me if I had been drinkin' any.
And I said, "Yes, I been drinkin' a mite."

And then that doctor said, "Well, Jed, I might just as well tell
you now that if you don't want to lose your hearin' you've got to
give up drinkin'."

"Well," said Uncle Jed, "I thought it over; and then I said
'Doc, I like what I've been drinkin' so much better than what I've
been hearin', that I reckon I'll just keep on gitting deef.' "[21]

Roosevelt firmly believed that his policies would result in the greatest
attainable good for the greatest number of his people. He was convinced
that the people would support him if they were in possession of the facts.
He had a marvelous knack for building up humorous momentum in his
informal speeches simply by his manner of presenting ordinary facts.
He could reminisce in such a way as to convey his special affection and
regard for a region or a community and skillfully explain to his listeners
one or another New Deal measure of interest to them. Let us listen to him
talk to "my neighbors in Georgia":

Fourteen years ago a democratic Yankee, a comparatively
young man, came to a neighboring county in the State of Georgia,
in search of a pool of warm water wherein he might swim his way
back to health; and he found it. The place—Warm Springs—was
at that time a rather dilapidated small summer resort. His new
neighbors there extended to him the hand of genuine hospitality,
welcomed him to their firesides and made him feel so much at
home that he built himself a house, bought himself a farm, and
has been coming back ever since. And he proposes to keep to that
good custom. I intend coming back very often.

There was only one discordant note in that first stay of mine
at Warm Springs. When the first of the month bill came in for
electric light for my little cottage, I found that the charge was
eighteen cents per kilowatt hour—about four times as much as I
was paying in another community, Hyde Park, New York. That

[21] *Public Papers and Addresses, 1940,* p. 34.

light bill started my long study of proper public utility charges
for electric current, started in mind the whole subject of getting
electricity into farm homes throughout the United States.

So, my friends, it can be said with a good deal of truth that a
little cottage at Warm Springs, Georgia, was the birthplace of the
Rural Electrification Administration.[22]

From the time of the establishment of the Republic till the advent of
Abraham Lincoln, American Presidents subscribed, in slightly varying
degrees, to "a tradition of solemnity."[23] Lincoln initiated a sharp but
short-lived departure from that tradition. He was an inveterate story-
teller and to this day remains unsurpassed by any of his successors in the
area of what may be described as "public humor." Critics castigated him
as a "funny man," a clown, and a retailer of risqué jokes. FDR was far
more cautious in his use of humor, especially in his major, prepared
addresses. Master politician that he was, he remained conscious of the
peril of being regarded as a mere story-teller. His use of humor, while
natural and spontaneous, was also measured and adroit. As a result, he
came to be not merely respected by millions of his countrymen as a
leader and a statesman but also loved as a Happy Warrior.

There was no violence or cruelty in Roosevelt's speeches or his banter.
Nor was there any trace of self-deprecation. He was never angrily icono-
clastic or irreverent and was not a man to mock the flag, or mother, or
apple pie. He was not a vitriolic or even a caustic critic of American
manners and morals, and he never believed that the country was "going
to the dogs." An irrepressible optimist, he believed that whatever was
wrong with America could be set right by the people through democratic
processes. It was an article of faith with him that "the way to make
progress is to build on what we have, to believe that today is better than
yesterday and that tomorrow will be better than either."[24] He was a
sentimentalist and had a strong streak of nostalgia for the good old days.
But he was no stand-patter and he did not fear change. There was no
trace of cynicism or despair or disillusion in him. He was a joyous person
who looked to the future with hope.

III

Many stories reportedly told by FDR are to be found in works by
persons who had been close to him. Some had been noted down in diaries

[22] Address at Barnesville, Georgia, 11 August 1938, *Public Papers and Addresses, 1938*, p. 463.
[23] Richard B. Morris, "A Presidential Sense of Humor," *New York Times Magazine*, 30 April 1961, p. 47.
[24] Remarks while dedicating by radio the Will Rogers Memorial in Claremore, Oklahoma, *Public Papers and Addresses, 1938*, pp. 583–84.

after the lapse of a few hours—as, for instance, in those of William Hassett and Harold Ickes. Others had been set down in writing after the lapse of some years as, for example, in the recollections of Grace Tully. Persons like Samuel Rosenman, Raymond Moley, Rexford Tugwell, and Frances Perkins, who knew FDR well, have written big tomes in which they make passing references to his extraordinary capacity to laugh and to joke even in times of considerable strain.[25] Unfortunately, however, we get very few examples of such stories in these volumes.

It may, perhaps, be appropriate at this point to give a few examples of Rooseveltian stories that were reportedly committed to writing within a reasonably short time by those who had heard them. Let us first have some excerpts from notes that Mrs. Rosenman made after a weekend visit to the President's retreat, Shangri-la:

> During dinner he [Roosevelt] told story after story. . . . Many I had heard before but forgotten. He told each dramatically, and with every detail. . . . One story was of a famous English general who was killed in the battle of New Orleans. The English wanted to take him to England for burial—so they put him in a barrel of rum and lashed it to the deck. One of his descendants had shown the President his burial place in England. The President inquired as to the state of the body upon arrival. Descendant said, "It would have been all right, but some of the crew got thirsty and used an auger on the way over."
>
> The other story was about a wealthy Chicago widow who was on in years, but insisted upon seeing the world. So she went traveling about until she finally reached Moscow. There she died. Her family cabled and asked that her body be sent to Chicago for burial. When it arrived they opened the casket to take one last look at "Dear Mama"—and much to their horror found a Russian General, with white pointed beard, in full military regalia etc. They frantically cabled the Embassy in Russia, and received the following reply: "Suggest you close the casket and proceed with the funeral. Your grandmother was buried in the Kremlin with full military honors."[26]

Grace Tully once made a record of the following story that she had heard the "Boss" tell on a few occasions:

> During the World War in the Summer of '18, a new Navy destroyer left our shores for the coast of France. About 200 miles

[25] Rosenman, *Working with Roosevelt*; Raymond Moley, *After Seven Years* (New York, 1939) ; Raymond Moley, *The First New Deal* (New York, 1966) ; Rexford G. Tugwell, *The Democratic Roosevelt* (Garden City, 1957) ; Frances Perkins, *The Roosevelt I Knew* (New York, 1946).

[26] Mrs. Rosenman's notes are reproduced in Rosenman, *Working with Roosevelt*, pp. 352–54.

off the Irish Channel the commanding officer of this destroyer told one of the young lieutenants who had come into the Navy from civil life to "shoot the sun" at noon; in other words to determine the position of the ship. The young man "shot the sun," took his figures over to the chart board and after about 10 minutes the commanding officer noticed he was still scratching his head. He went over and said, "Lieutenant, I will take your figures and work out our position," and the lieutenant moved off.

About five minutes later the commanding officer, after doing a little figuring, summoned the lieutenant to come back and said, "Young man, take off your hat. This is a solemn moment."

The lieutenant said, "Why, sir?"

The commanding officer said, "My boy, I find from your figures that we are now in the middle of Westminster Abbey."[27]

Hassett recorded in his diary the following story that FDR had told him:

> An American Marine, ordered home from Guadalcanal, was disconsolate and downhearted because he hadn't killed even one Jap. He stated his case to his superior officer, who said: "Go up that hill over there and shout: 'To hell with Emperor Hirohito.' That will bring the Japs out of hiding."
>
> The Marine did as he was bidden. Immediately a Jap soldier came out of the jungle, shouting: "To hell with Roosevelt."[28]
>
> "And of course," said the Marine, "I could not kill a Republican."

Anecdotes like these are all too few in works by associates of FDR despite the fact that virtually all of them refer to his fondness for joking and story-telling. Such stories as are available may have varying degrees of reliability. One can never be sure how accurately Roosevelt's words might have been recalled and recorded by the chroniclers. "There is hardly a dependable record of a conversation in Franklin Roosevelt's whole life," says Tugwell.[29] An unexpurgated record of the flow of conversation at one of the poker parties presided over by FDR, if one were available, would enliven a drooping spirit. Fleeting glimpses of the merrymakers are to be found in the bilious pages of the Ickes diaries. One wishes that some other member of the group had maintained a "fun diary" of what was said on those festive occasions.

FDR sought to make the people around him feel that they belonged to what he described as "a Greek letter society." He emphasized that

[27] Tully, *F.D.R. My Boss*, p. 5.

[28] William D. Hassett, *Off the Record with F.D.R.* (New Brunswick, 1958), p. 175. Diary entry, 17 June 1943.

[29] Tugwell, *The Democratic Roosevelt*, p. 14.

what went on at their meetings should be regarded as "just between us girls." "This is very distinctly a club," he once told a group of editors who visited him at the White House, "and, therefore, we ought to regard it as such." No member of the group should "go back to school tomorrow morning" and tell the school about what happened.[30] On occasion, Roosevelt might name some one present at a meeting as "housemother" to keep the "girls" in line.

Even if a serious issue of national or international affairs was under discussion the "Skipper" could be depended upon to keep the proceedings lively and pleasant. Few were the opportunities that he let slip without perpetrating a pun. Those who worked with him "were never afraid to interrupt and tell him a joke or a funny story."[31] If a stranger had entered the room while such a session was in progress he could hardly have believed that the man in the wheel chair was the President of the United States. "Yet," as Ickes noted in his diary, "in spite of all his fun-making, no one ever presumed to treat him with familiarity, although everyone knowing how friendly and approachable he is looks on him as a real friend and most desirable companion."[32]

Whenever the spirit moved him—and it often did—FDR would suggest that the "gang" should work up a betting pool. The wager might relate to the date of adjournment of Congress or to the possibility of King Edward VIII abdicating. With mock solemnity he would warn his companions to be sure to report their earnings or losses on their income tax returns. "Pa" Watson, the jovial military aide, received one fine morning a document signed by Roosevelt informing him: "You are hereby appointed Chief Bookmaker to the Dictator."[33]

FDR was an immensely successful politician, but he had talents that could well have enabled him to become a good actor. He once summoned Speaker Sam Rayburn and several other Congressmen (including young Lyndon Baines Johnson) to the White House. Fixing a cold look on the Speaker, Roosevelt said sharply that he had heard some very serious reports about the House of Representatives. "I am very sorry to inform you, Sam, that these reports involve you." Tension mounted in the room as the President continued: "My report is, Sam, that you are getting too old!" As "Mr. Sam" gasped, a grinning Roosevelt called for drinks and, handing a Stetson hat to the Speaker, he demanded that he should try it on for size. Only then did Rayburn realize that the occasion was really a birthday party in his honor. As Rayburn tried on the Stetson, Roosevelt quipped: "President Wilson used to say that in Washington some men grow and others swell. I am sure 'Old Sam' wears the same size hat

---

[30] Press conference, 20 April 1939.
[31] Rosenman, *Working with Roosevelt*, p. 24.
[32] Ickes, *Secret Diaries*, I, p. 240. Diary entry, 7 December 1934.
[33] Roosevelt to Edwin Watson, 13 April 1937, FDRL.

today that he wore the day he came to Congress some thirty years ago."[34]

Sometimes FDR came up with a bit of mimicry that seldom failed to amuse his audience. "I still have a bid of co'd id my dose," he once told reporters who enquired about his health.[35] On another occasion he broke into Hoosier lingo, leaving none of his listeners in any doubt that he was parodying Wendell Willkie. He could portray both the affected English accent of a salesman at Abercrombie and Fitch as well as that of the dear old lady who once entertained him at breakfast in a stately English mansion. Felix Frankfurter might have had very mixed emotions if he could have seen a portrayal of him by his dear "Frank." According to Roosevelt, Frankfurter had, on his way to the White House, stopped at Vice-President Garner's office and imbibed several stiff "three finger" shots of Cactus Jack's excellent bourbon. After additional libations at the White House, Frankfurter appeared to remain in perfect control—but, as FDR acted it out, his usual rapid-fire talk gradually gave way to very slow delivery and careful enunciation.[36]

Many were the pranks and practical jokes that Roosevelt played on his friends. Apparently his career as a prankster began when he was a very little boy. As he narrated to Hassett what was probably his first effort in the field, all he did was to slip a packet of seidlitz powder into a glass used by his German governess. He had then patiently stood outside her door as no good little boy should and before long had been rewarded by a shrill cry from the governess. The fraulein reported ill the following morning. FDR's doting father, shrewdly guessing what had hapened, sent for his son and warned him that he should "consider himself spanked!"[37] Even in his Presidential years Roosevelt remained impish in spirit, but his pranks were directed only at cronies and friends who shared his interest in merrymaking. The reader is invited to peruse two anecdotes in the present work entitled "The President is Missing" and "Joe Kennedy at the Shriners' Parade" as examples of pranks described in detail by Roosevelt himself.

The prankster in the White House was himself once the victim of a hoax perpetrated by a Harvard undergraduate. Soon after he became President he received a letter on the stationery of Lowell House, Harvard University, signed by R. P. Lucas who described himself as the Secretary of the House Committee. Mr. Lucas solemnly informed Roosevelt that his Committee had decided "to proffer you, as a slight token of our esteem for you, both as a President of unusual ability and profound farsightedness, and as a Harvard man, the dedication of the heretofore unnamed carillon of Russian Bells, at present installed in the tower of our House.

[34] Tully, *F.D.R. My Boss*, pp. 168–69.
[35] Press conference, 11 March 1941.
[36] Ickes, *Secret Diaries*, II, p. 602. Diary entry, 19 September 1937.
[37] Hassett, *Off the Record with F.D.R.*, p. 9. Diary entry, 31 January 1942.

We propose to name them, with your permission, the Franklin Delano Roosevelt Bells." Lucas added that the President could communicate his decision directly to the Master of the House, Professor Julian Coolidge.

FDR thought that the letter was "awfully nice" and promptly informed the Professor that he would be "delighted and, it goes without saying, greatly honored." Coolidge was baffled by the President's letter. A quick check brought out the fact that there was no one by the name of "R. P. Lucas" in Lowell House. The bells had been donated to Harvard by a certain gentleman and Coolidge had no authority "to put into execution the really charming suggestion contained in this young man's letter." "The fact is," he wrote to the President, "you have been made the victim of what the French call 'a mystification,' in other words, a piece of undergraduate pleasantry."[38] Roosevelt took the "mystification" in good spirit, but did not reform his own ways!

In spinning yarns about his fishing exploits FDR was a past master. Asked what he had discussed with two cabinet members who had accompanied him on a fishing expedition, he replied that they had "a good many arguments; in fact one practically every hour . . . as to whether if the fish had come into the boat, whether it would not have been the biggest."[39] His stories were sometimes very elaborate. Describing the sequence of developments in minute detail, he would build up the tempo step by step for the big climax—or anti-climax. "I did not fish as much as some others did, otherwise I would probably have caught the most fish and the biggest fish," he would assert.[40]

Long before Cassius Clay, FDR laughingly acknowledged: "I am best." He staked out this claim not only in the field of fishing but in the spheres of political prognostication and public relations. "I am a damn good guesser," he asserted, referring to his forecasts of election results. "I have come to the conclusion that when I am through here I am going to syndicate myself. It is cheaper than taking a poll and more accurate than any poll; that is pretty good. I am best."[41] He wrote to Frankfurter that many interesting stories could be developed on the basis of information available in governmental agencies but that the task was being inadequately performed. "I am thinking of resigning this job and taking on the job of Public Relations man for the Government," he declared. "Incidentally, I could do a swell job with Supreme Court decisions. There is a heart throb in most of them . . . ," he added.[42] He told a large group

[38] "R. P. Lucas" to Roosevelt, n.d., March 1933; Roosevelt to Julian Coolidge, 20 March 1933; Coolidge to Roosevelt, 24 March 1933, FDRL.

[39] Press conference, 5 December 1937.

[40] *Ibid.*

[41] Press conference, 15 September 1936.

[42] Roosevelt to Frankfurter, 1 May 1942, in Max Freedman, *Roosevelt and Frankfurter: Their Correspondence 1928–1945* (Boston, 1967), p. 658.

of Senators and Congressmen who met him on the train platform in Washington to welcome him on his return from a two-week fishing trip: "I have come back with all sorts of new lessons which I learned from the barracuda and sharks. I am a tough guy. So, if you come down and see me as often as you possibly can, I will teach you some of the stunts I learned."[43]

The man who spoke with such zest was a cripple who had to lock his legs into heavy steel braces before he could be helped to stand on his feet. An enthusiastic sailor and fisherman, it was an ordeal for him to get in and out of a fishing boat. The boat, with an armchair in the stern, would be brought alongside the naval vessel in which he was cruising. A companionway would be lowered from the ship and two men would carry him sideways down the companionway. They would hand him to two others who would swing him around into his armchair in the fishing boat.[44] The sight was far too painful for his friends to behold, unmoved, but FDR smiled and joked through it all as though he had not a care in the world.

Nobody ever heard a word of complaint from Roosevelt about his physical handicap, and there was never any show of self-pity on his part. Greeting Baruch cheerfully as he emerged from an elevator FDR said: "Well, you see Bernie, with these elevators and things a man doesn't need legs."[45] The man who could never hope to keep pace with an eight-year-old child would often say without any trace of self-consciousness, "I have got to run." He could laugh heartily at something and proclaim that "it was funny as a crutch." Not able to play golf himself, he could watch his companions play and keep up a running fire of comments, admonitions, and exhortations. He accused them of growing soft and allowing their waistlines to expand unduly. He would solemnly warn that he would "put in some kind of Swedish exercises out in the front of the Executive offices, and I will lead you—from a chair!"[46]

IV

The sunny side of Roosevelt's personality deserves further study. The present volume is a modest offering in that direction. Readers are entitled to know at this point that I am not an American. I am a native of India who lives in India and who happens to be a student of American affairs. I have a research interest in the Roosevelt years. I first became aware of the frolicsome side of Roosevelt's personality when I read, sev-

[43] Informal remarks to a Congressional Delegation, 13 April 1934, *Public Papers and Addresses, 1934*, p. 182.
[44] Described in Ickes, *Secret Diaries*, I, p. 449. Diary entry, 27 October 1935.
[45] Baruch, *The Public Years*, p. 354.
[46] Press conference, 18 February 1941.

eral years ago, the volumes edited by Elliott Roosevelt entitled *F.D.R. : His Personal Letters*. There are some amusing letters in that collection.[47] I had occasion subsequently to examine a substantial number of FDR's letters at the Franklin D. Roosevelt Library at Hyde Park and other manuscript collections and the human side of Roosevelt began to impress itself forcefully on my mind.

The personal letters of a very busy President cannot but be brief. Nevertheless, the enlivening touch of a happy story-teller can be seen in flashes in several of Roosevelt's letters to persons of whom he was fond. FDR liked to quote the dictum of Ralph Waldo Emerson that "the only way to have a friend is to be one." Even when they were in some distress or discomfort his friends found it natural to write to him in a jovial tone. A retired naval officer, hospitalized for an eye ailment, reported to the President that he had been "shanghaied" by the Navy Department and rushed to the hospital "because I was seeing double—not so bad as being unable to see at all, but rather inconvenient; otherwise I am fine." Back came a characteristic response from Roosevelt: "What is this silly business about seeing double? In the old days you held your liquor pretty well." On another occasion Roosevelt learned that Senator Carter Glass of Virginia had had six of his teeth extracted and that his dentist had experienced some difficulty in getting sufficient gold to make the required plates. He promptly wrote to the Senator assuring him that "the Attorney General will overlook the gold hoarding of which . . . you undoubtedly have been guilty."[48]

Professor Julian Coolidge of Harvard University had once taught mathematics to young Roosevelt at Groton. Writing to him on one occasion, the President made the charge that "my worthy House Master . . . tried his best to teach me something many decades ago." The Professor replied with feigned indignation that he could not understand the innuendo in Roosevelt's comment. "I have naturally attributed your present success to the mathematics you learned from me thirty-five years back," he added. Wrote FDR to his old preceptor:

> Referring to the mathematics days, do you remember your first day's class at Groton? You stood up at the blackboard—announced to the class that a straight line is the shortest distance be-

[47] Elliott Roosevelt, *F.D.R. His Personal Letters* (2 vols., New York, 1950). Among other volumes of correspondence containing similar material may be mentioned Carroll Kilpatrick, ed., *Roosevelt and Daniels: A Friendship in Politics* (Chapel Hill, 1952); James Roosevelt and Sidney Shalett, *Affectionately, F.D.R.* (New York, 1959); and Freedman, *Roosevelt and Frankfurter*.

[48] Lt. Commander George C. Sweet to Roosevelt, 26 July 1940; Roosevelt to Sweet, 29 July 1940; Roosevelt to Carter Glass, 12 December 1933, FDRL.

tween two points and then tried to draw one. All I can say is that I, too, have never been able to draw a straight line. I am sure you shared my joy when Einstein proved that there ain't no such animal as a straight line!

The Professor paid the ultimate tribute to his pupil when he wrote to him: "I am willing to grant that the ability to write a note such as yours adds more to the gaiety of nations than the ability to write mathematics such as Einstein's."[49]

FDR and the journalist Herbert Bayard Swope carried on a game, each trying to find out unwary errors in the use of words that the other might be guilty of. On 9 January 1934, for instance, the President communicated to Swope the charges that had been framed against him:

> The Typographical Union has lodged complaint under their code against you for submitting copy to the *New York Times* containing the word "ouhemeristic." A hearing will be held by me at your convenience. It is respectfully suggested that a jail sentence can be avoided if hereafter you will provide a dictionary of your own copy to all typesetters. . . .
>
> P.S. By the way—what does the darn word mean anyway?

On another occasion it was Swope's turn to twit the "Boss." "I got it on you at last," he wrote. "You said 'Argentinian,' in your speech. There ain't no such word. So you owe me a drink." Reacting in self-defence, FDR hit out strongly at the "Purist":

> When did you get that way? Navy people never go wrong and there is still an English shipping company founded by Dr. Johnson who wrote the dictionary which named its ships "Brazilian," "Uruguaian," "Chilian" and "Argentinian."
>
> I suppose you read Funk and Wagnalls—but after all can you pit Mr. Funk or Mr. Wagnalls of Chicago against Dr. Samuel Johnson who got it direct from Shakespeare and Chaucer? The latter two always said "Argentinian." They used to visit that country in their dreams.
>
> Anyway, why shouldn't you and I coin new words? . . . .[50]

One of FDR's favorite Congressmen was Maury Maverick of Texas. The Texan once informed the President that in a speech the latter had pronounced the word "augury" in a rather unusual fashion. Instead of saying that "the celebration was a good augury," he appeared to be

[49] Roosevelt to Julian Coolidge, 20 March 1933; Coolidge to Roosevelt, 24 March 1933; Roosevelt to Coolidge, 3 April 1933, FDRL.

[50] Roosevelt to Henry Bayard Swope, 9 January 1934; Swope to Roosevelt, 14 October 1940; Roosevelt to Swope, 17 October 1940, FDRL.

saying that "the celebration was a good orgy." Maverick was worried whether some of those who had heard the President might have been offended. Replied Roosevelt:

> I thoroughly and completely disagree with you. If the public had known that at the corner-stone laying we all had "a good orgy" there would have been millions of votes in it. People love orgies. They don't give a continental about auguries. I suggest that Plank No. 1 of the Philadelphia Platform read as follows: "We advocate bigger and better orgies."[51]

The letters that the President exchanged with William Allen White, editor of the *Emporia* [Kansas] *Gazette*, were almost always in a humorous vein, even when they discussed serious themes. "You and I," he wrote to White, "are often in the same fix as my Dutchess county brickyard colored 'pusson' who took $4.00 from the Republicans and $2.00 from the Democrats and almost voted the Democratic ticket on the ground that it was the more honest but ended by staying away from the polls altogether after he was given a pint of liquor by the Prohibitionist leader." White used to send the President friendly warnings on a variety of themes. "Watch out for your health," he cautioned the President. "Politics will take care of itself if you keep your dauber up." Roosevelt responded that nothing was likely to touch either of them because of their "serene nature." "If you have felt your nerves getting a little bit on edge, take up stamp collecting—it is never too late," he advised the editor. White grimly predicted what might be in store for Roosevelt if he persisted in "doing a swell job" in the White House: "You will fool around here for the next two or three years and get yourself branded on the right hip in the Hall of Fame as a statesman if you don't watch out."[52]

What does a President do when a formidable Solon bears down upon him and flings at him so dangerous a missile as a fable? Roosevelt was confronted in that fashion by Senator Key Pittman of Nevada, a passionate advocate of currency inflation by a substantial increase in the coinage of silver.

[51] Roosevelt to Maury Maverick, 20 April 1936, FDRL. The President had used the phrase in his speech at the cornerstone laying ceremony for a new building for the Interior Department. Reporting Maverick's comments, FDR wrote to Interior Secretary Ickes that "it would have tickled the much needed humor of the nation if the copy of my speech had actually carried the statement that the celebration was a good orgy." Roosevelt to Harold L. Ickes, 20 April 1936, FDRL.

[52] Roosevelt to William Allen White, 14 June 1938; White to Roosevelt, 1 March 1938; Roosevelt to White, 14 March 1938; White to Roosevelt, 11 July 1941, FDRL.

Senator Key Pittman to the President: There is an ancient fable that runs something like this:

> There was a breed of monkeys 'way back in the Malay jungle. There were only a few of them, and they had lived in a very small space during all their generations. There was only one thing that they would eat, and that was a little pomegranate—a little golden pomegranate. And then along came a big fire that destroyed the entire area where these golden pomegranates grew. The little monkeys were starving, and other monkeys did their best to get them to eat other pomegranates. There was a beautiful silver pomegranate, just as delicious as the gold pomegranate which all of the other monkeys in the Malaya Peninsula had grown fat on; but the little golden monkeys would not eat anything but the little golden pomegranates. And today they are all dead.

The President to Senator Pittman: I remember that fable about the monkeys and the pomegranates but the true story runs this way:

> It was perfectly true that the little monkeys got on very well with their little golden pomegranates. After the big fire destroyed the golden pomegranates, the little monkeys discovered vast quantities of silver pomegranates. They liked them so well that they ate dozens and dozens of them and that is why all the little monkeys are dead today! [53]

In June, 1940, when a controversy raged over the question of the nation's attitude toward the European war, Mayor Fiorello La Guardia of New York made a fighting speech at a meeting of the Associated Harvard Clubs on the need to extend full support to the President. Reporting to Roosevelt, the Mayor said that a prominent Harvard graduate, who had once been FDR's law partner, had stated at the meeting that while Harvard men were "an independent crowd" and had criticized the President in the past, they were now ready to endorse the idea of national unity. FDR expressed his gratitude to La Guardia "for restoring my speaking acquaintance with my fellow Harvard graduates." "What I love particularly," he added, "is the suggestion that these Harvard men 'are rather an independent crowd.' I am willing to grant that their minds open a crack or two in great national emergencies." [54]

Invitations from university presidents to accept honorary degrees amused Roosevelt a great deal. Once a president informed FDR that he could choose any kind of doctorate that he wished from his institution. Roosevelt replied that since he already had an LL.D., an L.H.D., and a Litt. D., his one unfulfilled ambition was to be made a Doctor of Veteri-

[53] Key Pittman to the President, 17 April 1934; Roosevelt to Pittman, 24 April 1934, FDRL.
[54] Roosevelt to Fiorello La Guardia, 15 June 1940, FDRL.

nary Medicine![55] Informed that a carillon in Harvard University was not likely to be named after him, FDR wrote to an old friend in that institution that he would "much prefer to have a puppy dog or a baby named after me than one of those carillon effects that is never quite in tune and which goes off all hours of the day and night. At least one can give a paregoric to a puppy or a baby!"[56]

The President enjoyed giving and receiving gifts from his friends and took advantage of such opportunities to engage in jovial correspondence. When Press Secretary Steve Early sent him a bottle as a Christmas gift in 1944, FDR informed him that it had been "carefully placed in my 'special closet' with a skull and bones tag on it." Acknowledging a gift from a North Carolina friend of a pajama suit reportedly made from "nylon human escape parachute cloth," Roosevelt wrote: "I hope when I wear them that I do not start counting ten and jump! If I have any bad dreams, I will blame them on you." Colonel "Pa" Watson, thanking FDR for the gift of a fine leather folder, wrote that it was already a prize possession in the Watson retreat at Charlottesville. "What is all this I hear about your referring to the new home in Charlottesville as 'The Watson Retreat'? No F.F.V. General ever retreats!" Roosevelt retorted.[57]

Included in the present volume is a small selection of materials from the Roosevelt correspondence. It is earnestly hoped that the reader will not miss the thrilling account of a geographical expedition sponsored by FDR in search of the Cherable Isles, with Archibald MacLeish, Librarian of Congress, and David Mearns, Superintendent of the Reading Rooms, as the intrepid modern counterparts of Lewis and Clark. Full documentation is also provided of the scandalous Watson-Grayson Affair, which, according to questionable Rooseveltian evidence, culminated in a court martial in the White House presided over by the Commander-in-Chief himself. Patient readers will find out for themselves how the Chief Executive responded to a variety of emergencies, such as getting a single coffee bean as a Christmas gift from comedian Fred Allen, and receiving high-level intelligence reports concerning the unwashed condition of professors and officers at the US Naval Academy at Annapolis.

It is possible that some of Roosevelt's humorous letters were drafted by others. Presidential aide William Hassett was sometimes pressed into service to draft humorous epistles or letters with a human touch for Roosevelt's signature. At one time the letters that Hassett drafted for despatch to certain widows evoked such enthusiastic and verbose re-

[55] Narrating the story in a letter to a friend, FDR added that the college president "was so mad that he almost withdrew the honor." Roosevelt to David Morris, 13 June 1940, FDRL.

[56] Roosevelt to Julian Coolidge, 3 April 1933, FDRL.

[57] Roosevelt to Stephen Early, 31 January 1944; Roosevelt to O. Max Gardner, 2 February 1942; Roosevelt to Edwin Watson, 16 January 1941, FDRL.

sponse that FDR presented him a pen with a card inscribed: "For Bill—on his birthday—to write more often to his widows." On another occasion Roosevelt called on Under Secretary of State Sumner Welles to prepare "a brilliant or a Rabelaisian answer" to a long letter from a Rumanian damsel.[58]

While the problem of determining the authorship of some letters does exist, it appears to the present writer that the stories contained in them are essentially Rooseveltian in their style and content. However, how can one get in those brief passages the true flavor in generous measure of the conversation of that blithe raconteur? Where, then, can one turn for more satisfying fare—for the yarns and the gay banter that Justice Douglas recalls so nostalgically?

V

In my continuing search for authentic examples of Rooseveltian banter I was gratified to find some among the excerpts from FDR's press conferences printed in the thirteen volumes of the *Public Papers and Addresses of Franklin D. Roosevelt* edited by Samuel Rosenman. I found that only 220 of the 998 press conferences held by the President were included in the work. I also noted Rosenman's statement in his foreword that only "the more important excerpts have been included" and that "minor editing" had been done on the stenographic record.[59] I decided

[58] See, for instance, the memorandum from Steve Early to Hassett, 25 January 1938, FDRL, giving detailed instructions for the preparation of a letter to be signed by Roosevelt and addressed to "Senator Russ Young, Dean of the J. Russell Young School of Expression for use at the special convocation of the School Friday evening." Also "Introduction" by Jonathan Daniels in Hassett, *Off the Record with F.D.R.*, p. xiii; Roosevelt to Sumner Welles, 15 April 1941, in Elliott Roosevelt, *Personal Letters*, II, p. 1141.

[59] "Foreword" by Samuel Rosenman, *Public Papers and Addresses, 1941*, p. x. I found that Rosenman had, on occasion, tended to take some liberties with his material. For instance, he omitted certain passages without indicating that he had done so. I shall cite a case in point. At a press conference for members of the Negro Newspaper Publishers' Association on 4 February 1944, Roosevelt described his brief visit to Gambia in Africa and said, *inter alia*: "It is just plain exploitation of those people. There is no education whatsoever. A few missionaries. With all due deference to the missionaries, if they wouldn't try to live in the best houses in town they would be better off." The light-hearted comment about missionaries is typically Rooseveltian and is to be found in the transcript of the press conference. It is, however, not to be found in Rosenman's version and no indication is given that two sentences have been omitted. On this problem, see Samuel B. Hand, "Rosenman, Thucydides, and the New Deal," *Journal of American History*, LV (September, 1968), pp. 334–48.

to examine the original transcripts of the press conferences and I soon struck "pay dirt."

The present volume contains mostly a selection compiled from the transcripts of the press conferences. (A much smaller number of letters and excerpts from speeches has also been included.) The transcripts, running into several thousands of pages, constitute the only available, accurate source of the conversations of Roosevelt.

In Roosevelt's days press conferences were highly informal. The President was in a position to speak in an entirely relaxed fashion, since he faced no electronic contraptions that could carry his every word and gesture to virtually all living rooms in the country. Indeed, even his words could not be directly quoted unless he authorized reporters to do so. Today's press conferences are highly stylized shows: the President, as the star of the show, is groomed to present himself before millions of his countrymen as the shining embodiment of virtue, honesty, integrity, courage, wisdom, sobriety, and so on. The reporters, as the supporting cast in these shows, have to appear pretty and proper. A reporter has to bear in mind the possibility that not only his "missus" and neighbors but also the editor or owner of his newspaper may be watching his performance. The glare of klieg lights and the whirr of cameras are not conducive to banter and playfulness. Neither Roosevelt nor the White House correspondents of his time had to operate under such constraints.

FDR regarded the correspondents as "a great big bunch of kids" and he enjoyed teasing them in friendly fashion. He was quite willing to permit correspondents considerable latitude in the same direction. The situation was made to order for banter, witty exchanges, and laughter. Roosevelt used banter as a device to spread cheer and goodwill, to avoid answering a question, and, on occasion, to provide an illuminating insight. Story-telling in his sessions with the gentlemen of the press was not always for fun. Many were the occasions when he told a story to explain his position and to win support for his point of view. FDR's allegories concerning "Dr. New Deal and Dr. Win-the-War" and on lending a garden hose to the neighbor whose house was on fire are well known. These, as well as a number of others, are included in the present work. As can be seen, these stories, touching the most significant aspects of his domestic and foreign policies, were his tools to build support among newsmen— and through them the public—for the causes he believed in.[60]

[60] The present work does not purport to be a study of FDR's press conferences as such nor of his relations with the press. The best available study on the subject is the chapter on Roosevelt in James E. Pollard, *The President and the Press* (New York, 1947), pp. 773–845. See also Merriman Smith, *Thank You, Mr. President* (New York, 1946), *passim*; and Charles Hurd, *When the New Deal was Young and Gay* (New York, 1965), *passim*. Hurd was White House correspondent for the *New York Times* during FDR's first term, while Smith was assigned to the White House beat by United Press in the fall of 1941.

Chroniclers of the Roosevelt era have not paid adequate attention to the President's close association with a very important but secret institution of higher learning in the nation's capital—the Russell Young School of Expression. The motto of this famous institution was *Non Bono Publico* and it adhered strictly to a "no co-ed policy." "Our dear School believes in laughter, pleasantry and fun," proclaimed its venerable Dean.[61] He was none other than veteran correspondent Russell Young, a "scholar" who was always respectfully addressed by Roosevelt as either "Dean" or "Senator." The "campus" of the School was the White House itself, but the annual convocation, featuring the "poison ivy chain procession," was held in the "old campus"—the Mayflower Hotel. Regular membership in the School was restricted to White House correspondents; occasionally, however, carefully screened outsiders were permitted to qualify for the diploma of the School.

FDR professed to be deeply loyal to the School because he was its first graduate. He was rather nervous when, in May, 1936, he heard that the Dean had a message for him. "A message from the DEAN always arouses curiosity. Oftentimes it struck very terror to the heart. I have to this day distinct recollections of my own emotions long years ago upon receipt of the simple summons: 'The Dean wishes to see you.' It was rarely good news. Often it was very bad news," he wrote.[62]

Roosevelt was relieved when he learned that he had completed all the prescribed requirements for a doctorate. The impressive scroll presented to him carried the following citation:

THE RUSSELL YOUNG SCHOOL OF EXPRESSION

Know all men by these presents that Franklin Delano Roosevelt having fulfilled the prescribed course of study and having complied with all the rules and regulations and being of exemplary moral character and having by meritorious effort, perfect enunciation, diligent application, sublime poise, graceful gestures, rarefied rhetoric, soporific sophistry and unlimited vocabulary earned the accolade of

THE	SILVER	TONGUE
Summa cum Laude	Magna cum Laude	cum Laude

is hereby invested with the degree of Doctor of Oratory in extraordinary convocation and all the rights and privileges thereinto appertaining

Conferred by and with authority invested in the J. Russell Young School of Expression

by act of the Continental Congress

[61] "The Dean Speaks Again," Announcement for the 1943 Convocation, FDRL.

[62] Roosevelt to J. Russell Young, 27 May 1936, FDRL.

Welcoming the "belated recognition" accorded to him, Roosevelt wrote that he wished he had had an "unlimited vocabulary" in his encounters with Deans in his earlier years. "How many times have I been mute, silent, speechless, dumb, in the presence of the Dean, only to recover an unlimited and reinforced vocabulary when I related the experience with the Dean to my buddies who waited outside," he added.[63]

Loyal alumnus of the School that he was, FDR continued to dedicate himself, along with the faculty and other members of the institution, to advanced study and research in the School's area of specialization— Applied Frivolity. As late as 25 May 1943 we find Roosevelt writing to the Dean that he wished he could attend a convocation of the School wearing his Oxford cap and gown. "But, perhaps it is just as well I am not coming, as I should demand the admission of women to the school," he added.[64]

In the course of his many years in the White House there were few occasions on which FDR failed to "keep his cool" in his dealings with White House correspondents. He did make uncomplimentary references to columnists whom he once described as "an unnecessary excrescence on our civilization."[65] Reporters took issue with his argument that they were sometimes forced against their will by the controllers of their newspapers to slant their stories. Nevertheless, Roosevelt retained to a greater extent than perhaps any other President the affection and goodwill of White House correspondents. He got along famously even with Walter Trohan, who represented a newspaper that was a bitter opponent of Roosevelt, the *Chicago Tribune*. "Trohan comes up here to every press conference and politely spits in my eye. He doesn't seem to mind when I spit back," FDR once told Mike Reilly, head of the White House Secret Service detail.[66]

Roosevelt developed a genuine affection for George Durno despite the fact that he was a Hearst man working for International News Service. On the ground that the corpulent Durno (235 pounds) was obstructing the view of others standing around his table during press conferences, the President accorded Durno the privilege of sitting on a special chair. But he would also repeatedly incite the formidable and irrepressible May Craig to pre-empt the chair and proceed to offer his sincere sympathy to Durno. Almost invariably he played a little game with reporters while opening press conferences. Assuming a most innocent air he would announce, "I don't know a thing," or "There is darn little news." He would then trade a joke or two with reporters standing near him. He would often comment on the "pale" looks of the newsmen and speculate whether their condition was really due to overwork—or gin. But the gaiety and

[63] *Ibid.*
[64] Roosevelt to Young, 25 May 1943, FDRL.
[65] Press conference, 22 December 1944.
[66] Michael F. Reilly, *Reilly of the White House* (New York, 1947), p. 88.

playfulness were never allowed to interfere with his seriousness, skill, and determination in pursuing his objective.

In 1935 a Congressman asked that the transcript of a press conference should be made available to him, but FDR refused to comply with the request. He told reporters that if he had done so, a precedent would have been set and the result would be to "put a sort of subconscious cramp in my style." "It is entirely extemporaneous on my part," he continued, referring to his remarks and quips in press conferences. "I don't think ahead of what I am going to say. It is a bit slangy and I think that if I once agreed, I would be worrying about the language I was using and the fine points that ought to be made."[67]

Thus what we have in the transcripts of the press conferences—verbatim records made by highly competent stenographers—is genuine Roosevelt stuff—uncramped, extemporaneous, and a bit slangy. Perhaps the reader who peruses the selections from the transcripts that are presented in this work may get an idea of one dimension of FDR's personality that does not emerge sharply in the learned treatises on Roosevelt and his era. Only a man with tremendous inner resources could have faced the problems of the time with the ebullient self-assurance that Roosevelt usually displayed. One of the phrases that he frequently and happily used was, "It's all right!" A few weeks after his entry into the White House he told reporters, "I hope you are all having a good time; I can stand it and if you can stand it and the American people can stand it we are all right."[68] It was an attitude and an approach to life that he retained till the end.

VI

On 2 March 1945, at a press conference immediately after his return from the Yalta Conference, the weakening President—with but a few weeks left to live—spoke gaily of "the nice fishing trip" that he had taken in the company of the three representatives of the wire services. "They seem to be happy, and I hope everybody else is—like *I* am. That's about the only news I have got," he quipped.[69]

No such breezy response could ever come from a grouchy or grumpy soul. While turbulent winds swirled around him and even when they seemed to assume the proportions of a hurricane, FDR could remain smilingly imperturbable. "Nobody can get my goat," he once asserted. "I am too old a hand to have people try to get my goat. It doesn't work."[70] In him the "strenuous life" was harmoniously blended with the joyous

[67] Press conference, 8 May 1935.
[68] Press conference, 5 July 1933.
[69] Press conference, 2 March 1945.
[70] Press conference, 28 July 1942.

life. When that tireless flatterer, Felix Frankfurter, once attempted to compare him to Oliver Cromwell, FDR filed a strong demurrer. Wrote Roosevelt:

> I have been compared with Kerensky, Judas Iscariot, Cesare Borgia and Hitler but never Cromwell. Almost every day I wish to decapitate some new Charles I, but I restrain myself and I guarantee never to become as dour and sour as old Oliver.[71]

FDR was greatly amused when persons pleaded with him to embark immediately on particular courses of action and warned him of the dire consequences that would befall the country if the nostrums they proffered were not accepted. In response to one such plea from his long-time friend, Secretary of the Treasury Henry Morgenthau, Roosevelt responded: "AW HEN! The weather is hot and I am going off fishing. I decline to be serious even when you see 'gremlins' which ain't there."[72]

It is this spirit that permeates the Roosevelt banter as portrayed in this work. The gay, gallant, and confident captain at the helm of affairs realizes the importance of convincing his crew that there "ain't no gremlins." But when he does find a gremlin, carefully and smilingly he goes about the job of dealing with it.

I realize that not all the items that are included in this volume may appeal to all readers. What I may regard as amusing may appear to some others as quite insipid. I hope that the many references that are to be found to certain bottled stimulants, and anecdotes on such basic themes as "laying," may not make the noses of some readers more blue than they normally are. If FDR's rendering of the "Prophecies of the Grandson of an Old Bachelor" makes them somewhat uncomfortable, let them turn to his tale of the Hyde Park tramp, the story of old farmer Pete, or the legend of "An Old Gentleman from over in Shiloh." Many such characters are to be found in FDR's Fantasyland! For the sportsman there are fishing stories and there is also offered the ancient and famous "Copha" recipe—for the benefit of "all housewives, male and female," as Roosevelt put it.

Among American Presidents only Abraham Lincoln had talents superior to those of Roosevelt as a raconteur and story-teller. Lincoln's laughter was depicted as "boisterous" and "joyous," but he often gave

---

[71] Roosevelt to Frankfurter, 4 October 1934, in Freedman, *Roosevelt and Frankfurter*, p. 237.

[72] FDR's letter was in reply to a communication that he had received from Morgenthau on 27 July 1943. "The whole atmosphere is one of doubt and uncertainty which I think will very greatly prejudice your ability to make recommendations on taxes to which Congress will give serious heed," the Secretary had written. Quoted in John Morton Blum, *From the Morgenthau Diaries: Years of War 1941–1945* (Boston, 1967), p. 67.

the impression to others of being "a laughing man of sorrows."[73] In contrast, Roosevelt was seldom seen in a melancholy mood but almost always as radiant, confident, and cheerful. James Randall's perceptive characterization of Lincoln as a story-teller can with equal validity be applied to FDR:

> By easing into a story Lincoln could change the climate of an interview. He could carry the ball, shape the trend, and control the direction of a conference.
>
> ... The by-play of laughter was part of Lincoln's knack of being good company. It was an attribute of his magnetism. . . . Though his published works were usually serious, dignified and well polished, humor served him as a kind of popular language. More than that, it was an actual resource in thought and deliberation; for the man of humor is superior in mental tools. He does not stop with the obvious stereotype or the conventional stock phrase. He takes another look at a problem, turns it over and gives it a new relevance.[74]

Roosevelt was not a professional humorist and it would, therefore, be quite inappropriate to compare him with men like Charles Farrar Browne, Henry Shaw, Mark Twain, Finley Peter Dunne, and Will Rogers. His humor and banter must be viewed in the context of the enormous cares and anxieties that rested on his shoulders as President of the United States. It is not without significance that the era of Roosevelt witnessed a notable resurgence of the comic spirit in America. The 'thirties, says Jesse Bier, in his study of American humor, witnessed a "supreme minstrel show" featuring the "most rambunctious, sustained, and diversified comic talent we ever had."[75]

In the decade of "crushing depression and global mischief," American humor came into its own on every front—W. C. Fields, the Marx Brothers, Charlie Chaplin, Fred Allen, George Burns, Will Rogers, Robert Benchley, James Thurber, H. L. Mencken, Ring Lardner, Don Marquis, and all the rest of them. But no other person, no jovial mirthmaker or solemn politician, could steal the show from the most charismatic President that the United States had ever had. He made no mean contribution to the creation of a mood of optimism, a conviction that

[73] David Donald, *Lincoln Reconsidered* (New York, 1961), pp. 151–52.

[74] J. G. Randall, *Mr. Lincoln* (ed., Richard N. Current, New York, 1957), pp. 237–39. On Lincoln's "laughter," see also Carl Sandburg, *Abraham Lincoln* (New York, 1954), pp. 561–74. For some stories told by Lincoln or attributed to him see Bill Adler, comp., *Presidential Wit from Washington to Johnson* (New York, 1966), pp. 47–65. FDR leads in Adler's collection with 37 pages while Lincoln comes second with 18.

[75] Jesse Bier, *The Rise and Fall of American Humor* (New York, 1968), pp. 278–79.

difficulties would pass, and that momentous challenges could be met and surmounted. That mood was indispensable not merely for the flowering of the comic spirit but for the very survival of American democracy.

The words that he used in paying homage to the memory of Will Rogers—"a man who helped the nation to smile"—can truly be applied to Roosevelt himself:

> . . . I doubt if there is among us a more useful citizen than the one who holds the secret of banishing gloom, of making tears give way to laughter, of supplanting desolation and despair with hope and courage. For hope and courage always go with a light heart.

> There was something infectious about his humor. His appeal went straight to the heart of the nation. Above all things, in a time grown too solemn and somber he brought his countrymen back to a sense of proportion.

> With it all his humor and his comments were always kind. His was no biting sarcasm that hurt the highest or the lowest of his fellow citizens. . . . And when he wanted to make a point . . . , he used the kind of gentle irony that left no scars behind. That was an accomplishment well worthy of consideration by all of us.[76]

Roosevelt's attitude to life offers a valuable lesson to us. If a man of his physical handicap, if a leader burdened with problems of immense magnitude, could go through life with a gay twinkle in his eyes and sunny laughter on his lips, what excuse do we have to practice bellyaching and to moan over the ulcers that we imagine we are developing because of our fancied cares and anxieties? Think about it!

It is with real cheerfulness that I present to you a jovial prankster and a master raconteur[77] who was also President of the United States and world leader of the first rank—Franklin Delano Roosevelt.

[76] *Public Papers and Addresses, 1938*, pp. 583–84.

[77] Certain persons may regard FDR's banter as somewhat "unbecoming." Tugwell, for instance, notes with obvious discomfort that Roosevelt was "mildly addicted to practical joking and to a kind of involved humor of expression." George Allen, self-styled humorist and court jester to Presidents, writes that FDR was "most charming when he was most serious and least so when his mood turned playful. . . ." Allen complains that Roosevelt laughed only perfunctorily at his jokes and retaliated with "bad jokes" of his own. There was, perhaps, an element of "professional jealousy" in Allen's evaluation! Allen adds that the practical jokes that Roosevelt played on him had "probably something to do with my lack of appreciation of the jokes."

According to Arthur Schlesinger, Jr., FDR's humor was "slapdash, lacking wit and consisting mostly of corny remarks which no doubt sounded funnier at the time than they do in cold print." However, the few examples that he provides do not represent Roosevelt at his best.

By far the harshest appraisal of FDR comes from Dean Acheson.

While his meetings with the President were gay and informal, "they nevertheless carried something of the relationship implied in a seventeenth-century levee at Versailles," he writes. Acheson—tweeds, moustache, and all—expresses a strong preference for the "respectable, dignified, and bourgeois" style of British royalty. "It is not gratifying to receive the easy greeting which milord might give a promising stable boy and pull one's forelock in return," he says. I leave it to each reader to judge for himself whether he would prefer Acheson's company in a highbrow soiree to a "children's party" for friends presided over by FDR. Tugwell, *The Democratic Roosevelt*, p. 361; George E. Allen, *Presidents Who Have Known Me* (New York, 1950); Arthur M. Schlesinger, Jr., *The Coming of the New Deal* (Boston, 1957), p. 580; Dean Acheson, *Morning and Noon: A Memoir* (Boston, 1965), pp. 164–65.

II

ROOSEVELT'S REMINISCENCES

EUTHENICS

2 August 1933

APPOINTMENTS SECRETARY MARVIN MCINTYRE: We are all invited down to Henry Morgenthau's[1] Saturday evening for the Dutchess County clambake. Have you been invited?

THE PRESIDENT: I think I was, but I have another party on.

CORRESPONDENT: You could take both of them in.

THE PRESIDENT: No, because then you spoil both of them.

CORRESPONDENT: We understand you are going to be invited out to Vassar Friday afternoon.

THE PRESIDENT: This is wholly off the record. What I want to do is to go out to Vassar and go to the School of Euthenics. Did I ever tell you the story of the School of Euthenics? This is one thousand per cent off the record. When I was elected to the Board about 1924 and went to my first meeting in the Commodore Hotel in New York, there was present the Board of Trustees consisting of perhaps eight or ten eminent gentlemen and women from very prominent families. President McCracken presided

---

[1] Henry Morgenthau, Jr., was FDR's friend and neighbor. He was appointed Secretary of the Treasury in 1934.

at the Board of Trustees. He got up and announced various gifts that the College had had, and among others he announced the gift of the new Euthenics Building. I need not tell you the name of the donor other than to say that he was well known to us all and very beloved by all of us. Whereupon, being very innocent, I said, "Mr. President, would you mind telling me what the purpose of this building is or, I should say, what are euthenics? I never heard the word in my life." Well, McCracken got up and he waved at a lady sitting beside me. She was a very wonderful looking lady, she looked like a million dollars and had on half a million dollars worth of jewelry. So the lady looks at me and puts a lorgnette to her eyes and says, "Perhaps if Mr. Roosevelt were familiar with his Greek, he would realize that the word, 'euthenics,' comes from 'eu,' meaning 'well' and the word, 'thenics,' meaning 'the sense of living.' In other words, it means 'the sense of good living.' " And she sat down.

I was properly and completely squelched. Then one of my fellow trustees alongside of me leaned over and said, "What she means is 'home economics.' "

The building was given by a very marvelous lady who was, I think, connected with the Cadillac Motor Company out at Detroit. Well, I went down to see the building in its first summer of operation. I drove into the grounds and there, on the grass plot, I saw, oh, there must have been twenty long-haired men and short-haired women in a circle on the grass. In the middle of the circle were two unfortunate children, one about one year old and the other about two years old, and the motions of the children were being watched to see what they meant. So, if you want a real thrill, go down and the watch the Class in Euthenics.

THE MERIT SYSTEM

4 September 1935

CORRESPONDENT: You were speaking of Grover Cleveland. Hasn't he the record of the White House also for vetoes?

THE PRESIDENT: Yes. Of course that was caused mostly, in those days, by the very large number of what they called private pension bills.

CORRESPONDENT: Civil War pensions?

THE PRESIDENT: Yes.

CORRESPONDENT: You are getting a bunch of them.

THE PRESIDENT: Yes. These that come are mostly for individuals—private. All you had to do in those days was to get hold of John Henry Ketcham, who served in Congress here from 1864 to 1910 or 1908, with one term out. He was beaten once. The old boy was the Colonel of the Dutchess County Regiment, and all you had to do was to get hold of him and he would introduce a private pension bill and he nearly always got it through.

CORRESPONDENT: That kept my father in cigars for quite a while too, pensions.

THE PRESIDENT: A great thing. The old boy was very deaf. Of course, before the Civil Service days, he would go in to the Secretary of the Treasury and he would say, "Mr. Secretary, I have a beautiful, nice girl from Dover Plains who has come down here and I want you to give her a job."

The Secretary of the Treasury would say, "She has to take her place on the list and the list is pretty long. It would probably be a year or a year and a half before she could be placed."

And he [the Congressman] would say, "Thank you, Mr. Secretary, I will have her report right away. She will report within the hour. Who do you want her to report to?"

And the Secretary would say, "I can't take her."

"That is perfectly grand, Mr. Secretary. She will be here in an hour."

And she always got there; no getting away from that.

He had a great combination. He was a great friend of Chauncey Depew's [New York Senator] and he had a game all through this district. Whenever any family of Democrats was growing up, father, a Democrat, four or five or eight or ten children—we had a family in the village, father and mother Democrats, and there were ten children. The first one got to be eighteen or nineteen years old and he drives in with a horse and buggy one day and says, "Don't you want that boy to get a good job?" He had three places—he had all the places in the world: he had the Government in Washington and the Customs in New York, and today when I come in on a steamer, I can always find a Dutchess County boy. There are lots of them. They are up around the top now. And then there was the New York Central. . . . Ketcham—John Henry Ketcham. He was a great friend of Chauncey Depew and could place anybody on the railroad.

"IN FULL FAITH AND CONFIDENCE"

18 September 1935

Reporters wanted to know whether FDR had made up his mind in regard to the composition of the Coal Labor Board. Nearly sixty names had been mentioned and the President was to nominate three. Roosevelt told them a story apparently to suggest that they could, "in full faith and confidence," depend upon him to make only such choices as would promote the public interest.

THE PRESIDENT: Phelps [Adams] wrote a story last night in the [New York] Sun in which Phelps was unusually accurate! . . . It made me think of telling you a story about the Constitutional Convention that was held at Poughkeepsie in 1788. It was an awfully interesting thing and very few people have dug into it. The reason I know of it was because my great-great-great-grandfather was a member of it.

CORRESPONDENT: Isaac Roosevelt?

THE PRESIDENT: Yes. It took nine states to ratify. Seven had ratified it. New York and Virginia were holding their conventions. Obviously New York was the key state because if New York did not ratify, you would have had New England on the one side and Pennsylvania and the South on the other side, with this split right across the middle of the colonies, so it was literally a critical thing.

So the New York delegates were divided—there were 47 or 48 of them—and they were divided into two groups, one led by old man Clinton, Governor of the State from the formation of the State Government, and the other was led by Hamilton. In other words, there was a Clinton crowd and a Hamilton crowd. All the delegates were for the Constitution. But the Clinton crowd were in the majority, a very definite majority, and they would not ratify the Constitution without a Bill of Rights, and there was no Bill of Rights in it.

So they met in Poughkeepsie, at the site of the present Court House, and they sat there week after week, and there were some interesting speeches and debates. The Clinton crowd would not vote to ratify it. The Hamilton crowd, and my great-great-great-grandfather was a member of it—I think they only had about 20 or 22 votes—and they had a complete deadlock. The Clinton people said that they would not ratify without a Bill of Rights and the Hamilton people said, "We are all for a Bill of Rights. Now, there is a clause in the Constitution that allows it to be amended. Let us ratify it and then seek an amendment afterwards."

Well, the thing dragged on and the Clinton crowd would not yield, and finally a fellow named Malark Fond Smith who was a delegate from Dutchess County . . . made a speech. "We are all agreed that there should be a Bill of Rights but, after all, if we do not ratify the Constitution there won't be any Union." . . . And he said, "I propose a formula and that is that we, the delegates here, ratify the Constitution in full faith and confidence that an amendment or series of amendments will be immediately adopted providing for a Bill of Rights."

On that, the Hamilton people swung enough Clintonian delegates to ratify the Constitution, and they were all set.

That was done right after the speech and at that moment, in came the horseback rider saying that Virginia had ratified. So Virginia beat us to it by about three days.

New York, having been straightened out on the Bill of Rights, ratified by a close vote—ratified in full faith and confidence—that the Bill of Rights would be added to the Constitution.

. . . He [Malark Fond Smith] found the formula and after the very first session of the Congress, the Bill of Rights bills were introduced—the Ten Amendments.

... That was a very nice formula: "in full faith and confidence."

JOE KENNEDY AT THE SHRINERS' PARADE

6 November 1935

FDR described to reporters his plans to proceed to New York by car to attend a dinner at the Masonic Temple and to participate in certain ceremonies as a Shriner.

STEVE EARLY: Will the dinner be at the Masonic Temple?

THE PRESIDENT: Yes, just a very small dinner with the officers of the Grand Lodge. . . . Yes, only ten or fifteen at the dinner, and then the ceremonies after that. We will get through between ten and eleven and then I will go to the train and be back in Washington at 8:30 the next morning. . . .

CORRESPONDENT: Do you have an active part in the ceremonies, or are you merely going to be present?

THE PRESIDENT: I don't know.

CORRESPONDENT: I saw something in the New York papers that you were going to induct.

THE PRESIDENT: Probably assist in it.

CORRESPONDENT: What degree is he taking, the Third Degree?

THE PRESIDENT: Third Degrees—Franklin and Jimmy. Elliott[1] went in before I went down to Washington.

CORRESPONDENT: Are you taking Jim Farley along with you, Mr. President?

THE PRESIDENT: I had him at the Shriners, you remember that? him and Joe Kennedy.[2]

(Farley and Kennedy were Roman Catholics and Catholics do not seek to become Masons or Shriners.)

Did you ever hear of the hoax I pulled on Joe Kennedy?

... This is off the record. I said to Joe before the Shriners' Parade, "You know, I am all alone. Why don't you come and join me at it."

He said, "My God! I go to the Shriners' Parade?"

I said, "Sure, Jim Farley is coming." I didn't know whether he was

---

[1] FDR's sons.

[2] Joseph Kennedy, first chairman of the Securities and Exchange Commission. An ardent supporter of the President and a contributor to the Democratic Party, Kennedy subsequently served as US Ambassador to Great Britain.

but he did. And he [Kennedy] said, "Jim is coming? Is that a command?" And I said, "Sure."

And so Joe arrives and Jim Farley too. It was a terribly rainy night; it did not last very long, only about a quarter of the parade.

They went back—Joe had been sliding behind the police all the time so that the photographer wouldn't get him—and he went up to Hyannisport. I waited about two and half weeks and at the end of July I sent him a telegram. I picked any old name out of the telephone book, John Turner or something like that: "HONORABLE JOSEPH P. KENNEDY. IN ACCORDANCE WITH OUR DELIGHTFUL CONVERSATION THE NIGHT OF THE SHRINERS' PARADE, WILL IT BE CONVENIENT FOR YOU TO GO THROUGH THE CEREMONY THE FIRST WEEK OF SEPTEMBER? A LARGE AND DISTINGUISHED GATHERING WILL BE HERE TO WELCOME YOU. PLEASE WIRE AS QUICKLY AS POSSIBLE TO ADMIRAL CARY T. GRAYSON"[3]—(Cary did not know anything about this either)—"WE COUNT ON YOUR PRESENCE AND THE CEREMONIES WILL BE MADE AS EASY FOR YOU AS POSSIBLE. JOHN TURNER."

I sent this off and Joe got it there and he had a fit because that night, when he was leaving the White House in the rain, after the Parade, one or two high-muck-a-mucks in the Shrine said, "Can't we give you a lift" and so they gave him a lift and Joe said, "My heavens! What did I say that night. I know I was perfectly sober. What could I have said?"

And then said, "I wonder if this is a hoax." So he got hold of a secretary and said, "Run this thing down."

They checked and found the telegram had been sent from the Willard Hotel. I did not let it go out of the White House.

He [Kennedy] told the wife and children and the whole Kennedy family went up through the roof and they remained up through the roof all of August.

He tried to find out about it and he called Cary Grayson and Grayson said, "I don't know anything about it except that I got a message that I might get a telegram from you, that I would be called up later to find out if I had. I have had no call nor a telegram."

"Well," said Joe, "are you a Shriner?" and Cary lied like a trooper and said, "Of course I am a Shriner."

About the twenty-fifth of August I was talking to Joe on the telephone from the White House—he was still up on the Cape and at the end of the conversation I said, "By the way, Joe, are you going to be down here the first week in September?" Joe said, "You blankety blank blank." Just like that and to the President of the United States.

CORRESPONDENT: He finally got wise?

THE PRESIDENT: Yes. He had a bad month. So this Christmas I am sending him my red fez, all wrapped up with blue ribbon.

[3] Chairman of the American Red Cross and an old friend of FDR.

SEE AMERICA FIRST

12 June 1936

Roosevelt was tireless in urging Americans to cultivate "the excellent custom of getting acquainted with the United States." Travelling around the country and seeing things at first hand was "a mighty good habit," he said. It would inculcate love of the country, and foster a commitment to safeguard its scenic wonders. The first excerpt gives a story he narrated to an audience in Dallas, Texas, in 1936 and the second some comments he made in a radio address to the Forum on Current events.

THE PRESIDENT: I spoke this morning about getting to know the people. I got that idea from another President of the United States away back about the year 1905. A young lady that I was engaged to, also a member of the family, and I were stopping in the White House, and the then President Roosevelt—this was after supper—was visibly perturbed and was stamping up and down in front of the fireplace in the Oval Room upstairs. The various members of the family did not know what was the matter with T. R., and finally somebody said, "What is the trouble tonight?" "Oh," he said, "you know that bill for the creation of a large number of national parks? I am not going to be able to get it through this session because there are a lot of people up there that cannot think beyond the borders of their own States." And then he clenched his fist and said, "Sometimes I wish I could be President and Congress too."

Well, I suppose if the truth were told, he is not the only President that has had that idea.

And somebody said, "What would you do if you could be President and Congress too for just a few minutes?" He said, "I would pass a law or a Constitutional Amendment"—and T. R. was always a little bit vague about the difference between laws and constitutional revisions—"I would pass something making it obligatory for every member of the House, candidate for the House, candidate for the Senate . . . to file a certificate before they can be elected certifying that they had visited in every State of the Union." And he said, "That same thing should apply to every high public official in Washington."[1]

[1] Radio address to the Forum on Current Events, 5 October 1937.

5 October 1937

THE PRESIDENT: The professor and student in a university, the newspaper editor and the reporter, the man in public life and his local constituent, can and do learn greatly by much reading, the study and the discussion cover all sides of any given question. But the result of it all is almost inevitably tinged with provincialism or narrowness if it is not supplemented by "field work." By "field work" I mean not merely personal observation of the actual practice involving the immediate problem in the home town, but also observation in a field which covers the entire nation.

I knew a man once who, after graduation from college with a Bachelor of Arts Degree, kept right on by taking a degree in Science, a degree in Law, a degree in Medicine and several graduate degrees in other subjects. When I knew him he was forty-five years old and had been at college for more than a quarter of a century. He was a walking encyclopedia but had never been outside of his home town, and he was about the most bigoted, narrow-minded, unsophisticated and generally impossible person I have ever met.

... That is why, in the utmost good humor, I hope that in the days to come our educated and thoughtful citizens will make some special efforts to know their own country better.

... And in their travels, may I repeat a suggestion which I once gave to a young man in New York who thought he knew it all. I said, "Take a second-hand car, put on a flannel shirt, drive out to the Coast by the northern route and come back by the southern route. Don't stop anywhere where you have to pay more than $2.00 for your room and bath. Don't talk to your banking friends or your Chamber of Commerce friends, but specialize on the gasoline station man, the small restaurant keeper and farmers you meet by the wayside and your fellow automobile travelers."[2]

[2] *Public Papers and Addresses, 1936*, pp. 214–15; *Public Papers and Addresses, 1937*, p. 412.

THE ROOSEVELT WEDDING
17 March 1937

From Warm Springs, Georgia, FDR conveyed his greetings to the Charitable Irish Society of Boston and the Hibernian Society of Savannah on the occasion of St. Patrick's Day.

THE PRESIDENT: I have a particular tenderness for St. Patrick's Day for, as some of you know, it was on the seventeenth of March, 1905, that a Roosevelt wedding took place in New York City with the accompaniment of bands playing their way up Fifth Avenue to the tune of "The Wearin' of the Green." On that occasion New York had two great attractions—the St. Patrick's Day Parade, and President Theodore Roosevelt, who had come from Washington to give the bride away. I might add that it was wholly natural and logical that in the spotlight of these two simultaneous attractions the bride and the bridegroom where almost entirely overlooked and left in the background.[1]

[1] *Public Papers and Addresses, 1937*, p. 134.

"I AM FEELING VERY PEACEFUL"

6 April 1937

CORRESPONDENT: . . . today is the twentieth anniversary of our entry in the World War. Have you any reflections on the general situation today, in contrast?

THE PRESIDENT: Yes, I was thinking today how much more peaceful I am than I was on the 6th of April, 1917. As I remember it, I got to bed that particular night about four o'clock in the morning. I spent most of the day in sending telegrams to every ship and every naval station on every ocean and putting into effect the contracts that we had made in the Navy for various war materials.

I always remember one particular episode: The Navy, at first under Paymaster General Cowie and then under Paymaster General McGowan had started in the previous fall, because they thought that things looked like War, and they had made contracts with every known company for supplies and materials of all kinds from steel down to potatoes that we would need in case of war in the Navy.

About four days after the declaration of War, about the tenth of April, I was sent for by Joe Tumulty[1] to come over here to the White House. I came and there was the President, Barney Baruch, the Secretary of War and the Chief of Staff.[2] The President said, "Roosevelt, I am very sorry but you, in your zeal, you have cornered the market in a great many essential supplies and you have got to give up 50 percent of it to the Army."

The Navy did a great job because actually on the 2nd of April, when the President determined on his message to the Congress, and within a few minutes of the time that we got the flash that he was going to the Congress to ask for a declaration of war, we had sent a code telegram to all of these contractors which meant, "Go ahead with that order."

So today I am feeling very peaceful compared with twenty years ago.

[1] Joseph P. Tumulty, Secretary to President Woodrow Wilson.
[2] Bernard M. Baruch was a member of the Advisory Commission of the Council of National Defense. The Secretary of War was Newton D. Baker and the Chief of Staff was General Peyton C. March.

FDR: MILITARY HISTORIAN

25 February 1938

CORRESPONDENT: Has it been brought to your attention of late that the Army and Navy have been studying the vulnerability of battleships under so-called aircraft fire? . . . .

THE PRESIDENT: When I was a small boy somebody invented—this was back about 1885—invented a torpedo boat and nations began to build very, very fast little boats—torpedo boats. If you want to see one, there is one that runs today between Indian Head and Washington. It was built back in that year. She is about 100 feet long and, for those days, was very fast. I think she could do 24 or 25 miles an hour. There was a school of thought at that time that said, "The battleship is finished; the torpedo boats will wipe every battleship off the ocean."

The next thing that happened is what happens in time of war. You find an antidote. The torpedo boat destroyer came along. It was built to keep off torpedo boats and protect the battleship, which it did. Yet the torpedo boat was regarded by a great many people at the time as the one thing that was going to change the course of warfare.

Then came the submarine and the exponents of the submarine said that that would put every battleship and every surface ship out of commission. You remember that. When we got in the World War, the submarine for the first three years had a very distinct edge over surface ships but, as the war went on, antidotes for the submarine were developed and before the war was over the balance between offense and defense was restored.

You can go even further back, at the time of the Civil War. The "Monitor" was supposed to put every other type of ship out of business. The "Monitor" defeated the "Merrimac" type of ship[1] and lots of navies all over the world began building monitors. The only trouble was that it couldn't go to sea when it blew. And so you can go through the whole history of warfare; always when a new weapon is invented an antidote immediately appears.

The same thing is true of aircraft today. They are a component part—both on land and sea, but there are antidotes to the offensive airplane. The antidotes are the anti-aircraft guns and the defensive airplanes.

The whole thing balances and if you read and study the history of war through the ages you will find that no one weapon has ever become supreme.

[1] The "Merrimac," renamed by the Confederates as the "Virginia," was armored with iron plate and carried a deadly cast iron rod attached to its stem. It played havoc on the Union's wooden ships till it met its match in the "Monitor," an ironclad with a revolving gun turret.

THE WARM SPRINGS STORY

24 November 1938

THE PRESIDENT: . . . when I come to these Thanksgiving parties I think of the past. I think of the early years at Warm Springs a long time ago—fourteen years ago, when I first came.

... When I came down this year I learned of the death of two very old friends of mine, Mr. Persons and Mr. Colbert. A great many of you did not know them, and yet I remember a September of 1924, when I turned up here and occupied the only cottage, with one exception, that was open. The hotel was closed. Everything was closed and most everything was falling to pieces. Most of the roofs leaked and when you went to bed at night it sounded like thunder, because the squirrels were rolling nuts overhead. In those days it was pretty hard foraging for food. We did not have any wonderful store to go to as you have now. It was hard to get wood and food, and sometimes you had to travel ten miles to get a chicken for supper.

There were two people who were neighbors of ours, Mr. Persons and Mr. Colbert, and almost every evening someone would knock on the door and then their heads would come around the door and say: "Do you need some kindling-wood? Can I get you some eggs tomorrow?"

They were that kind of neighbors, and we are going to miss them a good deal.

You know this place would not have been possible if it had not been for that kind of reception and hospitality that I received. . . . They were the kind of people who extended the kind of hospitality that made me want to come back, and that is why the following spring I came back, and the influx of people began to arrive.

That is when Fred Botts was carried off the train. . . . And we thought he was going to look like a skeleton, or die of tuberculosis before night. We did not have any doctor down here and I acted as doctor. I did not know what to do and so I fed him cream. It put flesh on him. We got him in the pool and he was scared to death, and in about a week he began to walk in the pool, and that is one of the things we discovered, that people can walk in water when they cannot walk on land. And that, as you all know, has been increasing year by year.[1]

[1] Address at Thanksgiving Dinner, Warm Springs Foundation, Warm Springs, Georgia, 24 November 1938, *Public Papers and Addresses, 1938*, pp. 611–12. Roosevelt read out a telegram that he had received from comedian Eddie Cantor: "May you and yours have a happy Thanksgiving. I am thankful that I can live in a country where our leaders sit down on Thanksgiving Day to carve up a turkey instead of a Nation."

THE ACQUISITIVE HABIT

4 February 1939

FDR spoke informally at a dinner for the Trustees of the Franklin D. Roosevelt Library, Inc., Washington, D.C. He said that in that assemblage of "presidents of universities and leaders of learned societies and historians of world renown," he experienced the diffidence of the amateur. But not for long![1]

THE PRESIDENT: I felt that way a little until a few minutes ago it occurred to me that I probably occupied an important historical position at an earlier age than any of you because, when I was twenty years old, I was elected the librarian of the Hasty Pudding Club in Cambridge, Massachusetts. That was the beginning of a great many years of what my family has called the bad habit of acquisitiveness.

When I was the librarian of the Hasty Pudding Club, I had a small fund at my disposal—I think it was $400 a year—to buy books for the Hasty Pudding library. Probably the man who is more responsible for my collecting instincts than anybody else . . . was an old man named Chase, who ran the bookstore for N. J. Bartlett and Company at Cornhill in Boston.

I went to Mr. Chase and I said to him, "I have this fund; I know nothing of what I should buy." And he said, "I am going to give you a course in liberal education on books of all kinds." And I proceeded to buy under his guidance, first for the Hasty Pudding Club and the following year for the Fly Club, books that in those days were very cheap but on which, if they were to be sold tomorrow, either Club would realize a very handsome profit. For example, I bought a complete set of Dickens' Christmas books for $28. What would they bring today, not just first editions, but first issues? You know what that was. That was the beginning.

One of the first things old man Chase said to me was, "Never destroy anything." Well, that has been thrown in my teeth by all the members of my family almost every week that has passed since that time. I have destroyed practically nothing. As a result, we have a mine for which future historians will curse as well as praise me. It is a mine which will need to have the dross sifted from the gold. I would like to do it but I am informed by the professors that I am not capable of doing it. They even admit they are not capable of doing it. They say that they must wait for that dim, distant period . . . when the definitive history of this particular era will come to be written.

I always remember an episode in 1917. It occurred at the White House. I was Acting Secretary of the Navy and it was the first week of March. It was perfectly obvious to me that we were going to get into the War within the course of two or three weeks depending entirely on when the first ship flying the American flag was sunk by the unlimited submarine warfare of Germany. I went to see the President and I said, "President Wilson, may I request your permission to bring the Fleet back from Guantanamo, to send it to the Navy Yards and have it cleaned

[1] *Public Papers and Addresses, 1939*, pp. 117–18.

and fitted out for war and be ready to take part in the War if we get in?"
And the President said, "I am very sorry, Mr. Roosevelt, I cannot allow
it." But I pleaded and he gave me no reason and said, "No, I do not wish
it brought north." So, belonging to the Navy, I said, "Aye, aye, sir" and
started to leave the room. He stopped me at the door and said, "Come
back." He said, "I am going to tell you something I cannot tell to the
public. I owe you an explanation. I don't want to do anything, I do not
want the United States to do anything in a military way, by way of war
preparations, that would allow the definitive historian in later days—
these days—to say that the United States had committed an unfriendly
act against the central powers." I said, "The definitive historian of the
future?" He said, "Yes. Probably he won't write until about the year
1980 and when he writes the history of this World War, he may be a
German, he may be a Russian, he may be a Bulgarian—we cannot tell—
but I do not want to do anything that would lead him to misjudge our
American attitude sixty or seventy years from now."

COUSIN HINCKLEY OF UTAH

23 April 1939

Senator Elbert Thomas of Utah informed the President that he had
discovered yet another flock of "fifth cousins—once removed" of Roosevelt and among them were the prolific Merrills and Hinckleys. "This
makes you related to literally thousands out our way," Thomas wrote.

THE PRESIDENT: Thank God for my kinship with the state of Utah!
I am proud of my relatives. The genealogists fail to discover that I have
another relationship with the Hinckley family—and thereby hangs a
tale. My great grandmother, Mrs. Lyman, who lived in Northampton,
Massachusetts, carried on a constant feud with her cousin, Mrs. Hinckley. One day they had a bitter altercation after church service. Mrs.
Hinckley lost her temper completely and said, "Why, Mrs. Lyman, your
very name begins with a lie." Mrs. Lyman drew herself up with great
dignity and replied, "Mrs. Hinckley, I acknowledge the soft impeach-
ment but I would infinitely rather have my name begin with a lie than
end with a lie like yours."

All that, however, was in the so-called good old days. From personal
experience I am convinced that my cousins in Utah have totally abandoned the habit of prevarication.[1]

[1] Elbert Thomas to the President, 18 April 1939; the President to
Thomas, 23 April 1939, FDRL.

GIN IN MAINE

11 August 1939

FDR spoke of his forthcoming cruise to Campobello. Only a few reporters were to join him on his destroyer, while the rest were to stay in a nearby town in eastern Maine. Roosevelt offered a discourse to the reporters on the important theme of the liquor situation in Maine.

THE PRESIDENT: Well, I hope that all your marks are good, not only of those of you who are going on the destroyer but those of you who are going up to live in eastern Maine.

CORRESPONDENT: You mean in Eastport?

THE PRESIDENT: Yes, George[1] wasn't there, but it was something that happened the last time we were there. . . . Well, this is off the record, but away before prohibition, even before the World War, the Navy used to kick like a steer, in fact they issued an order that no more ships were to go into Eastport because the liquor was bad. It was literally true because Maine is dry. They had the damnedest liquor.

I remember once, up the Coast, we ran out of liquor and I think we ran into Rockland and went shopping. We went up to the hotel and I leaned over the counter and said a few kind words to the clerk.

I said, "Where can I get some gin?"

He said, "Right in the drugstore, next door. Just give him this card." He said, "Talk to the old man at the rear of the drugstore."

I went to the drugstore and I said to the old man, "I want six bottles of gin," and he said, "Right."

I said, "How much?"

"Oh," he said, "do you want the best gin?"

I said, "Sure."

He said, "Ninety cents a bottle."

Well, gin was cheaper then than it is now, so he gave us the gin with nice labels, and I took it back on board and that evening we made ourselves a Martini and everybody said, "How," and "Down the hatch," and —well, we had to spit it out!

We found out afterwards that it was gin that was made out of the heads and tails of codfish. Did you ever hear of such thing? It was fish gin. It was the most horrible thing I have ever tasted and I think it was about 210 proof.

Well, that was the sample of what you would get and up at Eastport they would give you straight denatured alcohol into which they put a little brown sugar or something to color it up and it was the damnedest thing.

[1] Correspondent George A. Durno of International News Service.

. . . Yes, quite a town. . . . I will tell you, Dick,[2] you had better bring your own liquor with you!

[2] Correspondent Richard L. Harkness of the National Broadcasting Company.

NAUTICAL INNOCENCE

17 November 1939

FDR indicated that Senator Burton Wheeler might find himself in deep waters if he persisted in his desire to investigate alleged faulty designing of certain ships—especially since naval architects and engineers would befuddle him with such concepts like "metacentric height" that nobody understood! Roosevelt referred in this connection to the unhappy experience of another Senator in the past.

THE PRESIDENT: Some newspapers may, quite correctly, remember what Senator [William Alden] Smith of Michigan questioned at the time the "Titanic" went down. You remember that one? Don't you know the story?

Well, the "Titanic," you know, scraped an iceberg and the ice tore out her plates along the starboard side in a sufficient number of watertight compartments to prevent her staying afloat. A ship, you know, is divided across, across the middle.

An investigation was held by the Senate of the United States, or a Congressional Committee. Senator Smith of Michigan said to one of the officers who had been saved, "Didn't your ship have watertight compartments?"

The officer said, "Yes, Senator."

"If so, why didn't the passengers go into the watertight compartments and be saved?"

PRESIDENTIAL AIDE WILLIAM HASSETT: And there was the opening question, "What is an iceberg made of?"

THE PRESIDENT: Yes; that's right; that is true.

HASSETT: He retired from public life!

THE UNFINISHED STORY
OF THE HYDE PARK TRAMP

12 January 1940

Correspondent Earl Godwin handed over to the President a clipping of a UP story featured in a newspaper of the Midwest. According to the story, an individual who described himself as the "President of the Hoboes Union" had stated that Roosevelt would be renominated for a third term and re-elected. The chieftain of the hoboes had declared that his assessment was based on "back door information"—information that he had received at the back doors of American homes.

THE PRESIDENT: I love it!

GODWIN: Isn't it wonderful—"back door"?

THE PRESIDENT: Well, that sounds like the United Press. . . . The A.P. is much too respectable to write news about hoboes.

. . . Some day I will have to tell you a story about a tramp, an old-fashioned tramp up at Hyde Park, who claimed to be a nephew of James Madison. He had one of the most fascinating stories you ever heard. It was when I was a boy. Madison's nephew, and probably he was.

CORRESPONDENT: At Hyde Park?

THE PRESIDENT: Yes. He was a great friend of Chauncey Depew. He had free railroad passage, et cetera. He went to Florida every winter—

(Unfortunately Roosevelt got sidetracked at this point and never got around to finishing the story of the old-fashioned tramp who claimed to be Madison's nephew.)

ON SOVEREIGNS AND PASSPORTS

5 February 1940

A report had been issued on the Federal Deposit Insurance Corporation. FDR referred to stories on the report in the financial pages of newspapers.

THE PRESIDENT: . . . in the old days—I mean, way, way back—my father always kept $500 in gold . . . because he said you never can tell when you need money in a hurry. Of course, in those days the banks were not insured and most of the paper money you had was bank notes. You could never tell whether the bank notes you happened to have were not of a bank which had closed up the day before. So he always kept that gold. On some days when the family ran short he would trot out some gold pieces.

In those days nobody ever had passports. When we went abroad in the early 80's and 90's nobody ever thought of having a passport—it is an amazing thing but nobody ever thought of keeping a passport. I never had one until the World War. And everybody kept on the bottom of his handbag or valise about twenty or thirty pounds in gold—English sovereigns which were accepted everywhere in Europe.

Now you have to get a passport and a letter of credit and God knows what.

THE TREES AND THE MANSION ON
THE VANDERBILT ESTATE IN HYDE PARK

5 February 1940

CORRESPONDENT: Have you heard anything more about the Vanderbilt estate and if the Government is still interested in it as a park?[1]

THE PRESIDENT: I have not heard anything for about a month, but, as I understand it, the title searchers are going on and it is hoped that this spring it will be taken over by the Government. . . .

Well, I will tell you a story and you cannot use it. . . . Of course I remember the place when it was owned by old John Langdon. There was a house on it—it was not the original house—built about 1840, when people were all crazy about the Italian villa type architecture. You know that [type] along the river here; it is a brick house, with a tower on one end and two stories here and one story and three stories there et cetera. It looks like a train of cars.

I think it was old Dr. David Hazzard who built the old Italian villa. It was a nice house in those days, painted brown on top of the brick, and plenty of rooms, very high ceilings, and it really went pretty well with the landscaping; it did not stick out.

Of course, I also think of the place having historical value because of the Bards, who built it originally and brought trees from all over the world. Old Dr. John Bard and Samuel Bard, a great naturalist, brought trees from Honolulu, Norway, France, England, Scotland, and Dr. Hazzard, who followed, brought trees from Russia and Siberia. So it was a real arboretum and some of those trees came from almost every part of the world and were marvelous specimens. They are undoubtedly the best specimens in the United States, trees from Japan and China.

I have always thought of it as being a very beautifully landscaped place, with marvelous samples of trees, and I thought the Government ought to own it. So this Board came up from Washington, . . . this Advisory Committee, with one or two architects, one or two landscape gardeners and three or four eminent historians on it. I told them about it and said quite casually, "Of course there is on it a marble mausoleum [the Vanderbilt mansion] that does not go with the Hudson River country at all. It cost a million and a half dollars and I don't know what we are going to do with it. But, I think, in spite of it, the place itself and the trees are worth taking over."

They came back to Washington and said, "The trees are lovely"—but that the Government ought to own it because of the mansion!

I said, "My God, why?"

[1] The Vanderbilt estate, located about three miles north of the Roosevelt property, was offered to the Government by Mrs. James L. Van Alen, niece of Frederick Vanderbilt.

They said, "Well, it is probably the best example of the millionaire period in American history that can be found in the United States. It was built in the year 1899 or 1900. It was designed by Stanford White and Charles McKim, of McKim, Meade and White. It is an enlarged version of the Petit Trianon at Versailles and inside there are some of the most beautiful rooms anywhere in the world today. There are all kinds of lovely panelling that came out of European palaces and some very wonderful old furniture that came out, again, of European palaces. There are a great many tapestries that are almost priceless and, because we have luckily been getting away from that millionaire period of American history, it should be preserved as an example, just in the same way we hope that somebody will come along someday in the Hudson River Valley and give to the Government a marvelous example of Victorian—you know, those God-awful things we have around here occasionally, the house with towers and windows that go like that [indicating], perfectly terrible stuff from our point of view today, that Victorian architecture, but it ought to be preserved for history, for people to go and look at just as much as one of the old New England colonial homes or Virginia country places or things of that kind. We want to get a complete, rounded picture."

They went on and said, "We ought not to stop there. We ought to get something like the amazing and God-awful Pullman [Palmer?] Palace in Chicago, with brownstone and towers and minarets all over it, just to show the period."

So, they have listed the place up here as being of ultimate historic interest.[2]

[2] The Advisory Board on National Parks, Historic Sites, Buildings, and Monuments recommended the designation of the Vanderbilt estate as "representative and illustrative of its period, of national significance in the economic, sociological, and cultural history of the country."

A LESSON DEARLY LEARNT

3 May 1940

FDR discussed how technological innovations could profoundly change accepted notions of military capabilities of various war-making devices. He recalled an article that he had written in the *North American Review* in 1914 about the potential role of submarines and the inevitable development of anti-submarine devices. He then proceeded to tell a story.

THE PRESIDENT: Well, the article was published—I think it is in the September number of 1914. And this is just a sidelight for some of you who, like myself, have written for pay.

I supposed that George Harvey [editor of the *Review*] would send me a check for this article. It was the lead in the *North American Review*. And no check came.

Well, finally, way on in October, I got a letter from George Harvey saying, "Dear Mr. Secretary: At a meeting of the Board of Directors of the North American Review a resolution was passed thanking you—thanking you for your splendid leading article in the September number and, in token of their esteem and appreciation, they have voted to send you the *North American Review*, free, for one year."

I learned a lesson. I use the contract method now!

THE LEGEND OF AN OLD GENTLEMAN FROM OVER IN SHILOH VALLEY

5 June 1940

A press conference had been arranged for representatives of the American Youth Congress in the State Dining Room of the White House. In the course of his remarks, FDR touched on the problem of "slanted" news and the faith of many people in the truth of the "printed word." The remarks led to a story and we find Roosevelt conjuring up yet another character from out of the land of fantasy.

THE PRESIDENT: . . . there is all the difference in the world between straight news, honestly written, factual, and a whole lot of people—of course not confined to editors—but there are a lot of other people who make comments to the general public sometimes not in accordance with their own conscience. I illustrated that to the editors and publishers by a remark that was made to me by one of the nationally known commentators.

I said to that commentator, "I believe that in your column, three days out of six, you are consistently taking a crack at every known kind of social reform or betterment program of the Government that we have been trying to put through in the last seven years. Why is it?" I said, "I have known you for a great many years and you are not as anti-social or unsocial personally."

"Well," he said, "of course I am not; of course I am not. But I can sell my column if I take this line that I have been taking now ever since you have been President. I can sell my column to sixty papers and if I commented the way I really feel, I would not have any clients left."

Now that is a sort of human interest story, but it also goes to show that an awful lot of people in this country believe an awful lot of things they are told because they see it in print—and I can illustrate that—because they see it in print or because they have been told by somebody they respect. And I can illustrate that by telling you a little story about the 1928 campaign:

Al Smith had been placed in nomination and duly nominated and I believed that Al had made a fine governor and put through a great deal of legislation that was really of definite social benefit. That fall, in September, I went down to Warm Springs.

One morning, when I was sound asleep, it was around about daylight, about 5 o'clock, somebody banged on the shutters and kept on banging on the shutters. So I got into a little wheel chair and went over, opened the shutters and there was an old gentleman from over in Shiloh Valley. And I said to him, "I do not want any eggs this morning; I do not want any chickens—I got plenty in the larder. Why, in God's name, do you waken me at this time of the morning?"

He said, "Mr. Roosevelt, I did not come to waken you at this time of the morning. I don't want to sell you chickens and eggs. We are all upset over in Shiloh Valley."

I said, "Why?"

He said, "Oh, we are all upset about you."

I said, "Why?"

"Well," he said, "we people over in Shiloh Valley, we are sort of old-fashioned and we believe the written word. We believe the written word."

I said, "Yes, and what happened?"

"Well, the preacher on Sunday, after church, he gave us a lot of handbills and . . . if what those handbills say is true, we do not see how you can be supporting this fellow Smith."

I said, "Why not?"

"Well," he said, "we could not go along with Smith. We have been Democrats all our lives; we never voted anything but the Democratic ticket. And we cannot go along with Smith. We don't see how you can because when you first came down here to Georgia we thought you were a damned Yankee but," he said, "we got to know you. You haven't got any horns. You did not go through Georgia with General Sherman and, well, we like you and we respect you and you understand us. And, what we can't understand is why you, a friend of ours, can be for Smith."

Just because of this written word—the written word.

I said, "Let me see it." So he goes down into his pocket and hauls out a couple of posters, handbills, and the first handbill says, in large type at the top, "Do you know that if Al Smith becomes President you will be living in adultery with your own wife! Because"—a great big BECAUSE —"the Roman Church does not recognize any marriage as valid unless it has been performed by a Roman priest."

So I said, "That is pretty bad, isn't it?" I said, "Funny sort of thing. That fellow Al Smith has been Governor of New York for eight years and, after all, a question of marriage is purely a state question. It is not a Federal question. "And," I said, "I think I am still legally married to my wife even if Smith has been Governor of New York for eight years."

I said, "let's look at the other one." It said, "Do you know that if Smith becomes President all your children will be illegitimate?" And then the same reason, that the only legitimate children are children that are baptized into the Roman Catholic Church.

I said, "I have got five pretty husky kids. . . . I have every reason to believe that they are still legitimate."

Well, that is just an illustration of a form of being credulous and believing all sorts of things that you are told or that you read in the printed word, without going any further, any more than this old man from over in Shiloh Valley did. He did not go down into the facts of the case. He believed what he read and there is an awful lot of that in this country, not only among the uneducated—because they are mostly uneducated people over in Shiloh Valley—but also in much more highly educated circles in every state of the Union.

HOW OLD JOE DANIELS
OUTWITTED THE CRAFTY CONTRACTORS
3 September 1940

FDR enjoyed travelling by train. He was in a relaxed mood as he chatted on this occasion with reporters in the Presidential train, in a journey from Charleston, West Virginia, to Washington. Roosevelt discussed naval contracts and the problem posed by collusive bidding by contractors. He recalled an experience in 1913 when he was Assistant Secretary of the Navy and Josephus Daniels was his chief.

THE PRESIDENT: It is an amusing story. Back in 1913, just after Joe Daniels and I went in there, we found three or four battleships that needed armor contracts. The previous price had been $460 a ton and the new identical price from these three companies was $520 a ton, and the cost of construction and the cost of labor had not gone up in the meantime, so old Joe Daniels sent for them. I loved his words.

He said, "Gentlemen,"—there were three of them—he said, "this I am afraid, is collusive bidding for you, all three, to arrive at exactly the same figure. I am afraid I have got to throw the bids out and ask for new bids."

And one of them stepped forward and said, "Mr. Secretary,"—with a perfectly solemn face—"Mr. Secretary, it was a pure coincidence."

And Daniels said, "Well, the bids are all rejected and we will open new bids at 12:00 o'clock tomorrow. Sharpen your pencils, think it over during the night and don't have another coincidence."

Which was rather nice. And then came the other part of the story.

About—oh, they came in the next day with identical bids again, still $520. They had the same coincidence in the night.

Daniels sent for me and when I came to him he had a newspaper under his hand.

He said, "Do you see who has landed?"

"Who?"

He said, "Why, Sir John Hatfield."

I said, "Well, who in hell is Sir John Hatfield?"

"Why," he said, "he is one of the three or four great armor plate makers in England and makes a lot of armor plate for the British Navy." He said, "Can you take the train right away?"

"What do you want me to do?"

"Go up to New York, see Sir John Hatfield and ask him if he will take this order for this armor at $460 or less,"—which was the previous year's price.

I went up and saw Hatfield.

He said, "Give me the specifications, although I know them more or less offhand, and I will send a cable and let you know tomorrow."

I said, "Wait a minute now. The Secretary and I are using you, quite frankly, we are using you to force down the American price. We do not want to buy this in England if the American producer of armor will come down to $460 a ton."

He said, "I know that; you do not have to tell me that."

I said, "In other words, if you bid $460 a ton and the Americans do not come down to the price, you get the order, but if they do come down to the price, we will give them the order."

He said, "It is all right with me."

The next day I got a telegram, "Firm offer making all the armor plate you need for $460." So we sent for the three gentlemen and showed them the telegram from Hatfield and Daniels sent them out and the next day we got all our armor plate from them for $460 a ton!

NOTHING BUT THE TRUTH!

3 December 1940

The press conference was held on board the special train proceeding from Washington to Miami, Florida. Correspondents knew that Roosevelt intended to go out on a cruise and they insisted on knowing his travel plans. On a previous occasion FDR had given them, as his destination, the fictitious names of non-existent islands. But, on this occasion, he promised to tell them nothing but the truth. The mood brought on by his playful return to honesty led Roosevelt to narrate the sad tale of Herbert

Bayard Swope, a well known writer of the *New York World* in earlier years.

THE PRESIDENT: How are your seagoing legs, and how are you? [Turning to a newswoman] If you were in sailor clothes I might take you along! Sit down here.

CORRESPONDENT: Couldn't you tell us where you are going?

THE PRESIDENT: I wish I knew. Well, I'll tell you. The last time I told you about some phoney islands that weren't on the map. This time I won't deceive you at all. We are going to Christmas Islands to buy Christmas cards then we are going on to Easter Island to buy Easter eggs! . . . .

CORRESPONDENT: Mr. President, if you are going to put in at one specific island we might be able to fly down there.

THE PRESIDENT: That always reminds me—it really wasn't a trick. It concerns Herbert Bayard Swope, who at that time was really one of the top men on the old *World*—

[It was] during the summer of '19; and we carefully worked up the . . . boat flight to Europe. It was to be the first continuous regular flight of planes across the ocean. We fitted three of them at New York. There were an awful lot of stories—everybody wrote it up. . . .

We sent a ship to Newfoundland to fuel them up and another to the Azores to fuel them up. About two days before they were to push off I received a telegram from Herbert Bayard saying, "Do you really think these ships will get through and is it important enough for me to go down to Lisbon to cover it?"

I thought it was a big story, wired back and said, "Think it of utmost importance. Strongly recommend you go to Lisbon and be there by Thursday,"—because it was always possible they would have got to Newfoundland, refueled, refueled at the Azores the next day and got to Lisbon the next.

Herbert Bayard packed up and went to Lisbon. The weather was bad and it was a dreary place.

He gets down there—and the three boats, due to stress of weather, were held up in New York, expecting to go the next day, then the next day and the next day. They were there for 5 days.

At last they hopped and got as far Newfoundland, where the fog shuts in and they were ready to hop the next day.

Herbert Bayard cabled me, "When are they leaving?"

They were 5 days in Newfoundland, then hopped off and only one of them got safely to the Azores. The other two were in the ocean.

The plane at the Azores busted an aileron and took two full weeks to get to Lisbon,—and every day Herbert Bayard would sit on the end of the pier.

He never forgave me!

HENRY CABOT LODGE

27 January 1941

The President read with considerable interest an article by Harold Ickes, Secretary of the Interior, on the Progressive Party. He wrote to Ickes that he had never been able to understand the faith that the founder of the Progressive Party, Theodore Roosevelt, had in Senator Henry Cabot Lodge of Massachusetts.[1]

THE PRESIDENT: I was one of those who helped to organize the Woodrow Wilson Foundation in 1922 or the beginning of 1923, as I remember. I was the temporary chairman and at Wilson's suggestion, we undertook to set up a jury to decide on who should receive the annual awards. We decided to ask President Emeritus Charles W. Eliot [of Harvard] to be the foreman of that jury and we sent Houston[2] to see him.

First of all the old gentleman raised a terrible row at the idea of having women on the jury as well as men. But Houston managed to straighten this out with him.

Lodge, who was still alive, was continuing his destructive tactics and Houston said to Eliot:

"Mr. President, you must have known Lodge very well as he has been on various governing boards at Harvard for many years. What is your estimate of him?"

President Eliot replied as follows:

"Yes, Houston, I have known Cabot intimately since he was a small boy. In fact, I saw him grow up because his father's house was next to my house in Nahant. Of Cabot, I should say that I have never met a less generous person—except possibly Cabot's father."

As a matter of fact, in thinking back, I am inclined to the belief that President Eliot was right but that as long as Mrs. Lodge was alive Henry Cabot Lodge's lack of generosity was made up for in part by Mrs. Lodge's influence on him. All of us in the family loved Mrs. Lodge. It was not until after her death that the pettiness in Cabot came so clearly to the surface.

[1] The President to Harold L. Ickes, 27 January 1941, FDRL.

[2] Franklin Houston was Secretary of the Treasury in the Wilson Administration.

THE MANY BIRTHDAYS OF SAINT ROCCO

Hyde Park, 27 June 1941

CORRESPONDENT: Do you think you will be Washington on the Fourth [of July]?

THE PRESIDENT: I haven't the faintest idea. Somebody said it was supposed to be unusual. Hasn't anybody been in Washington on the Fourth?

CORRESPONDENT: Not if they can help it, Mr. President. . . .

THE PRESIDENT: What is that famous fellow—you ought to know. He is quite a saint to all the Italians, who fire off fireworks all the time. This is off the record.

CORRESPONDENT: [Saint] Rocco.

THE PRESIDENT: Yes. When I was Governor of this State . . . he had a birthday two or three times a year! Perfectly incorrigible. Right close to the Executive Mansion, and every time that Rocco came along, each church—there were one or two churches quite near—got up a special celebration for him, and they were firing off these great big bombs in the park which is about a block from the Executive Mansion—keeping us awake till three o'clock in the morning—and the poor old bishop of the diocese, he had no effect, because financially the churches were in a hole all the time; they had to be helped by the diocese—they were shooting off their money in fireworks!

This is all off the record, but I think on the Fourth of July it isn't a patch on this old fellow Rocco. . . . Just see to it that we don't pass Poughkeepsie on St. Rocco's Day!

WOULD THE GATES OF HEAVEN OPEN FOR FDR?

19 August 1941

Congress had adopted a bill for the construction of a new building for the War Department on a site in Arlington. Roosevelt did not like the suggested location.

CORRESPONDENT: Mr. President, here is a real trivial question. Can you say anything about the new War Department building in Arlington?

THE PRESIDENT: . . . I think it ought to be of interest to everybody. I haven't got the bill yet. . . . My present inclination is not to accept that action by Congress.

. . . When I first came down [to Washington] in 1933, I said I didn't think I would ever be let into the Gates of Heaven because I had been responsible for desecrating the parks of Washington.

Back in the fall of 1917, the Navy Department needed space, and I took up with President Wilson the possibility of building a temporary building—wooden building—down here on the oval.

And he said, "Why do you select that site?"

I said, "Mr. President, because it would be so unsightly right here in front of the White House, that it just would have to be taken down at the end of the war."

"Well," he said, "I don't think I could stand all that sawing and hammering under my front windows." He said, "Can't you put it somewhere else?"

So I said, "Of course. Put it down in Potomac Park."

"Well," he said, "Put it down there and we will get rid of it."

. . . that located it in the park—then came up the question of the dangers of a wooden building. And the President decided it should be a fireproof building; and I got hold of the Turner Construction Company, and they did a perfectly amazing job as you know. Well, that was finished in the Spring of 1918. That is 23 years ago, and the building is just as solid as the day it was built. There was nothing temporary about it; and then it was so good that we went ahead and put the Munitions Building right alongside.

It was a crime—I don't hesitate to say so—it was a crime for which I should be kept out of Heaven, for having desecrated the whole plan of, I think, the loveliest city in the world—the capital of the United States.

Now, a part of that plan of course, as it developed over the years, created the great National Cemetery. Er—General Lee's old place. And Arlington is known and loved throughout the length and breadth of the land.

. . . And here it is—under the name of emergency, it is proposed to put up a permanent building, which will deliberately and definitely, for one hundred years to come, spoil the plan of the National Capital. . . . I think that I have had a part in spoiling the National Parks and the beautiful waterfront of the District once, and I don't want to do it again.

UNCLE DAN'S HANDS

22 August 1941

Relations with Japan were deteriorating fast. And then the crabs entered the picture!

CORRESPONDENT: Mr. President, we understand that you cut off imports of crab meat.

THE PRESIDENT: Crab meat?

CORRESPONDENT: We get a lot from Japan. I wonder if that has any particular reference to—

THE PRESIDENT: [Laughing] I never heard of it. On that crab meat, I will have to tell you—this is off the record—a very amusing story.

Old Dan Roper, when he was Secretary of Commerce, had under him the Fisheries Bureau, and one day in Cabinet I said, "Dan, have you got any news for us today?"

"Yes, indeed I have," says Uncle Dan, "Crabs."

I said, "What?"

He said, "A most amazing thing. I am very much worried. You know, up there on the coast of Alaska they have these wonderful crabs." And he said, "That big across." [FDR indicated with his hands a width of about thirty inches.]

I said, "What?"

Well, he was measuring somewhere—twenty-four to thirty inches across. Literally with his hands.

"Oh, no," I said, "You're exaggerating."

"No," he said, "I tell you they are that wide across."

And I said, "Dan, Dan, you're exaggerating."

"No," he said, "my people tell me. I have never been there—they are that big across!"

And he wouldn't yield one inch as to the size of this crab.

I said, "What about it?"

"Well," he said, "the Japs are coming there, just up to the three-mile limit, and they are catching these crabs."

I said, "Dan, you must be exaggerating."

"No, the Japs are catching these crabs. On the boat they catch them they have a crab factory."

I said, "What?"

He said, "They do everything to that crab."

I said, "Dan, they are as big as that?"

"I tell you it is as big as that." And he said, "They take them on the boat with all these nets that catch them. . . . They process them right on the boat. Take the meat and boil it, whatever it is, and they do all the canning on board."

. . . Whenever I hear about crabs I think of Uncle Dan's hands.

A SURPRISE VISIT TO THE STATE DEPARTMENT
26 August 1941

Roosevelt commented on the accumulation of paper in government offices. Non-essential government records, he thought, should be in a big, separate, records building while only current and important materials should be in the Departments concerned. However, he added, "the tendency of any Department is to hang on. It's—it's not merely acquisitive, but it is retentive."

THE PRESIDENT: I always think of this retentive spirit. I went over, in pursuance of this subject—two or three years ago—to the State Department one afternoon—after all the people had gone home—because they assured me that in the State Department over here they only had very current records. Nothing more than four or five years old. Everything else was stored.

Well, frankly, I didn't believe it, and I went over there, and I got into a wheel chair, and I wheeled through various rooms, and came to a closed door which had been separated off.

One of these great doors was opened up, and there was a great, big, long room—oh, I suppose six or eight people had worked there in the course of the day—nobody there, they had all gone home. And along the sides of the room and stacked out into the middle of the room were hundreds of square feet of filing cabinets.

So I—at random I said, "Open that one."

And in there it happened to be a case that was devoted to consular reports of the years 19–1907 to 1911, on the "History and Future of the Mongolian Pony." It's very nice, but it wasn't exactly current, or of great importance at that particular time. It was a record story, and it ought not to have been in that building which was the State Department—yelling for more space!

HOW MONSIEUR ROOSEVELT NEARLY LOST THE FIRST WORLD WAR

24 October 1941

THE PRESIDENT: During the World War, in the spring—early summer of 1918—we were getting an awful lot of men over to Europe. . . . an awful lot of men to keep secret, and we were pretty happy about the whole thing. They were actually being landed.

And we had a policy, as you know, of complete secrecy about numbers and that lasted all through the . . . early summer of 1918. And everybody was asking the same question: "Why this secrecy? Does it mean an awful lot of men, or are they behind schedule?"

Well, I got over to Paris in early July, and they had a meeting of the . . . Inter-Allied Naval Council, and of the Army end of it, and they talked a couple of days as to whether the time hadn't come to do a little boasting. So . . . we came out with a big splurge announcing that we had got—I don't know what it was—a million and a quarter men, actually in France. And I was deputed to receive the French press and tell them that the Navy, in co-operation with the British and the French, had very greatly cut down on submarine sinkings, and that our Navy had a complete line of anti-submarine aircraft patrol the whole length of the west coast of France, Bay of Biscay, et cetera. . . .

Of course I personally had a little episode that was very funny. I received the French press at eleven a.m. in the . . . Hotel Meurice. And the people in charge of it had prepared one end of the room as a bar, with all the champagne and hors d'oeuvres, et cetera, that you could put on it.

Well, I went in there. It was a great, big room. And the French press arrived at eleven a.m., and they were all in full dress suits, with white ties. And they weren't the working newspapermen—a few were—nearly all of them were the redacteurs—the editors—of the papers, and they were seen. They were having the privilege of being received by "Monsieur le Ministre." Apparently it created the most awful furore.

Well, I had a translator there, and started. . . . He couldn't translate it; so I sat on the edge of the table, and in perfectly awful French told the story.

"Well," I said, "go ahead and ask questions."

Well, that was something that they had never heard of in the newspaper business in France—asking questions of a "Ministre." Unheard of.

So they asked a few questions, and I answered them as far as I was allowed to. And then at the end, one of these editors in the full dress suit said, "Monsieur le Ministre, is it really true that in Washington the members of the Cabinet receive the press once a day?"

I said, "Yes. Twice a day." Whereupon I thought nothing of it.

Next morning I went around to breakfast with old man Clemenceau,[1] and as I went into the room, Clemenceau came at me just like a tiger—with his claws out.

He said, "Ah, you overthrow my government. You overthrow my government. You lose the war."

Well, I was horrified. I said, "My God, what have I done?"

He said, "The French newsmen, they come—they want to see me—they want to see me and my cabinet once a day, and some of them say twice a day. I will resign first!"

So I darn near overthrew the government and lost the war!

[1] Georges Clemenceau, French Prime Minister and Minister for War, 1917–1920.

THE BLIMP AND FDR
31 October 1941

An extremely serious incident had taken place on this day. The President informed reporters that the destroyer, "Reuben Jones" had been sunk by German submarines. It was likely that casualties might be heavy. (One hundred and fifteen men lost their lives.) Even on such a day FDR could not only remain unruffled but tell the story of his ride in a blimp.

Roosevelt told reporters that during the World War submarine sinkings by Allied action were not always announced though losses sustained by the Allies were acknowledged.

THE PRESIDENT: Of course, there are perfectly obvious reasons for that. Everybody knows, when they come to think about it.

I always remember one episode in the World War. I went out—summer of 1918—in a French . . . blimp, out over the Bay of Biscay. We took a ride and I ran the thing. I was sitting in an armchair, and pulled a stick up and down, and turned a wheel right or left. Anyone of you could have run it—it was perfectly fascinating. We were up four or five hundred feet above the surface. I was out a couple of hours.

And the next day, . . . that same blimp thought she saw . . . the shape of a submarine, way down on the bottom—off a place called Penmarch Point. Well, there had been a German submarine operating off there—oh, for several months—and she had sunk quite a lot of ships that were going into the mouth of the Loire river. And everybody was trying to get her. She would be on station a week or ten days, and then go back to Germany and refuel; then return to Penmarch Point.

This blimp saw this shape, down on the bottom about a hundred feet below the water, and dropped a buoy over it; came back, and one of the planes went out and dropped depth charges. And I think some of the sub-chasers went out and dropped depth charges all around the buoy.

Well, some oil came up, and the people who had done it said, "Hey, We've got a submarine. We've sunk a submarine."

Well, of course, we were awfully, awfully careful, and we didn't claim that submarine at all. It wasn't claimed as a "get."

After the war was all over—months later—they sent some divers down, and sure enough it was a submarine—they got her! But we didn't know at the time.

Now, of course, obviously, the Germans didn't know what had happened to that ship either. She might have been wrecked. She might have been sunk. She might have been captured. The fact was that she was missing, and that's all that Germany knew. Which, of course, had a pretty . . . important effect on the morale of the crews of other submarines.

It just didn't come home!

WHEN THEY BEAT ROOSEVELT'S DAD

3 November 1941

FDR raised the question whether the curricula in American schools were sufficiently "practical" to enable boys and girls to cope with the complexities of modern life.[1]

[1] Informal remarks to a conference of Dutchess County Teachers, Hyde Park, New York, 3 November 1941, *Public Papers and Addresses, 1941*, pp. 456–57.

THE PRESIDENT: Take my own memory of schools in this township of ours. A great many years ago, when I was a boy, my father was one of the school trustees for many years, and he used to take me, when I was eight or ten years old, to sit outside the little old schoolhouse in the village to hold the horses. And I remember one day he came out of the school saying, "Well, they beat me."

He said, "They voted me down. You know I have tried to put a course in carpentry into this school for a long time."

Carpentry for the boys. But nobody had ever heard of teaching carpentry to the boys, and besides that a course in carpentry would not have brought any money in from Albany, from the Board of Regents. So, in place of carpentry, the School Board voted a course from which they got many dollars from Albany—a course in comparative anatomy.

Then I got back home, and my father said, "I wanted to have a course in the basement of the school, for the girls, in cooking and sewing."

My dear mother was very much interested in that. They turned it down. Nobody had ever heard of teaching cooking and sewing to girls. They were supposed to pick it up at home. Some of them did, but a lot of them didn't. And in place of that—they could get no money for that—they put in a course in German and French literature.

. . . today almost every school in this State, and most other States, is teaching a lot of practical things that were not taught in the earlier days. But I wonder—in view of the complexity of our civilization—whether our schools are keeping up with the growth of that complexity.

LET THEM SEE THE WHEELS GO ROUND
3 November 1941

Relations with Japan were worsening rapidly. On 16 October the Japanese cabinet headed by Prince Konoye fell and General Hideki Tojo formed a new government, setting its course on the road to Pearl Harbor. From intercepted Japanese secret despatches Roosevelt knew that a crisis was fast approaching. But he was as breezy and relaxed as ever while he chatted with reporters in his study in the Roosevelt Library at Hyde Park. His major engagement of the day was to be a visit to the local high school.

THE PRESIDENT: I don't think they will let you people in, will they in the high school? . . . .

CORRESPONDENT: Sure hope so.

THE PRESIDENT: I think they let only high school graduates in! Maybe you have your certificates with you! It's all right. . . .

CORRESPONDENT: Are you going to touch on local issues this after-noon in your speech, Mr. President?

THE PRESIDENT: Not local issues. I am going to talk about a thing in education that I have always talked about a great deal and this morning a little bit that way. I have talked about it for thirty years and that is: giving boys and girls in high school a little bit more firsthand knowledge of how, and where, and why the wheels go round.

. . . I'll use an illustration of the fact that the average boy and girl doesn't know anything about the procedure of local law. They don't know what a Justice of the Peace does, what his duties are. They don't know what the police force does in Poughkeepsie—we hope! They don't know what the Supreme Court in Poughkeepsie does. They have never been to a court room.

Well, that happened to me! I always think of my own experience. I got through school, and college, then went three years to a law school, and was duly admitted to the Bar of the State of New York. And in 1907, or in there somewhere, I went into a great big law office as a sort of a glorified office boy.

And the day after I got there I was told to go up to the court and answer a calendar call. Now, mind you, I was a full-fledged lawyer, duly certified. I didn't know what a calendar call was. I had never been in a court room, and yet I was a lawyer. Never been in a court room! And then the next day I was sent up to record a deed in the County Clerk's Office. Well, I hadn't the foggiest idea about the recording of a deed. I had to learn all these practical things. Never been in a County Clerk's Office!

I had never been in a big factory, mind you, at the age of—what?—twenty-five. Didn't know what a factory meant, where the stuff came from, and the different individual processes, and the selling process. Had to learn that long after I had graduated and was in a profession.

I am going to use some of these examples this afternoon. The general idea [is] that in the high schools—take this County as a perfectly good example, it is a practical thing to take around high school students and let them see the wheels go round. Of course, the County highway system, the Sanitation, County health people, what a Surrogate's Office does, and so forth and so on. . . .

CORRESPONDENT: What does a Surrogate's Office do?[1] I want to be there for it.

THE PRESIDENT: You will never get there until you are dead! It's all right.

[1] A Surrogate is a probate court judge in charge of probating wills and administering estates.

THE HYDE PARK INDIANS

3 November 1941, Hyde Park.

CORRESPONDENT: There's a slight argument among the boys this morning on how old is the tree in front, out there. . . .

THE PRESIDENT: . . . it is rather an interesting one. I had a tree man here about twenty years ago with a similar tree, about the same age.

And he counted the rings and figured out that the tree started to grow about 1640, which is three hundred years, and then he advanced the extremely interesting theory—the tree obviously grew under field conditions. In other words, not in a forest—in those early years—because the lower limbs started out at a very low level, and branched out fifty or more feet on all sides of the tree. So it must have been an open space. It meant necessarily almost that this was a field, and if it was a field, then it was an Indian field. Therefore there was an Indian encampment, or village, right here. . . . the only fields in the East in those days were Indian cultivated fields.[1] Everywhere else were woodlands.

CORRESPONDENT: Is that a hickory? . . . .

THE PRESIDENT: White oak. They are all white oaks. And I think it is rather an interesting thing. Of course, we find all kinds of arrowheads.

---

[1] FDR had an abiding interest in the history of the area where he was born and raised. On the occasion of laying the cornerstone of the Franklin D. Roosevelt Library in Hyde Park in 1939 he spoke of the trees and the Indians and reminisced about his own boyhood. He said:

Half a century ago a small boy took especial delight in climbing an old tree, now unhappily gone, to pick and eat ripe sickle pears. That was about one hundred feet to the west of where I am standing now. And just to the north he used to lie flat between the strawberry rows and eat sun-warmed strawberries—the best in the world. In the spring of the year, in hip rubber boots, he sailed his first toy boats in the surface water formed by the melting snow. In the summer with his dogs he dug into woodchuck holes in this same field, and some of you are standing on top of those holes at this minute. Indeed the descendants of those same woodchucks still inhabit this field and I hope that under the auspices of the National Archivist, they will continue to do so for all time.

. . . We know from simple deduction that these fields were cultivated by the first inhabitants of America—for the oak trees in these fields were striplings three centuries ago, and grew up in open fields as is proved to us by their wide spreading lower branches. Therefore, they grew in open spaces, and the only open spaces in Dutchess County were the cornfields of the Indians.

Public Papers and Addresses, 1939, pp. 580–81.

Right on the driveway we dug up a deer bone—a shin bone that had been made into a needle. And we have quite a lot of arrowheads and things that are dug up. It's rather good.

CORRESPONDENT: Isn't it one of our oldest parts of America up here—in terms of history then? . . . .

THE PRESIDENT: Yes, yes. This County did not get settled until 1690, something like that, so it couldn't have been a white man's field. Of course the other side of the river was settled about 1640, over in Ulster County.

TELL THEM THE TRUTH?

6 January 1942

THE PRESIDENT: I remember in the 1920 campaign, when I started out West on my first trip, I realized that there was quite a lot of trouble among the cattle growers of the West. They had been encouraged to add to their herds, to get all the new calves that they possibly could. And the whole West was flooded with calves and cows.

And I knew that I would run into trouble, and the reason was that the people who had lent them the money—the banks, which had been encouraged by the Treasury Department—they were calling loans.

So I wrote a letter to the Secretary of the Treasury, Mr. Houston, and said, "Now what will I say in my speeches to these cattle growers?"

And I got back a letter—imagine my using it in the campaign—saying, "Dear Mr. Secretary, tell them the truth. Tell them that they have to be the vicarious sacrifice for a restoration of the country to normal financial positions."

Well, I didn't use it!

THE HONEST BRITISH

9 June 1942

FDR explained that the newly-established Combined Food Board would strive to bring about equitable distribution of available food supplies among Allied countries.

THE PRESIDENT: I always think of a story a great many years ago—in 1918. I was staying at a country house in England, to which a number of the British Cabinet had been invited. And they spent all Saturday evening indoctrinating me on all the terrible hardships that people in England had gone through. They hadn't had this to eat or that to drink, and so forth, for a long, long time. They hadn't had any butter, and they hadn't had any bacon, and so forth. They had to really tighten their belts enormously. And I was being indoctrinated because I was the first "near" Cabinet member to go to the other side in the war.

And the next morning I was late for breakfast, and sat down, and suddenly realized that all the food was on the sideboard, like most British breakfasts. And I went over to it, and the first hot dish I took the cover off was just piled high with bacon. So I filled my plate with bacon and sat down.

And the hostess said, "What! Only—only bacon?"

I said, "Yes." I said, "You know, at home I have gone without bacon for a year and a half, in order that you good people might have it!"

There are all kinds of things of that kind where we can get, I think, a more even distribution.

THE ADMIRAL'S MALADY AND
A LADY'S SIXTH SENSE
12 February 1943

Shortly after his return from Casablanca, Roosevelt held a press conference for members of the American Society of Newspaper Editors. He congratulated them for having done "a grand job" of keeping secret his visit to North Africa. "Of course, you didn't all know just where I was," he added.

THE PRESIDENT: But my old Chief's wife [Mrs. Josephus Daniels] guessed that I was in Africa. She was just about the only one that did. The Chief said that she had always had—Mrs. Daniels always had—a sort of sixth sense on things like that. So I wrote him back to tell Mrs. Daniels that I had always known that in the old days.[1]

Oh, back around 1913–14, we had in the Navy a very clever and brilliant Rear Admiral by the name of Bradley Fisk. Well, Bradley Fisk had no "terminal facilities,"—otherwise he was extremely able.

[1] On 28 January 1943 Josephus Daniels had written to FDR: "You know that my wife is the second Sherlock Holmes. Shortly after you left, and it was 'norated' that you had gone away on some official visit, and when most people supposed you were making another tour to look at the American arsenal, my wife asked one day: 'Where do you think Franklin has gone?' My imagination is not as good as hers. Neither is my foresight, so I asked in Yankee fashion: 'Where do you think?' She replied that you had gone to North Africa, and she was so confident that she was one of the few persons not surprised at all when it was announced." Text of the letter in Carroll Kilpatrick, ed., *Roosevelt and Daniels: A Friendship in Politics* (Chapel Hill, 1952), pp. 210–11.

The first thing that reminded the Chief was when we were coming back from Baltimore—or Annapolis—one day in the trolley car, sitting side by side. . . . There up on the hill was a sign. And he said, "Read that. That's the truest—the truest sign that has ever been put up in this country."

And the sign said, "FISK TIRES"!

Well, old man Fisk, about—oh, five or half-past, when the Secretary was thinking of going home, almost every day would bring him a long twelve or twenty-page typewritten technical article on armor, or some new form of machine gun, or something like that, which no layman could possibly understand, and tell the Secretary he had to read that because he wanted action on it in the morning.

And I knew what he did with them, but I wasn't always sure!

So he went away one day. And Bradley Fisk came around to see me, and he said, "I have got to have action on about three different documents that I left with the Secretary."

I said, "Where are they?"

"I don't know. I can't find the documents on his desk."

I picked up the telephone. I called up Mrs. Daniels, and I said they were lost, and she said, "Hmm—"—thought a minute—"I think I can find them."

I think you know in those days most of the politicians wore those long, full-tailed cutaway coats.

And she said, "I am going up to his closet. I think they are in the right-hand rear tail of his spare cutaway coat."

And they were! We got them back.

So she did have a sixth sense as to where people had gone, and where people kept things.

LATTER-DAY SAINTS: CLEMMIE AND WINSTON

4 January 1944

In a letter addressed jointly to "Clemmie" Attlee and Winston Churchill, the President stated that according to a story in the *Deseret News* of Salt Lake City, "there is a definite link between Clemmie and the Mormons" and that Winston himself was "a sixth cousin, twice removed" of a founding father of the Mormon Church.[1]

THE PRESIDENT: All of this presents to me a most interesting study in heredity. Hitherto I had not observed any outstanding Mormon characteristics in either of you—but I shall be looking for them from now on.

[1] The President to Clement Attlee and Winston Churchill, 4 January 1944, FDRL.

I have a very high opinion of the Mormons—for they are excellent citizens. However, I shall never forget a stop which my Father and Mother made in Salt Lake City when I was a very small boy. They were walking up and down the station platform and saw two young ladies each wheeling a baby carriage with youngsters in them, each about one year old. My Father asked them if they were waiting for somebody and they replied, "Yes, we are waiting for our husband. He is the engineer of this train." Perhaps this was the origin of the Good Neighbor Policy.

WHO DISCOVERED CARUSO?

19 January 1944

THE PRESIDENT: When I was in college, in my senior year, I went down with my roomate on one of those . . . German cruises down through the West Indies. And we got down to Caracas and stopped there. And my roommate and I went up to the clerk of the hotel and said, "What's doing tonight? We want to go to a café, some place where they have dancing." I don't know what they would call it today, but probably a different name.

And the clerk said, "Oh, you can't do that. You have got to go to the opera."

My roommate and I said, "We didn't come to Caracas to go to the opera."

He said, "But you must. Everybody is going to the opera, they are giving *Pagliacci.*" Well, I had been to the opera with my mother several times, I said, "I have never heard of *Pagliacci.*"

"But," he said, "the great artist is singing."

I said, "I don't care."

"But," he said, "It's Caruso."

I said, "I never heard of him," and yet at that time Caruso was considered the greatest tenor in all the world, he had sung at Caracas before, in Buenos Aires, in Rio and in Lima, I think. He was one of the great singers known to all South America.

So because there was nowhere else to go, we went to the opera. And he was perfectly marvelous.

After we got back to New York, I talked to some of my musical friends about Caruso and *Pagliacci,* but they had never heard of him. Years later, Caruso was taken on by the Metropolitan Opera Company in New York, and of course became the greatest tenor of all times. But I have always said that my roommate and I discovered Caruso.[1]

[1] Toast at a State Dinner for the President of Venezuela, 19 January 1944. *Public Papers and Addresses, 1944,* pp. 46–47.

THINK ABOUT THAT WHEN
YOU HAVE YOUR NEXT MARTINI!
6 May 1944

Towards the end of March, 1944, FDR was weakened by recurring bouts of fever. He then decided to "disappear" from Washington for a few weeks and had a restful vacation at "Hobcaw Barony"—the estate of financier Bernard Baruch located near Georgetown, South Carolina. On his last day at the "Barony," Roosevelt chatted with the representatives of the three major press services—Merriman Smith of the United Press, Douglas Cornell of the Associated Press, and Robert Nixon of International News Service.

THE PRESIDENT: One thing that strikes us all about this part of the country down here is the enormous amount of land that is vacant. I have made a number of drives about the country. I love the place—love going through the woods. . . . It's the general feeling of everybody that this part of the country will support a great many people . . . and . . . certain industries locally—like this thing that smells over here! [He was referring to a pulp mill in Georgetown.]

CORRESPONDENT: Can you smell it over here?

THE PRESIDENT: Yes, but don't put that in.

After the first night down here, "Pa" Watson came in to see me at breakfast-time.

I asked him, "Did you do that?"

He said, "What do you mean?"

I told him, "That odor."

He said, "I didn't do it"; and I told him it must have been him, his room is just overhead.

CORRESPONDENT: We bought three bottles of incense, but it only aggravated things.

THE PRESIDENT: They have promised to eliminate that smell after the war. This is the second such experience I have run into. At Campobello it was the same thing. In the morning when they light the fires in the factories at Eastport, the odor will knock you out of bed. They make fertilizer out of fishheads and tails—guano.

Speaking of smells, I want to say a word about Vermouth. It's something for you to think about, when you have your next Martini.

Some years ago, I was going down the Italian continent [*sic*], got to Turin. We rode out to an Italian camp, about six or eight miles out of town—there were two Italian generals in the car. We got out of town, and I smelled this awful thing.

"What is that?" I asked.

They said, "It's all right." Worst smell I ever smelled!

He said, "Vermouth."

We drove past it. Over in back of a small building there was a pile, where they did the last process of fermentation—a pile as high as a house —of decaying figs brought in from all parts of Italy and taken and thrown on this pile. Then they track them down. The pressure starts the fermentation. That is what Vermouth is made of. Think about that, when you have your next Martini!

MAYBE THE LIEUTENANT WANTED VEAL

6 May 1944

THE PRESIDENT: I have signed a number of bills and other regular papers. . . . Got a lot of things out. . . . The only things I have to sign are courts-martial.

Speaking of courts-martial, I want to tell you a story about a Marine court-martial case at Guantanamo.

You know a court-martial in any of the services is a very solemn affair. They had appointed down there a major general, a couple of colonels, two or three majors as members, and a judge advocate of the court. They had also appointed another officer to the defense.

The accused was a second lieutenant, a youngster who had, I think, been in the service six months or so. He had been sentenced to dismissal.

. . . It came on down to me. I picked it up to read it and the more I read of it, the more I laughed.

The youngster had gone out from Guantanamo—Guantanamo is a U.S. naval reservation surrounded by Cuba—he had taken a party out on patrol, to patrol around the edges of the eastern side of the reservation.

About two miles out, they ran across some cows. The cows obviously were strays. There was a good deal of question as to whether the cows were on the Cuban side or the American side. One calf was limping very badly. After a conversation some members of the patrol felt that this calf was suffering a great deal. That was a perfectly correct assumption. The second lieutenant told the sergeant that he would take the responsibility, that he thought the calf should be put out of its misery.

So the sergeant shot the calf.

Now, they happened to have in this patrol the company cook. The cook butchered the calf. The result was the whole company had veal for about three days. Perfectly delicious veal, butchered by the company cook!

The story came to the ears of the major general that one of his officers had shot a calf. The result was the kid got a court-martial—and all that a court-martial means in time of war. The court was held. The record built up into a pile of documents. It finally got to the Major General

Commandant. . . . They approved it. It was all lined up to ruin this kid's life—to dismiss him from the service. Maybe he did want the veal! But it was funny—the great question was about his decision whether or not this calf ought to be put out of its misery!

So I took the recommendation that had been prepared for my signature, reading: "Approved. The sentence will be carried into effect";— and instead of signing it I wrote thereon,

> The sentence is approved, but it is mitigated, so that in lieu of being dismissed the accused will be placed on probation for a year, subject to the pleasure of the President.
>
> This man must be taught not to shoot calves.
>
> Franklin D. Roosevelt

It went back to the Marine Corps Headquarters. And they were wild. They thought I was trying to be funny with the Marine Corps.[1]

[1] Perhaps FDR was influenced in reaching his decision by memories of his own experience in Germany many long years earlier. Little Roosevelt had offered an explanation for an action of his that was on a par with the ingenious defense put forth by the Marine second-lieutenant of Guantanamo. He had been riding his bicycle and had run over a goose. When he was "arrested" for the offense FDR explained that he did not actually run over the goose. "The goose really committed suicide by sticking its neck into the spokes of the wheel." William D. Hassett, *Off the Record with F.D.R.* (New Brunswick, 1958), p. 200.

GOOD OLD DAYS IN EUROPE
7 June 1944

THE PRESIDENT: . . . I traveled over a large part of Europe on a bicycle, without a passport. I never carried a passport.

And I came to a barrier across the road, and a man came out, yawning, and wanted to know where I came from and where I was going.

I told him I was an American; and he said, after a few minutes of a few, very simple questions, "Have you got enough money to live on?"

I said, "Yes. I have ten pounds on the handlebars of my bicycle."

Thereupon, he waved me through the barrier, and said, "Hope you have a good time."

There was a good deal of intermarriage, interchanging of ideas and friendship between the Nations of Europe then. Yet in the last fifty years that has all gone. It is a very sad thing about Europe, that that spirit has gone. It has become so nationalistic.[1]

[1] Toast at a State Dinner for the Prime Minister of Poland, 7 June 1944, *Public Papers and Addresses, 1944*, p. 162.

AND EVERYWHERE THE ADMIRAL WENT, THE "LOW" WAS SURE TO GO

15 August 1944

Here is a grand Roosevelt story. FDR was returning to the capital in a special train after over thirty days of travel that took him to California, Hawaii, the Aleutians, Alaska, and Washington. As the train rumbled through North Dakota, he sat with a few reporters and happily spun his tale of the little cloud.

THE PRESIDENT: Shortly after leaving Honolulu, clear blue sky, calm sea, no wind, there appeared over the horizon a cloud as small as a man's hand. It saw us and approached slowly.

It turned out to be one of those rather rare animals known as a "low." The party was on deck, and as soon as the "low" saw us it recognized Rear Admiral Wilson Brown, U.S.N., and headed straight for us.[1]

We cannot shake it off.

It smiled all over, circled us several times and took a position just off the stern. It followed us all night and the next day and the next.

After three more days, we reached Adak, where it went ashore and played happily in the wake of Admiral Brown. With it came wind and rain fog.

We all realized that it was a nice little cloud but to be accompanied everywhere by a "low" was getting to be monotonous. Its presence became so persistent that the tug boats were prevented by it from pulling us off the dock. In other words, it was an annoying "low."

Our expert said it would pass us to the eastward and finally when it went off to gambol on the horizon for a few minutes, we got under way and had only been headed for Kodiak for an hour or two when the little "low" turned up again from nowhere and accompanied us. All the way to Kodiak it hovered around us, and while it was kind enough to run away while we caught a fish, there it was back again all the rest of the day, and all the next day, and accompanied us in to Auk Bay.

By unanimous cursing, we persuaded it to go away while we caught some more fish, and the sun actually came out. But having transferred to a destroyer, Admiral Brown seemed to be somewhat worried, and sure enough his little "low" appeared again that evening. He was so glad to see it that it never left us. We think he fed it surreptitiously under the table.

It was with us all the way down the Inland Passage day after day, and actually followed us into the Puget Sound Navy Yard. We pleaded with the Admiral to say good bye and leave it there. He said he would do his best, and we think he did do his best, but to no avail.

In the late afternoon we went to Seattle and boarded the train, and to

[1] Rear Admiral Wilson Brown was Naval Aide to the President.

our horror the next morning after we woke up across the Cascade Mountains, there was the little "low" following us. It kept on going all the way into Montana and the following day across Montana and into North Dakota.

What can we do about it?

The trouble is that it has lots of friends in the party. For instance, it has encouraged Admiral McIntire[2] to use a new word with almost every sentence. If we cannot see the horizon, we are told it is an occluded front. It seems to me that is a very long word to apply to a little lamb or a little "low." Anna[3] and the girls had never seen an occlusion. They think it is just a nautical term for bad weather, and we tell them that it is just an old Navy custom.

So here we are approaching the Twin Cities, and we have got the bright idea that Admiral Brown should continue to feed his little "low" and bring it with us all the way to Washington. Washington needs a little "low" and we must never forget that Wilson had a little "low" and write a new children's book about it.

[2] Ross T. McIntire, Personal Physician to the President.

[3] FDR's daughter. The "girls" referred to were Grace Tully and Dorothy Brady, members of his personal secretariat.

A PERFECTLY GRAND EVENING

7 November 1944, Hyde Park.

The Presidential election of 1944 was over. The polls had closed and the returns had started coming in. It looked as though the Champ was well on the way to another victory. His Hyde Park friends took out a torchlight procession and FDR came out of his house to greet them.

THE PRESIDENT: I see some youngsters up a tree which reminds me of earlier days, when I wanted to get away from the discipline of the family, and I climbed that very tree up where that highest youngster is now, and I disappeared and I couldn't be found. And they got everybody —I think they got the fire department up trying to find me. And I realized that I was causing a good deal of commotion, so I said "Yoohoo," or something like that, and I came down.

Well, I remember my first torchlight parade right here in 1892— Cleveland's election. And I was asleep, or supposedly asleep, right up in this window, a little room at the head of the stairs; and I was listening, and I didn't know what was the matter—a queer light outside the window, with people coming up on farm wagons—before the days of the automobile. It was Hyde Park—a large part of it—coming down here to have a Democratic celebration.

And I got up and appeared down here in an old-fashioned nightgown of some kind, on this porch, and I wrapped up in an old Buffalo robe that came out of a wagon. And I had a perfectly grand evening.

... And then there are all kinds of people that I remember, which only very old people like myself can remember. And I remember, once upon a time, I was fascinated by old Dan Barrett's brewery. And Dan, after meeting the train, which came in about twice a day in those days, used to bring people down here in his old bus, and I would go out there and I would talk to Dan Barrett by the hour. Now we have got a young Dan Barrett and he is down here on this place, here on the right.

The reports that are coming in are not so bad . . . and it looks as if I will have to come back here on a train from Washington for four more years.[1]

[1] *Public Papers and Addresses, 1944–45,* pp. 413–14.

FDR IN IMPERIAL GERMANY

23 February 1945. Aboard the U.S.S. "Quincy," en route from Algiers to Newport News.

CORRESPONDENT: . . . do you think Germany and Japan in the foreseeable future ever should be permitted to re-arm?

THE PRESIDENT: No. I hope for armaments to be decreased all along the line, including even the Big Five.

CORRESPONDENT: How soon?

THE PRESIDENT: I am not a crystal gazer.

. . . I went to school in Germany under the old Emperor William I. The railroad employees were not in uniform—wore uniform caps. The school children were not in uniform, did not march all the time. But it was not a military-minded nation then. That was way back in 1888 or '89. I was in school off and on until 1896.

The young Kaiser came in in 1899. At the time I left Germany, the railroad employees all over Germany were in uniform. The school children were in uniform. They were taught to march. And if you were living in a boarding house and needed more coal you would call up Darmstadt, the provincial capital. By the time I left, you were calling up Berlin if you needed more coal. That made all the difference in the world. The government was more centralized. German family life was a decent family life. Gradually they got militaristic.

Now, if a nation can do that in fifty years, why couldn't you move in the opposite direction? Why can't you move in a non-militaristic method?[1]

[1] Apparently FDR enjoyed reminiscing about his boyhood years in Germany. According to Hassett, the President told Ex-Empress Zita of Austria on 11 September 1943 that in Germany he had once been arrested four times in one day: "once for running over a goose, once for carrying a bicycle into a railroad station, once for picking cherries by the roadside, and once for riding his bicycle into a forbidden area after sundown—a good total for one day." He also spoke of the "mania for regulation" that came over Germany under Kaiser Wilhelm II. William D. Hassett, *Off the Record with F.D.R.* (New Brunswick, 1958), p. 200.

III

NEW DEAL ECONOMICS WITHOUT TEARS

BEER

2 June 1933

CORRESPONDENT: Do you expect with the increase from revenue from beer, et cetera, that the budget might be balanced by the end of the fiscal year?

THE PRESIDENT: I haven't heard a thing on beer for three weeks or a month. I don't know how it is running now. About three weeks or a month ago I said they were a little ahead of their expectations, but I haven't heard of it recently.

CORRESPONDENT: We have been keeping up our end here.

THE PRESIDENT: I got word from a very old brewer friend of mine. He said, "For God's sake don't drink any of my beer until next September—it is terrible."

MONEY

16 June 1933

CORRESPONDENT: Mr. President, on the public works proposition, how long will [it] be before no one can come in and ask you something?

THE PRESIDENT: Oh, gosh; until all the money is gone.

RECOVERY THROUGH RUM

20 September 1933

CORRESPONDENT: Anything on the rum situation in the Virgin Islands? Some plan on to open a sugar refinery?

THE PRESIDENT: I will tell you. It is just one of those amusing things. . . . I have forgotten who the originator was, but it was somebody who recollected the fact that my great-great-grandfather had been in the sugar business in New York around 1790. Of course in those days the sugar business was a West Indian business entirely, and he asked me whether, as a side line, he [the great-great-grandfather] had sold rum; and I told him that in all probability he had, although the ancestral records do not show it one way or the other.

He had a sugar refinery in what is now Franklin Square, directly back of the old World Building, and his house was directly opposite the refinery.

Well, from that this individual said, "You know, in those days St. Croix rum used to be the drink." Of course, St. Croix is part of the Virgin Islands. Then he made this suggestion, that he could do something when the Eighteenth Amendment was repealed to restore the fine qualities of the old St. Croix rum and that that might be a solution for the economic ills of the Virgin Islands. . . . It would help them to restore their economic prosperity, so the Secretary of the Interior is looking into it.

CORRESPONDENT: It isn't necessary to age rum. It can be used almost immediately. I mean it isn't fusel oil.[1]

THE PRESIDENT: It is a very happy thought to age it, just the same!

[1] Inferior liquor that has been insufficiently distilled.

DISTRESS IN KENTUCKY

21 September 1933

FDR told reporters that the Agricultural Adjustment Administration would purchase supplies of foodstuffs and staples and that these would be distributed to the unemployed through the Federal Emergency Relief Administration headed by Harry Hopkins.

THE PRESIDENT: You see, here is another thing: The supply of clothing . . . has been actually inadequate in a great many places in relief work. As a matter of fact they have not had any supply of clothing. For instance, there is a story, off the record. You know Miss [Lorena A.]

Hickok? She went down, for Hopkins' department,[1] I think it was some-where around southeastern Kentucky. She got into one of those mining towns and came around a corner of an alley and started walking up the alley. There was a group of miners sitting in front of the shacks, and they pulled down their caps over their faces. As soon as she caught sight of that she walked up and said, "What is the matter? Why are you pulling your caps down for?"

[They said], "Oh, it is all right."

"Why pull your caps down?"

They said, "It is a sort of custom to pull caps down because so many of the women have not enough clothes to cover them."

Now, we are going to buy a lot of cotton and have it processed and provide clothes. . . .

[1] Harry Hopkins, Administrator, Federal Emergency Relief Administration.

BARTER AGREEMENT

12 January 1934

Even an obtuse topic like a commodity agreement was no barrier to Rooseveltian mirth.

THE PRESIDENT: I think if you were to go and see Assistant Secretary Moore[1] you could get a story out of him. I got this at the Diplomatic dinner last night. You know there has been some discussion between us and Great Britain about swapping pork for liquor, and apparently Mr. Moore sent a very, very good Virginia ham to the British Ambassador and he got back a bottle of Scotch.

17 January 1934

CORRESPONDENT: Are you seeking any understanding with Great Britain on the currency and monetary program? . . . Or on trade?

THE PRESIDENT: No. The only thing I know about is the big whiskey deal.

CORRESPONDENT: Is the whiskey coming in?

THE PRESIDENT: Yes, and the pigs are going out.

[1] R. Walton Moore, Assistant Secretary of State.

THE RIGHT HAND AND THE LEFT FOOT

19 January 1934

FDR would talk seriously about a serious issue and the correspondents would listen most attentively. The President might wind up his solemn discourse with an impish crack that reporters could hardly have expected.

CORRESPONDENT: Has Roper[1] presented his report on stock exchange regulations?

THE PRESIDENT: He is bringing that in Monday, also the Securities Bill. . . . his Committee has been studying not only the stock exchange end but the securities end and the problem of the investment banker. For instance, a firm which is engaged in buying and selling securities, in other words, as a broker, is at the same time an investment banker, and at the same time runs an investment corporation. Now that kind of a firm has three functions and the question has come up as to how one firm can conduct all three functions at the same time without letting his right hand know what his left foot is doing.

[1] Daniel C. Roper, Secretary of Commerce.

PLEASE MAKE IT RAIN

9 May 1934

In a bid to raise farm prices the President authorized the ploughing under of every third row of cotton and the slaughter of several million pigs. He also initiated benefit payments to farmers for undertaking a reduction of acreage under cultivation. Farmers welcomed these measures but were worried about the possibility of a drought. A gentleman farmer from Waterloo, New York, complained that Roosevelt was apparently not doing his best with the "climate controller." "Please make it rain," he pleaded. "I have all my spring fitting done, all my oats (not wild ones) are sown. Now if the Administration does not make it rain my clover will not grow . . . and my little pigs need it. Please tell the weather man down there to use a little more discretion in his distribution of the sunshine."

THE PRESIDENT: You are right about the rain but the fault lies with Wall Street. They watered their stocks so liberally in past years that the Almighty is trying to average up the majority by withholding rain. Also He is trying to get even with you for raising little pigs! Don't you know that little pigs are unpopular with the Big Bad Wolf in the White House?[1]

[1] George C. Sweet to the President, n.d.; the President to Sweet, 9 May 1934, FDRL.

STOP BUILDING THOSE SILLY DAMS
3 October 1934

THE PRESIDENT: Not long ago a very important businessman of New York City came to see me to talk about the one thing that lay nearest to his heart, the balancing of the budget. Well, I told him I thought it was pretty important, and that we were going to get it balanced next year. Then I asked him if he had ever read the budget. He said, "No." I asked him how much he would save in the coming year if he could and he said, "Oh, two or three billions of dollars." And then came my question which always stumps people of his kind. I said, "Just where would you cut expenses?" He hemmed and hawed, and he hemmed and hawed some more; but he couldn't tell me where he would save money, although he was saying to the Nation, through the newspaper he owned, that it was perfectly simple to do it.

Well, I pressed him on it and finally he said this: ". . . you can stop building, right away, these silly public works like Fort Peck and the Grand Coulee and Bonneville Dam. Stop all this flood control business. Stop all this irrigation business."

When I suggested to him that his program would bring terrific hardship to several million families of Americans, he finally told me what his real philosophy of life was. He said, "All this business of helping people is ruining the country. Look at my taxes. I have to pay half of all my income in Federal, State and local taxes."

I happened to know what the gentleman's income was—four hundred thousand dollars a year. And that "poor" man thought that he was going to the poor house because, after paying his taxes, he only had two hundred thousand dollars a year left.[1]

[1] Informal remarks at Fort Peck, Montana, 3 October 1934, *Public Papers and Addresses, 1934*, pp. 397–98.

CRYSTAL BALL
12 October 1934

Correspondents could never be sure when FDR would throw in a big word or twist a word to suit his fancy.

CORRESPONDENT: Will there be any immediate or near future change in the gold policy?

THE PRESIDENT: I am neither a prestidigitator—

CORRESPONDENT: Yes, sir.

THE PRESIDENT: —nor an astrologist. Let it go at that.

THE COST OF LIVING

31 October 1934

CORRESPONDENT: Mr. President, can we take it, then, that you expect a continuing increase in the cost of living between January first and July first?

THE PRESIDENT: It will go up substantially, without much question. . . .

CORRESPONDENT: The averages for the first three weeks show rather surprising declines.

THE PRESIDENT: Whose chart are you going by?

CORRESPONDENT: The National Fertilizer Association.

THE PRESIDENT: It will be interesting to see how that compares with the National Perfumeries Association.

SELF-LIQUIDATING PUBLIC DEBTS

31 October 1934

CORRESPONDENT: Is there anything you can tell us on the public works program for the next year or the following year?

THE PRESIDENT: Only what I have read in the papers.

CORRESPONDENT: The papers say 12 billion dollars.

THE PRESIDENT: Some say 12 and some say 10 and some say 5. You pays your money and takes your choice! In fact, it depends entirely on which paper you read. That reminds me. One man came in the other day and said, "I hear you have a very ambitious public works program, self-liquidating on a 20-year basis." I said, "That is absolutely true. They are planting some black walnut trees in certain areas and it takes them that long to mature."

DON'T CALL IT GRAFT

7 November 1934. Hyde Park.

Roosevelt acknowledged that there were defects in the administration of the relief program. He contended that most of them could be traced to "the human element."

THE PRESIDENT: You take this morning, I was talking to Jim Townsend, who is County Chairman here. He knows this county extremely well.

I was talking to him about the people on relief in this county. Of course this was not from a political angle at all.

I said, "How many of them do you think are chiselers?"

"Well," he said, "I should say somewhere between 15 and 20 per cent."

I said, "So where are they?"

He said, "Here is where they come in: you will find in the relief office at Poughkeepsie that three or four of the girls employed there come from families who have plenty of money to get by with. The girls don't need relief. Then, they hired fourteen engineers and of the fourteen engineers only about three of them were engineers up against it."

I said, "Are there any more engineers up against it around here?"

He said, "Yes, there are lots of them." He told me about the eleven that could get by.

Then you get out into the towns and the human element comes into it. It does not make any difference whether it is a Democratic township or a Republican township. It comes through the supervisor and naturally they pick their friends first. It is a very difficult problem to handle as at present constituted.

Now, if that is true in Dutchess County, it is true in every state of the Union. It is not all Democratic and Republican politics, personal favoritism enters into it too. A great deal of personal favoritism. You will help your friends and build yourself up. The local fellow wants to be known as the man who hands out the jobs. It is perfectly natural.

. . . I said, "What is happening to the mental slant of those people on relief?"

"Well," he said, "it is bad, for the reason that if it is home relief, a grocery store order or cash, they will barely get by in their families; nobody works and they just bum around all day. There is nothing to do. It is very bad for them, obviously. We ought, if we can, to give them work."

I said, "How about work? A lot of them are on some kind of work."

"Well," he said, "I will give you an illustration. In the back part of the Town of Pleasant Valley here, they are putting in a mile of road. They are supposed to work 8 hours a day. Most of them work 5 days a week. But there is a general feeling on the part of everybody who sees that work that the people who are in charge of them almost give the order, 'Do not exert yourselves. Do not push yourselves. Spread it out as long as you can.' "

Now, that is a waste of money. They probably waste at least 50 per cent of the money spent for labor on that road. It is inefficient. . . . The result is that most of the relief money spent . . . won't come back to the nation in the form of permanent improvements.

. . . The objective, therefore, is twofold—threefold. First, to eliminate —don't call it graft—but to eliminate the 10, 15 or 20 per cent of the people who are on relief and who ought not to be on relief. The second thing is to put the money either into the kind of thing that will add to the national wealth even if does not come back to the Government or, secondly, into the kind of public works that will liquidate themselves and have the money returned to the Government so that it can pay off the debt incurred when it was borrowed.

Now, that involves a tremendous search problem, . . . and everybody is working on it.

JOE SAYS IT IS ILLEGAL

28 November 1934

THE PRESIDENT: Joe Day in New York is a very old friend of mine, and one of the best real estate men in the City of New York. He and I have been carrying on a very interesting correspondence. He started off by telling me that it was terrible for the Federal Government to go into slum clearance. He thought that private capital ought to do it.

I said, "Joe, this is all very well, but you have not eliminated the slums in New York."

He wrote back, "Give us a chance, I think we can."

I said, "At what cost per room per month?"

He said, "You have me there, we cannot do it for less than $12 per room per month."

I said, "How many families are in the City of New York that cannot afford to pay that?"

He came back and said, "We hope that with the return of prosperity there will be more."

I said, "That isn't any answer to my question!"

Now, the very simple fact is that in the City of New York there are probably a million people—there are probably two hundred thousand families alone—that is probably a rough guess—whose earning capacity brings them under the thousand dollar a year class. They probably ought not to pay, out of that thousand dollars or less, more, let us say, than a hundred and fifty, a hundred and forty or a hundred and fifty dollars a year for their rent. They cannot afford it because they have to eat and clothe themselves.

Now what does that mean if the cheapest rooms in the City of New York rent for $12 a room. That means that the whole family can afford to live only in one of those $12 rooms and no other room. They have to cook, to eat, and everything else in one room. If, on the other hand, you can get them rooms for $6 a month, the family can use two rooms.

What is the result? They are living today under the most terrible conditions. . . . They are able to get, on the average, perhaps two rooms at $5 or $6 a room. There is no sanitation, no light, no nothing. They are pretty terrible living conditions.

Now Joe says, "We are licked. Private capital could not afford to build for $5 or $6 a room. That is not enough."

That is his answer, "We are licked."

CORRESPONDENT: Is he convinced?

THE PRESIDENT: Yes, but he says that the Government ought not to go in. . . . He says it is not the prerogative of the Government. It is unconstitutional. Like the TVA. It is illegal. He says the thing, over a period of years, will work itself out some way!

STOPPING COLLISIONS ON A BAD CROSSING

9 January 1935

The Supreme Court had invalidated the "hot oil" provisions of the National Industrial Recovery Act. FDR argued that while the provisions might have been unsatisfactorily drafted, they had served the public interest.

CORRESPONDENT: Would you care to comment on the Court decision on the Oil Section of the National Recovery Act?

THE PRESIDENT: I think we might probably discuss the oil decision from the point of view of a parallel which occurred to me when thinking it over yesterday, in connection with a certain village in up-state New York that had a very bad crossing. There were two main highways there and an awful lot of people were being killed at that crossing. Under the village law that applied in this particular village the question arose whether they could employ a constable or not. Obviously something had to be done to prevent all of this loss of life at this crossing.

So they got the District Attorney of the county and the County Judge, and the Village Attorney to tell them whether they could have a constable at that crossing or not. They were advised that by passing a certain resolution in the Village Board they could get this constable. They did and the constable went on duty, and they passed another village ordinance resolution in the Town Board and put up red and green signal lights to implement [*sic*] the constable—and didn't have any more accidents. But one fellow got arrested for passing the light and took it to court.

After about a year and a half the court said, "Why, this particular resolution that was passed by the Village Council is badly drawn. It isn't constitutional or legal under the village law, and you have had that man on duty now for a year and a half illegally." They pointed out at the same time that it was perfectly possible to correct the particular resolution of the Village Council, which had been drawn up at the best advice they could get.

So the village went ahead and corrected the resolution and the constable stayed on duty. Of course, the net result was that they had had a year and a half of life-saving to their credit and yet the way was pointed out to them to accomplish their objective according to correct interpretation of the law by the court, and everybody was happy.

. . . Now, of course, you and I know that in the long run there may be half a dozen more court decisions on oil before they get the correct language, before they get things straightened and according to correct constitutional methods. . . . That's about the beginning of it and the end of it. It is just like stopping collisions in that particular crossing in that particular village.

AN IMPORTANT FINANCIAL ANNOUNCEMENT

25 January 1935

Assuming a very solemn air the President opened the press conference with a statement.

THE PRESIDENT: Well, I have a piece of very good news for you, a very important piece of news, something you are all deeply interested in and I might add that I owe my interest in this subject entirely to the interest that you gentlemen have taken in it. I have just written a letter to the Speaker, transmitting for the consideration of the Congress a supplemental estimate of appropriation for this fiscal year, to remain available for the following fiscal year also, for the Department of Agriculture in the amount of $480,000 for the control of the screwworm!

ECONOMIC EXPERTS

8 April 1935. On board the Presidential special train travelling from Jacksonville, Florida, to Washington.

Some of the White House correspondents were so much at ease with Roosevelt that they could swap stories with him just as they would with a neighbor.

On this occasion Roosevelt had recounted in a deliberately complicated fashion a story on interest rates that a newspaper publisher had once told him.

CORRESPONDENT: There is an interesting story to go along with that.

When the Hoover administration started to loosen up the gold restrictions, we went down to see [Secretary of the Treasury Andrew] Mellon and he said that it would not be a Lombard loan. Somebody said, "What is a Lombard loan?" Then he thought and he went off into a 20-minute explanation but nobody knew what he was talking about. Then somebody said, "We asked you about that Lombard." He did not explain it any better so they went in to see Ogden [Mills, Under Secretary of the Treasury] and, boy, did he go into it! What Andy said was child's play. But they still did not know what a Lombard loan was. They tried some of the wise men on the Hill without success, and so, finally, they had to go and write about this new bill. All they knew was that it was not going to be a Lombard loan, so they went over and picked up a big dictionary and it said that a Lombard loan is a loan made on any kind of security. That is all it meant, and they had gone all over town.

THE PRESIDENT: Well, that goes along with the average financial story which is written. I have never seen a financial story yet that made sense. . . . I have been reading a lot of financial literature on the trip and it really is awfully interesting. I brought down several books by English economists and leading American economists and there are two things that stand out. I suppose I must have read different articles by fifteen different experts. Two things stand out: The first is that no two of them agree, and the other thing is that they are so foggy in what they say that it is almost impossible to figure out what they mean. It is jargon, absolute jargon.

THE BEAUTIFUL THEORY

31 May 1935

On 27 May 1935 the Supreme Court, by an unanimous decision, had invalidated the National Industry Recovery Act. Many of Roosevelt's opponents hailed the decision enthusiastically. At his press conference FDR spoke at considerable length about the philosophy and accomplishments of the National Recovery Administration and challenged the contention that business could be depended upon to regulate itself in the public interest.

THE PRESIDENT: But fundamentally it comes down to this: You and I know human nature. In the long run can voluntary processes on the part of business bring about the same practical results that were attained under NRA? Can they do this? I mean, the good results? Of course there have been some bad ones. But I mean the good results. Can it be done by voluntary action on the part of business. Can we go ahead as a nation with the beautiful theory, let us say, of the Hearst press: "At last the rule of Christ is restored. Business can do anything it wants and business is going to live up to the golden rule so marvelously that all of our troubles are ended." . . . It is a school of thought that is so delightful in its naïvete!

THE BLUE EAGLE

12 July 1935

Roosevelt's sense of humor did not desert him even when he had to haul down the Blue Eagle, the emblem of the National Recovery Administration.

CORRESPONDENT: What is this? [Indicating an object on the President's desk.]

THE PRESIDENT: That is the new Blue Eagle. It just came out of an egg and we do not know who laid the egg.

THE THRIFTY PEOPLE

31 July 1935

THE PRESIDENT: There are a few things yesterday that come out clearly that I think are of some interest. They seem to be taken from the records of the Treasury. . . . For instance, it appears that the 58 thriftiest people in the United States—and of course we are all in favor of thrift, the thriftier you are the nearer you will come to being included among the 58—in 1932 they were all people so thrifty that they had a million dollars income a year or more and in 1932 they paid no tax to the Federal Government whatever on 37 per cent of their net income. . . . On 37 per cent of their net income they escaped taxation altogether, largely because the investments were in municipal or state or Government tax-exempt bonds. . . . Furthermore, it turned up in the figures that one family in this country had 197 family trusts. They are a very thrifty family. . . . I just jotted these things down because they seemed rather interesting. . . .

CORRESPONDENT: Won't that tend to increase the number of such trusts in the future if there is no provision against it in the bill?

THE PRESIDENT: It could. It is a form of tax avoidance. There is a very great distinction between tax evasion and tax avoidance. Tax avoidance means that you hire a $250,000 fee lawyer and he changes the word "evasion" into the word "avoidance."

THE PROFESSOR

4 January 1936

FDR told the correspondents that he would read a few pages of the Budget Message and explain the major issues.

THE PRESIDENT: This is just a family party. I think we should go through in an orderly way, the first few pages that describe the high points and then if anybody wants to ask any questions, Dan Bell[1] is here and will be able to answer them. I am a little bit like the professor who told his class, "I know very little about this but you know less." From personal experience I know that 70 per cent of you, at the maximum, know the difference between a dollar and a dime, so I might as well go through with it.

[1] Daniel W. Bell, Assistant to the Secretary of the Treasury on financial and accounting matters.

GOLD!

24 January 1936

CORRESPONDENT: . . . there is also some discussion up there [on the Hill] that the Government is going to establish a free gold market, whatever that is.

THE PRESIDENT: I think it sounds grand. . . . I think we will be all glad to go into a free gold market and help ourselves, if it is really free. Is there any catch in it?

$10 A DAY IS GRAND, BUT....

14 February 1936. Press conference for editors of business periodicals.

FDR contended that the people who harped on problems supposedly created by rising wage rates were failing to tell the whole story.

THE PRESIDENT: Heavens, when you pay $10 a day to the carpenter, that is awful! But how many days a year is he employed? That is a thing that has to go with it. . . . Well, a hundred days a year at $10 a day is not too much money for him at the end of the year.

What we have never worked out either, and what we want from all of you people, frankly, is the realization that this thing can be worked

out . . . without calling people names. Don't call the union names. I go
back to my old Navy experience. In those days we had what we called
sheet metal workers and they were getting what was, for those days, a
very high rate. They were getting $6 a day and it was not any more
skilled work than that of a machinist.

I said, "Why are you getting $6 a day?"

And they proved that they were only working a hundred days in the
Navy Yard a year.

The criterion on the labor question is not merely the hourly rate or
the day rate. We have to get away from that thought. It is how much a
man has taken into his pocketbook during the year.

You take the automobile industry: In the spring of 1934, when we
almost had the strike out in Detroit, . . . we got those boys in; they were
all young men in automobile factories who had been elected to represent
the men. They were not, any of them, old-fashioned professional leaders.
They did not know particularly well how to handle themselves.

I looked around and saw a boy about 35 and I said to myself, "That
boy has been in the Army or Navy." So I sat up and said, "Were you in
the war?"

"Yes, sir."

I said, "What were you in?"

"The Marines, sir."

"Were you under me?" I said.

"Yes, sir."

"Now," I said, "what are you?"

"Machinist, first class, sir."

Imagine a labor leader saying, "sir"!

I said, "What do you get now?"

"Dollar and a quarter an hour."

I said, "That is pretty good. At eight hours a day that is $10 a day?"

"Yes, sir."

I said, "Well, that is pretty good pay, isn't it?" I said, "How many
days did you work last year?"

"Sixty-seven, sir."

I said, "You only made $670 last year in an automobile plant in
Detroit?"

He said, "Yes, sir."

I said, "Own your own house?"

"No, sir; I have lost it."

"How much had you paid on it?"

"$2,000."

I said, "Then you couldn't keep up the payments on it and you lost
your house?"

"Yes, sir."

$670 a year! $10 a day is grand but forget that. The question is: How much did he get at the end of the year?

And then I got back to Chrysler and others and I said, "Listen, I have got some figures. How much was the average received by the automobile employee in Detroit in the year 1933?"

They said, "We do not know."

I said, "Well, I know. The average received by the automobile employee was exactly $690 in the year 1933. Well, American families cannot live on $690."

I got them to study the thing . . . and it has improved things very distinctly. This year we have them up to an average wage received for the year of $980. . . . So I set them a criterion to shoot for, of $1,250 a year average.

THE DISMAL SCIENCE
19 December 1936

Professor Joseph A. Schumpeter, the noted economist of Harvard University, informed Roosevelt that a dinner was being planned in honor of another veteran economist, Charles Taussig.

THE PRESIDENT: Thirty-six long years ago I began a more or less intensive study of economics and economists. The course has continued with growing intensity, especially during the past four years.

As a result I am compelled to admit—or boast—whichever way you care to put it—that I know nothing of economics and that nobody else does either!

This twofold assertion I am confident that Professor Taussig will be the first to approve and endorse.[1] . . . .

[1] The President to Joseph A. Schumpeter, 19 December 1936, FDRL.

THE KIDS WHO RAISED PERFECT CAIN IN TEACHER ROOSEVELT'S CLASS
15 April 1937

The growing militancy of Labor manifesting itself in the form of sit-down strikes in a number of places had evoked criticism from many editors. Asked to define his attitude towards the "epidemic," FDR responded with a story that was a plea for a patient, friendly approach towards Labor and a readiness to work out reasonable settlements of disputed issues.

CORRESPONDENT: We have had an epidemic of sit-down strikes and we still have an epidemic of smaller sit-down strikes at present. . . . Don't you think it would have been helpful if there had been an expression from you as to the sit-down strike? Would you like to inform us on that?

THE PRESIDENT: Yes. A great many years ago . . . I took a class of boys of the age of fourteen or fifteen and the first day in class—I had never taught a class before—these boys started raising Cain with me and I stood up behind the desk and I said, "Don't do that!" and to the next fellow, "Stand up in the corner," and to the next fellow who stuck a pin into the gentleman in front of him, I gave two demerits. Well, I did not get order in that classroom and for two or three days that class raised perfect Cain with me. The headmaster got onto it and he sent for me and he said, "You are pretty young in the game." He said, "When you go back in the class, take a pen or pencil and when they start throwing spitballs or sticking pins into each other, let them see you see them and jot down a name. When class is over, send for them one by one and say, 'Listen, son, you are trying to get into college. I don't give a continental damn whether you get into college or not. I am here to help you get into college, if you want to get into college. I don't mind your throwing spitballs but there are a lot of other boys in the class who want to get into college and your throwing spitballs is keeping them from achieving what is their ambition.' Reason with them and teach them, one by one, why they are hurting themselves and not you by raising Cain in the class."

Well, I tried it out and after a week of it I had the most orderly class in school because it was order based on a knowledge of the consequences, a knowledge of what it would do to them and a knowledge of what it would do to their fellow students. I never had any trouble after that.

Is the allegory sound? Incidentally, they are beginning to realize in an organization like the Automobile Workers, who have an experienced mentality of a fourteen or fifteen year-old, they are beginning to realize two things: first, that what they are doing is illegal—no question about that. They say so themselves—"It is a misdemeanor"—and they have been told by their representatives that that is not nearly as serious an offence as what some of the [corporation] lawyers have been doing ever since the Wagner Labor Relations Act went through. They [employers] have been receiving from the Chamber of Commerce of the United States, the National Manufacturers' Association and Liberty League lawyers pamphlets saying, "This [Wagner] Act is unconstitutional. Disregard it." Disregard a Federal statute! The boys . . . out in Michigan [automobile workers], they have been told it is not nearly as serious to trespass on somebody's property—that is a misdemeanor—as it is to violate a Federal statute.

You see what they have been taught; they have been taught the wrong thing. However, they are beginning to realize that a misdemeanor is a wrong thing and they are beginning to realize that sit-down strikes are damned unpopular and finally they will realize that labor cannot get very far if it makes itself unpopular with the bulk of the population of the country.

It will take some time, perhaps two years, but that is a short time in the life of a nation and the education of a nation.

NEVER LOUD

13 July 1937

CORRESPONDENT: Mr. President, what is your reaction to the House overriding your veto on the Farm Credit Bill?

THE PRESIDENT: How do you mean "reaction"?

CORRESPONDENT: Do you have any?

THE PRESIDENT: Oh, no; I never have reactions. Out loud, anyway.

MUCH AS I LOVE YOU....

10 August 1937

Roosevelt indicated that in view of declining prices he could not support a program of crop loans simply on the hope "that next January there is going to be some kind of better security behind the loan than there is today."

THE PRESIDENT: For instance, . . . suppose Earl [Godwin] came in and said to me, "I am making ten thousand dollars a year now but I want you to lend me a hundred thousand dollars."

CORRESPONDENT Godwin: Fine!

THE PRESIDENT: Yes, right. I would say, "That is fine, but I don't know whether on a ten thousand dollar salary . . . you are good for a hundred thousand dollar loan." And he would say to me, "I have got an awfully good prospect of getting a twenty-five thousand dollar job in next January." Well, I would say, "Have you a contract?"

He would then say, "No, I have a hope." And I would say, "As much as I love you, I cannot lend you a hundred thousand dollars on a hope."

Now, that is a pretty good illustration of my position on crop loans.

"IT IS A PIP"

15 October 1937

Some newspapers had carried reports concerning a slump in the stock market. At the press conference a reporter who apparently had been asked by his office to write a story on Roosevelt's reaction to the slump stood up with a piece of paper in his hand. An aide persuaded the reporter to hand over the note to the President who read it.

THE PRESIDENT: I think it is a pip. This is a Sunday piece. This is grand. That is what is called a psychological story to find out whether the slump in the market bothers me.

If he wants a psychological story he should hire Mark Sullivan[1] and then Mark can tell him all about it from the way I raise my voice or whether the tone of my voice denotes internal anger or not. I think Mark has been a scream lately as an expert on facial expression and tone of voice.

CORRESPONDENT: In connection with the market slump, have you read Winthrop Aldrich's[2] speech?

THE PRESIDENT: I haven't yet.

CORRESPONDENT: It is not long. He attributes the break largely to unwise and inconsistent legislation. Do you care to say anything about it?

THE PRESIDENT: Not on the record, but I will tell you an off-the-record story. . . . On the trip out West, about half-way across, I got a three page telegram from—I don't know that I should not tell you his name—it was Clarence Woolley, head of the American Radiator Company. He was upset about the stock market. In his judgment there was one thing to do immediately, and that was to reduce margin requirements. He went on for two pages about that and then he ended up with something like this: "As you know, I am not speaking for the big speculators, I am not even speaking for the medium-sized speculators, I am not speaking for any speculators. I am talking about the little man, the small investors, the people who are scattered all over the country, little bits of investors, the people you are most interested in, the kind of people who are carrying little brokerage accounts from ten to twenty thousand dollars."

CORRESPONDENTS: The paupers! . . .

CORRESPONDENT: Those on relief!

THE PRESIDENT: I think it is one of the best psychological stories I know, the attitude of those fellows who are thinking in certain terms—ten to twenty thousand dollars, poor little fellow!

---

[1] Columnist for the *New York Herald Tribune*, who was frequently critical of FDR and his policies.

[2] President of the Chase National Bank.

WHOM ARE THEY AFRAID OF?

21 December 1937

THE PRESIDENT: A fellow came in to see me from Philadelphia a little while ago. He has an exceedingly successful manufacturing business and he pays good wages. He operated under a collective bargaining system with great success. I said to him, "What do you think about the problem of raising the purchasing power of the people in this country in interstate industries that are below a decent level?"

He said, "I am absolutely in favor of a minimum wage law."

I asked him, "How about maximum hours?"

"I am absolutely in favor of preventing unholy hours."

I said, "Then you would be in favor of a national wages and hours bill?"

He said, "Yes."

I said, "Is that partly because you think it would prevent the South from competing with you?"

He said, "Oh, no; paying a living wage in the South isn't going to hurt the South, because by paying a little more they will get an equivalent increase in efficiency, and I think every industrialist, including most southerners, agree to that."

I said, "That is very interesting; so you are for a wages and hours bill?"

"Yes."

I said, "If I get you fifteen or twenty minutes on a national hook-up, will you tell that to the country?"

He said, "Oh, no, I couldn't!"

I said, "Why?"

He said, "My directors wouldn't let me."

I said, "In other words, a case of fear."

He said, "Yes, frankly, it is a case of fear—not fear of the Government but fear of my own associates."

Three days later a friend of mine from New England, who manufactures a kind of tools to be sold in country stores—screwdrivers and such things, rather heavy, substantial tools—came in. Most of his trade is in the rural districts in this country. I said, "How does your business fluctuate with crop prices?"

He said, "It fluctuates with them absolutely, up and down. The better the prices, the more I sell in the farming areas."

I said, "Are you in favor of stabilizing crop prices to keep them from dropping so low that the country people have no purchasing power?

He said, "I am in favor of a crop bill."

I said, "If I got you fifteen minutes on a Yankee network, will you say that over the radio?"

"My God," he said, "how could I do that? I would lose my friends! In other words, fear—fear of my friends, not fear of the Federal Government, of course not."

That is the psychology; and that psychology has been not only inculcated but fostered. . . .

"I NEVER THOUGHT OF THAT, MR. PRESIDENT"
4 March 1938

THE PRESIDENT: One of the objectives [of the Administration] is increased purchasing power for the people. . . . Some of my friends, who are in special lines of business, fine people, honest people, have come in to me and talked to me. They are people I have known by their first names for years, and I say to them, "By the way, what is your thought on the problem of the sharecropper and the tenant-farmer? I am sort of stumped by that but I think we ought to do something. What do you think we ought to do?"

Well, I have tried that on a good many people and the invariable answer from these perfectly fine businessmen I have talked to has been this: "What do you mean, Mr. President? What do you mean by the sharecropper problem?"

Well, I have explained to them and repeated and said, "What do you think we ought to do?"

The invariable answer has been, "I don't know anything about it. I have never thought of it."

And then I have said to them, "We have fifteen or twenty million Americans in this country who today have no purchasing power. There are fifteen or twenty million Americans falling into that category. They are farm tenants, sharecroppers. You fellows are making things, all kinds of things, automobiles, hardware, clothing, all the things that you see in a country store. Aren't you interested in giving those prospective, possible customers some purchasing power for the things you make?"

And then they have said to me, "Why, Mr. President, I have never thought of that. I never thought of that."

Today people are beginning to think of that. And that is the most hopeful thing at the present time. The most hopeful thing at the present time is that we are getting people to think about the rounded problem of Government and of the people of the country instead of just thinking along their own special line of business.

In that way, also, I am encouraged to think that we will get away, more and more, from what we call the pressure groups in the country, small groups coming down here with great vociferation and very often putting through legislation which is beneficial only to one particular group.

ONLY IN LATIN

29 March 1938

CORRESPONDENT: Any comment on the Supreme Court decision on the Public Utilities Holding Company Act?

THE PRESIDENT: No. I would have to do it in Latin if I do it at all. . . .

CORRESPONDENT: We will take a chance on it.

THE PRESIDENT: Just because you went to Notre Dame does not mean you know Latin.

THE "YES, BUT —" ATTITUDE

8 April 1938

At this press conference for editors and publishers of trade papers FDR charged that inadequate support was forthcoming from industry and business for programs like flood control and soil conservation aimed at protecting the nation's natural resources. He added that industry's attitude towards his policies relating to agriculture and to labor was neither helpful nor constructive.

THE PRESIDENT: What I miss in the trade papers, as I do in 85 per cent of the daily press, is any positive approval of any of these things that are intended to save the nation's capital. I find in what might be called "the opposition press" of all kinds the "yes, but —" attitude. They will say, "Oh, yes, we are in favor of flood control but we do not like this way of doing it. We would rather have someone else doing it." "Soil erosion? Oh, yes, it is a fine thing to have in this country but we object to the use of money for it."

With soil erosion goes the . . . very large business, the agricultural business, in which thirty or forty million people are engaged. . . . In that particular business, the farming business, nobody can have any permanent purchasing power for the things that your industries produce, if they have two dollar wheat one time and thirty cent wheat another time. You cannot have real purchasing power in the South if you have thirty cent cotton one time and four or five years after that you have four or five cent cotton. It just does not make any sense. It throws people out of work in the industries if the farming population cannot buy their goods. It means unemployment and the Government has to spend a hell of a lot of money for relief, and, if that sort of thing continues in this country, you are going to make for radicalism.

. . . That is why we have tried to get some kind of control over the big swings of crop prices. . . . I don't get from industry active, two-fisted support for such legislation. Now, that is my complaint. I do not get two-fisted support. If they had a better idea, it would be fine, but the people who oppose a crop control bill do not propose any alternative. It is like a typical editorial in the *New York Times*: "Oh, yes, we are in favor of maintaining good prices for crops but this bill is terrible. It is regimentation of the farmer." Period, end of the paragraph, end of the story!

Now, that is just plain unintelligent. It is just plain unintelligent and it makes for radicalism. Do you get that?

Now, come to some of the other things. On wages and hours, again take any one of four or five dozen big papers. "Oh, yes, we are in favor of good wages, but the Wages and Hours Bill, that is unthinkable." All right, I had one in the other day and I said, "I just read your editorial and that is just what you said. Now, I will give you three examples: one, a little factory in New England, paying girls four and a half or five dollars a week."

He said, "Well, conditions compel it."

I said, "When you had NRA, those girls were getting eleven dollars a week and the industry seemed to survive and the girls had purchasing power."

"Yes," he said, "that is right."

Well, was it bad when everybody was paying eleven dollars a week to those girls? No, it worked pretty well.

Well, number two: Down in the South there is a little old cotton factory that has spindles that date back to 1880, or something like that. A little group of people in the South found this mill in New England which had been closed for a couple of years during the period of 1927 and 1928, when most of the cotton mills in New England closed—it was in the 1929 panic. This little group bought all of those New England spindles that were already fifty years old and they moved them down to Georgia. They got an old factory and started up. Well, of course it is highly, completely inefficient. That type of factory ought not to be in existence. Well, they have managed to hang on by their eyelids since that by paying four and five dollars a week to the operators in the mill. . . , and they are going on, competing with properly equipped, modern mills that pay good wages.

. . . Let us take your lumber people in the South. . . . They spend, the Southern Pine Association, they spend thousands of dollars advertising all through the South and what does the advertisement read? It says, "Farmers to arms!" Now, you know it is not so good: "Farmers to arms!" They then say, "if this terrible Wage and Hours Bill goes through, you farmers will have to pay for your field labor a minimum of three dollars a day." Of course, there has never been any thought of including field labor in the Wages and Hours Bill.

And then, in the women's magazines and papers, they have full-page ads, "Housewives beware! If the Wages and Hours Bill goes through, you will have to pay your negro girl eleven dollars a week." Of course, you know if you come from the South, you can employ lots of excellent domestic help in the South for board and lodging and three or four dollars a week.

No law ever suggested intended a minimum wages and hours bill to apply to domestic help.

Now, that is an industry which is doing that advertising through trade papers. That is a pretty serious indictment. I don't bring these things out in the public press; I am just talking in the family, to a family group like this.

Now, why can't industry come out as a whole and furnish positive help in getting a reasonable floor and a reasonable roof? . . . It is always holding back. They say, "Yes, I am in favor of the principle but —". How many people really mean that—that they are in favor of the principle? I am beginning to be from Missouri! [1]

[1] Missouri's nickname is the "Show-Me State."

MILLIONAIRES IN SEARCH OF LOOPHOLES
8 April 1938

FDR often expressed indignation over the manner in which several wealthy men successfully practised "tax avoidance," taking advantage of every conceivable loophole in the law. In this press conference he bluntly asked editors and publishers of trade papers why they had neither condemned such practices nor given support to the Administration's proposals to promote equity in the incidence of taxation.

THE PRESIDENT: Take the question of taxes. I will give you a couple of very simple propositions to think over: Today it is the national policy, whether we like it or not—it is generally accepted by the people and you will never be able to change it—to maintain a graduated tax upon personal incomes. . . . Now, that being so, have I had any help from industry when I have sought to eliminate abuses of that principle? How many of your papers supported me last year when I tried to eliminate the Bahamas corporation, the incorporation of yachts, the incorporation of farms, et cetera and so on? Did any of you people come out and say, "By gosh, the President is dead right on that." These fellows are evading the law, perhaps not the letter of the law because it is awfully hard to draw a law that has no legal loopholes, but did you give me any support in regard to evasion of the spirit of the law? I ask you that question very seriously.

A great lawyer in New York . . . discovered what looked like a legal way. . . . He goes down to the Bahamas and for two hundred and fifty dollars incorporates a life insurance company in the Bahamas. He is in the upper brackets. He and four or five other people in the upper brackets go to the president of the new company—who is a law clerk in this man's office—and say, "I want to insure myself for a million dollars."

The president says, "Fine, here is your policy. Please pay us a premium."

Of course the amount of the premium was high, $100,000.

"Here is my check. Now, Mr. President—my managing clerk—I would like to borrow a million dollars on that policy."

So he . . . borrows a million dollars on that at a high rate and deducts that from his personal income tax!

Another big man—his wife happens to be extremely wealthy—that is legal, mind you, perfectly legal, and they have a lot of children, seven or eight children. He has been Governor of his state, this man; he has been a public servant. His wife makes him trustee for . . . five or six million dollars for the children, but it is a revocable trust. She can end it tomorrow and get all the securities back. She turns the securities over to her husband and then proceeds to borrow the whole amount back on the securities and deducts the interest on that loan from her income tax, which means that instead of paying roughly, four or five hundred thousand dollars a year net, her net is only eighty or a hundred thousand dollars.

Now, there is no moral indignation among you businessmen, among you people who represent them. Why don't you get some moral indignation with respect to taxes that are progressive, that are established?

. . . On undistributed profits: I know two brothers who inherited a business and ran it together, jointly, for quite a while. It is a good business and its actual value is about, by general consent and agreement, $10,000,000. One of these brothers got to be fifty years old and, with a good deal of common sense, he said, "I am getting $250,000 a year out of this business. I am not a high liver. I only spend about $50,000. I guess I will get out. I want to retire, see the world and have a quiet time." So his brother, in a perfectly friendly way, buys him out and now owns the business. Of course he still owes the $5,000,000 he borrowed to pay to the brother who got out.

The brother who got out went to Scudder, Stevens and Clark and said, "I have got $5,000,000 in cash. Give me a recommended list of investments." They said, a good sound list, which contained some Governments and municipals and first mortgage real estate and first mortgage railroads and some preferred and common stock. It was a perfectly sound distribution of a five million dollar investment.

He, of course, had no way of escaping his personal income tax. They were all corporations, a hundred different corporations. His net was $200,000 a year from these investments. On that he had to pay about 50 per cent—he has to pay $100,000 in income taxes.

His brother is still engaged in the business. His business made $200,-000 over and above the proper amount that should be applied to depreciation and put into surplus, and so forth and so on. He had $200,000 as his profit. But he did not declare it. He only wanted to use $50,000, so he left $150,000 in the treasury of his company and declared a dividend of $50,000 to himself. The net result [was] that his tax was only $10,000.

How is that equitable? The money of both those fellows was working, there is no question about that. In one case it was working in one mill and in the other case it was working through one hundred different corporations.

Now, do I find, among businessmen, any effort to help me to equalize that sort of thing?

Taking the case of a very rich man that you all know—we won't mention any names—he has a corporation that was worth about $150,-000,000. He knew that he was going to die. He got to be—oh, I don't know—sixty-five years old and he knew that his expectancy of life was to have another five or ten years. His corporation had an absolutely adequate surplus to carry on the business. Everybody knew that and he admitted it.

He said to himself, "By gosh, I might die and then my estate will have to pay a pretty heavy inheritance tax."

Now, an Englishman doesn't do that—the Government does not let him, but we do. So he started in and he put, out of the earnings of his corporation, he accumulated for the next eight or nine years $3,000,000 of additional surplus, unnecessary surplus. He dies and his heirs have, let us say, ten certificates of stock representing the entire ownership of this corporation, a fifteen million dollar corporation. They have to find $3,000,000 in cash; so they take two of these certificates and sell them to the corporation for $3,000,000, taking the $3,000,000 to pay the inheritance tax. Now, the surplus is decreased by that amount but they still own eight certificates which represent 100 per cent of the ownership of the corporation.

In other words, that accumulation for the purpose of paying an inheritance tax was accumulated not on the personal income tax rate but on the—at that time—12½ per cent corporation tax rate. Is that fair?

Now, that is the kind of thing that we are trying to eliminate, and that is all. But do I get any help on it? . . . I want to emphasize that from industry itself, this Government is getting lip service and that is about all, in trying to correct unfair trade practices. That is where you people —if you leave out the politics entirely; it is not a question of politics, it is a question of Government—if you get behind us and help on the establishing of fair trade practices up and down the line, we would go some place.

ORGANIZING SOUTHERN WORKERS
21 April 1938

The Wagner Act required employers to refrain from any action to impede the unionization of workers. The National Labor Relations Board set up under the Act was authorized to conduct elections to determine the choice of workers in respect of a bargaining agent. The Board was also to serve as a watch-dog against unfair labor practices by employers. The Act was a major landmark in the history of American labor legislation. The conditions that the Act was intended to remedy were graphically depicted by FDR in the following story that he told members of the American Society of Newspaper Editors.

CORRESPONDENT: Why does the National Labor Relations Board regard itself as a bunch of prosecutors instead of a fact-finding body?

THE PRESIDENT: Well, that is a statement, and I do not know that it is wholly justified. I think it is in some cases but on the other hand, there is another side to the picture.

Let me tell you a story that is known to four or five of you who are here tonight. There is a certain cotton mill in the South. The conditions in that cotton mill . . . are good. They are well above the average. As long as ten or twelve years ago the owners of this mill abandoned the company-owned house. Pretty nearly every operative in that mill owns or rents his own house. . . . Taking it by and large, the conditions of employment are good. They have had very little labor trouble.

Not long ago, the United—what do they call it?—the Cotton Textile Workers' Union, in pursuance of organization provided for in fact by the law—it is perfectly legal—they sent down to this town two organizers. Well, I happened to know one of them and that particular man is just as good an American as anybody in this room. He is a labor organizer but he is a damned good citizen. He took with him another man; I do not know him but his reputation is exceedingly good. They went down to this town with the specific purpose of seeking to create a union among the textile workers.

They got in town about ten o'clock in the morning and they went at the noon hour—they had a list of eight or ten of the operators. They were going to see them at the noon hour. So they went to the factory and they asked, "Where is so and so? Where can I find so and so?"

They were engaged in asking questions, when one of the mill police tapped him on the shoulder and showed his badge and said, "Come with me."

He said, "We have not done anything; we are outside and on the street and just asking to see some fellows."

"Oh, we know; come with me."

They were taken to the police station and locked up in a cell on the charge of vagrancy. Both of them had, oh, fifteen or twenty dollars apiece in their clothes. They said, "We are not vagrants; we came down here from such and such a city."

"But you are organizers."

"Of course we are organizers."

"Well, you are in a bad place."

They were kept in jail until five o'clock, just before dark.

And the judge came in and said, "What are you doing here?"

"We are down here to try to start an organization of the textile workers of this mill."

"That is what you think," he said. "Ten dollars fine and out of town before six o'clock and do not come back!"

They did not know what they were fined for but they paid the fine, and as they went out of the courtroom, one of the marshals or policemen, went up to them and said, "Which way are you boys going?"

They said, "We have to get out of town and we thought we would go to such and such a town, ten miles away."

"Well," said the policeman, "I will give you a lift; I turn off two miles short."

They rode with him and he said, "This is where I turn off." They got out and started to hike down the road.

They went about a quarter of a mile and out of a clump of bushes came some men with blackjacks and they got the worst beating up that any two people could get without getting killed.

They spent a week in the hospital and they were served notice by a man who brought the message, "Do not go into that town."

Now, these were authorities of that government, town and county.

Now, you do not get those facts and that is one reason why the National Labor Relations Board sometimes tries to bring out facts of that kind. It is their duty to do it. They have a perfect right to go into that town. It is their duty.

THE DUTCH IN ROOSEVELT

27 August 1938

FDR described to reporters his plans for a cottage to be built on the Hyde Park estate. He said he did not plan to have a telephone installed in the cottage. If, at any time in the future, he decided to have a telephone he knew exactly how to save money on the cost of installation. He used his story as the basis for a comment on the Rural Electrification Administration (REA).

The President: If you go out to buy telephone poles from the electric light company, they want $40 a pole. I have to have fifteen poles to get in from the road and it is $600. What I am going to do, I think, is to go down into the woods and cut fifteen hemlocks, strip them and put them into the barn for the winter so they will dry out and then, in April, creosote them and put in my own poles. Then of course the wire and the transformer will have to be put in by experts. But I can put in my own poles for about $10 a pole and that is a saving of $450. It is worthwhile.[1]

Well, as a matter of fact, of course that is the whole basis of the R.E.A. thing. The R.E.A. is being done in large part, of course, by the farmers themselves in a cooperative way. You can get poles out of the woods with your own labor and strip them and creosote them for $9 or $10 anywhere. All you need do is dig holes in the ground. You do not need experts to do that.

[1] FDR took pride in his frugality and thrifty habits. In a letter to a British friend he wrote: "In 1878 my Father had a tweed suit made in Edinburgh—that was four years before I was born. He wore the suit constantly until his death in 1900. I inherited it and wore it steadily until 1926, when I passed it on to my boy James. He still has it and wears it in the winter time when he is in the country. A good example of Scotch craftsmanship, aided and abetted by Dutch thrift!" Roosevelt to Arthur Murray, 13 May 1938, in Elliott Roosevelt, ed., *F.D.R. His Personal Letters* (New York, 1950), II, pp. 781–82.

LEARNING THE ART OF BLEEDING

7 October 1938

The President had discussed with Heywood Broun, noted journalist and head of the Newspaper Guild, the question of finding some useful work for newspapermen on relief. He had found it difficult to "invent" jobs for them. One possibility that had been suggested was that such newsmen could be associated with a project for the examination, selection, and publication of documents of historical interest that were lying around in county courthouses.

The President: We have here in Poughkeepsie, for example, WPA[1] projects which have done an excellent job in the County Courthouse in copying and listing the old records of this county and, I think, of the

[1] The Works Projects Administration had sponsored a massive emergency public employment program to provide work to about three and a half million unemployed persons on relief.

City of Poughkeepsie. But they have never been published and they can be published very easily under the auspices of the Dutchess County Historical Society, and the same thing is true in almost every county, and sold to libraries and collectors all over the United States, so as to bring back a portion of the cost of such projects.[2]

That is one suggestion I made to Heywood Broun and we are going to give it further study.

Here is something very interesting. . . . This is, I think, one of the most interesting of all historical documents. This is an indenture, in other words a contract, dated 1760, which is not so long ago.

> THIS INDENTURE Witnesseth, That Johanna Dwyer an Infant aged about eight years and an half Hath put herself, and by these Presents, by & with the Consent of Edward Dwyer and Elinor his wife her parents signifyed by their being parties to these presents doth voluntarily, and of her own free Will and Accord—

Get this picture, this child eight and a half years old putting herself as apprentice.

> put herself Apprentice to Elizabeth Wright of the City of New York, widow, to learn the Art of Bleeding and midwifery and after the Manner of an Apprentice, to serve from the Day of the Date hereof, for and during, and until the full End and Term of Eleven years & Six Months next ensuing; during all which Time, the said Apprentice her said Mistress faithfully shall serve, her Secrets keep, her lawful Commands everywhere readily obey: She shall do no Damage to her said Mistress nor see it to be done by others, without letting, or giving Notice thereof to her said Mistress: She shall not waste her said Mistresses Goods, nor lend them unlawfully to any: She shall not commit Fornication, nor contract Matrimony within the said Term: At cards, Dice, or any other unlawful Game, she shall not play, whereby her said Mistress may have Damage: With her own Goods, nor the Goods of others, without Licence from her said Mistress, she shall neither buy nor sell: She shall not absent herself Day nor Night from her said Mistress her service, without her Leave; nor haunt Alehouses, Taverns, or Play-houses; but in all Things behave herself as a faithful Apprentice ought to do, during the said Term. And the said Elizabeth shall use the utmost of her Endeavours to teach, or cause to be taught or instructed, the said Apprentice in the Art

---

[2] FDR was a founder of the Dutchess County Historical Society and took a keen interest in its program of publishing the historical records of the Hudson valley. He was excited and thrilled whenever he learned from his Poughkeepsie friends of discoveries of old records, as for instance, the records of the town clerks of Crum Elbow and Clinton.

of Bleeding and Midwifery and procure and provide for her sufficient Meat, Drink, Apparel, Lodging and Washing, fitting for an Apprentice, during the said Term of Eleven years and six months—

In other words, until she is nineteen years of age. No pay, remember.

and at the expiration thereof give unto the said Apprentice two Suits of Cloaths and during the said Term teach the said Apprentice to read and write.

I think it is an amazing document, right in this country in 1760, and yet when you come to think of it, as Heywood Broun remarked yesterday, that child of eight and a half was a good deal better off than many children of these days who are in canning factories or picking up crops, without board, lodging, food or anything else. It is a very interesting document.

OLD MOTHER FDR

14 March 1939

CORRESPONDENT: Senator Bridges[1] introduced a bill in the Senate to repeal powers granted you to issue three billion in greenbacks. Since you did not ask for the authority and have not used it, do you object to its repeal?

THE PRESIDENT: I do not know why it should be repealed at this time. Sometimes it is useful to have a club in a closet. It has not been used; I do not think it will ever be used. Perhaps you could use another simile: A little spare food in the back of the cupboard so that Old Mother Hubbard would not go there and find the cupboard so bare.

[1] Republican Senator Styles Bridges of New Hampshire.

WHEN THE UNIVERSITY PRESIDENT CRIED

30 March 1939

THE PRESIDENT: Two years before, the President of the University [of Alabama] came to Washington to thank me very much for some P.W.A. [Public Works Administration] money that had been allocated for two dormitories to replace the old dormitories that were unsafe. The law at that time provided that we could only use these grants to aid

State institutions to replace buildings that had fallen down or were burned down. The President of the University thanked me for the dormitories but, with tears in his eyes, said, "Mr. President, why didn't you give us the new library too?" I said, "But the application did not say anything about an old library which had either fallen down or burned down."

He said, "Mr. President, our library did burn down." I said, "When?" And he said, "In '64. General Sherman came our way." I believe we stretched the point and went back three-quarters of a century to the date of the arson, and gave him a new library.[1]

[1] Extemporaneous remarks at the Alabama Polytechnic Institute, Auburn, 30 March 1939, *Public Papers and Addresses, 1939*, p. 181. The Public Works Administration was set up in 1933 with Harold L. Ickes, Secretary of the Interior, as its head to initiate major public works.

CAN'T YOU HEAR THE WHISTLE BLOWING?

30 March 1939

Roosevelt spoke of the efforts initiated by his Administration to give Southern states a balanced economy and make them self-supporting.[1]

THE PRESIDENT: The first year I went to Warm Springs, fifteen, nearly sixteen years ago, I had a little cottage that was about a thousand feet from the old A.B. & A. tracks. The first night, the second night and the third night I was awakened out of a deep sleep by the sound of a very heavy train going through at pretty high speed and, as it went through the town, the whistle blew and woke everybody up. So I went down to the station and said to the stationmaster, "What is that train that makes so much noise and why does it have to whistle at half past one in the morning?" "Oh," he said, "the fireman has a girl in town."

I asked him what that train was and he said, "That is the milk train for Florida." Well, I assumed of course, knowing that the climate of Florida, especially South Florida, is not very conducive to dairy purposes, that this train on the A.B. & A. contained milk and cream from Alabama and Georgia. I was wrong. That milk and cream for Florida came from Wisconsin, Minnesota, Iowa and Illinois and was taken through all the intervening States of Indiana, Ohio, Kentucky, Tennessee, Alabama and Georgia in order to supply milk and cream and butter for Florida.

[1] Extemporaneous remarks at the Alabama Polytechnic Institute, Auburn, 30 March 1939, *Public Papers and Addresses, 1939*, pp. 182–83.

That gave me a feeling that something was wrong with the agricultural economy of these States of the lower South, because you and I know from what we have been taught and from the experiments that have been made that these States can produce perfectly good milk and cream.

A little while later I went down to the village to buy some apples. Mind you, this place is only 75 miles from here. I knew of the magnificent apples raised at the southern end of the Appalachian System. I had tasted them; no apples in the world were better. Yet the apples in Meriwether County, Georgia, the only ones I could find, came from Washington and Oregon.

I went to buy meat—and I know that we can make pastures in these States—and the only meat that I could buy came via Omaha and Kansas City and Chicago.

I wanted to buy a pair of shoes and the only shoes I could buy had been made in Boston or Binghamton, New York, or St. Louis.

Well, that was fifteen years ago, and there wasn't very much change in that system of economy until about six years ago. It was then we began to ask ourselves, "Why is all this necessary?" I think we have done more in those six years than in the previous sixty years all through these southern States to make them self-supporting and to give them a balanced economy that will spell a higher wage scale, a greater purchasing power and a more abundant life than they have had in all their history.

THE AMERICAN COW

16 May 1939

Roosevelt told reporters at a press conference on 12 May 1939 that the Navy had been buying a substantial quantity of foreign canned beef and saving money in the bargain. Asked whether beef from such foreign sources as Argentina was superior to American beef, FDR said: "No question about it. If you go off on a camping trip or a fishing trip, buy American canned beef and foreign canned beef and see which you like better. . . . We do not know why, but American cows do not make as good canned beef as some foreign cows."

CORRESPONDENT: There seems to be an idea in the West that you have impugned the honor of the American cow. Would you care to—

THE PRESIDENT: I have cast no aspersions on the virtue of the American cow or the valor of the American bull. . . . I would be the first to arise to the defense of American cattle!

. . . this whole question is a question of a certain kind of beef that comes in a can and the fact is that we, in this country, do not seem to use our highest grade beef for this canned corned beef, as other people do. . . . In other words, to come right down to it, we are not a canned beef eating nation. That is the simplest way of putting it. Have any of you people eaten canned beef in the last year—knowingly?

THE GEOGRAPHY OF BALANCING THE BUDGET
22 May 1939

THE PRESIDENT: I wonder if you have any conception of the number of businessmen and bankers and economists whom I talk with briefly or at length in any given month of the year. I wonder if you have any conception of the variety of suggestions and panaceas that they offer me. I wonder if you know the very large percentage of them who honestly, and in good faith, and very naturally, think of national problems solely in terms of their own business.[1]

. . . I sit in my office with a businessman who thinks the surest way to produce customers is to balance the Federal budget at once. I say to him, "How?"

Sometimes he says, "How should I know? That is your job." Sometimes he says, "Cut the budget, cut it straight through 10 per cent or, 20 per cent."

Then I take from my desk drawer a fat book and it is apparent at once from his expression that he has never seen or read the budget of the Government of the United States.

He tries to change the subject but I hold him to it. I say, "This budget is not all of one piece; it is an aggregate of thousands of items. I will, therefore, have to cut every item the 10 per cent or 20 per cent you ask or, if I do not do that I will have to cut some items very much more than 10 per cent or 20 per cent."

I point out the one and a half billion dollars for the Army and Navy. He pounds the desk and says in patriotic fervor, "Don't cut that item—not in these days."

I show him the item of a billion dollars for interest on the public debt. He owns some Government bonds, and he rejects any cut in his interest.

I show him the billion dollars item for war and civil service pensions. He says, "No, we couldn't get enough popular support to cut this."

I mention the billion dollars for running the permanent functions of the regular Government departments, and I tell him that they cost less today than under my predecessor. He readily agrees that the postmen and the G-men and the Forest Service and the customs people cannot be

[1] Address before the American Retail Federation, Washington, D.C., 22 May 1939, *Public Papers and Addresses, 1939*, pp. 345–48.

curtailed. The only people he would sever from the payrolls are the tax collectors.

That gets us down to a few other big items—totaling over four billion dollars to take care of four major things—payments for the benefit of agriculture, Federal public works (including C.C.C.), and assistance for our old people.[2]

. . . I come to the public works item. He suggests that that can be cut 50 per cent. I happen to know that his community is working tooth and nail to get a grant for a much needed new high school, and that his county suffered severe property losses from recent floods. I suggest that we start public works economy right there and not give the grants and that we defer building the school house or the levee or the flood control dam for twenty or thirty years.

In every case I find what I suspected. His local Chamber of Commerce, his local newspapers are "yelling their heads off" to have those projects built with Federal assistance. And I say to him: "Consistency, thy name is geography. You believe with the United States Chamber of Commerce that Federal spending on public works should cease—except in your home town."

. . . And so, at the end, my visitor leaves convinced, in nine cases out of ten, that I am not a complete and utter fool, and that balancing the budget today, or even next year, is a pretty difficult if not an impossible job.

   [2] The C.C.C.—Civilian Conservation Corps, established in 1933, sought to take unemployed youngsters off the streets and to put them to work in national parks, forests, and reclamation projects.

AN ELIZABETHAN PRECEDENT

3 January 1940

FDR was explaining his Budget proposals, adding his own inimitable running commentary on items of interest.

THE PRESIDENT: Then going back to Page XIII we have the item "Financing the maintenance of certain services." This is something that is really important, . . . on this old rivers and harbors situation.

In England, where they have been at it a great deal longer than we have, back in the days of Queen Elizabeth they organized a Government corporation called Trinity House, which we would call an authority in these later days. Trinity House was a corporation that was given its capital by the British Treasury and it was run by shipmasters and shipping houses. It began a great system of lighthouses and buoys and dredging out of channels . . . . [It] was given authority to impose tonnage taxes and port dues and things of that kind to offset the expenses they were under for annual maintenance of the channels that they had to keep on dredging out, like the channel going into Liverpool, which is a long muddy, sandy channel requiring constant dredging. I am not dead sure, but I think the lifesaving stations in England were also run by Trinity House.

The net result is that that system has run over four hundred years and the maintenance of all navigational aids, including the dredging of channels, is covered almost one hundred per cent out of the receipts that Trinity House gets from ships which use these channels.

If you go yachting on the coast of England and drop anchor in some little two-by-four harbor on the coast of Devonshire, along comes a fellow in a boat, with a Navy cap on. He rows out and he says, "Good evening gentlemen. What is your tonnage, please?" And you tell him the tonnage of your schooner and he says, "One night?" You say, "Yes." He says, "It will be six pence, sir."

For two nights it will be ten pence, and if you spend a week there you will get a further reduction. In that way the users of all the channels and harbors around the British Isles pay for these facilities which the Government provides for them.

Now when it comes to digging a new channel or putting in a new set of buoys or building a new lighthouse, that is a capital expense. That comes out of the Treasury.

... we are spending $50,000,000 a year for the maintenance of our rivers and harbors and channels and buoys and lighthouses and lifesaving stations, et cetera, and we are getting nothing back from the users. ... Well, that is one thing we ought to start to do.

A SHOCK FOR THE ECONOMIC ROYALISTS
9 March 1940

FDR liked a cartoon in the *New Yorker* by Frank Beaven that showed two gentlemen lounging in their arm chairs in the club and damning Roosevelt.[1]

THE PRESIDENT: ... Your two gentlemen in armchairs in the club remind me of George Earle's[2] story of what happened in the Rittenhouse Club in Philadelphia in the Fall of 1935 (I think it was) when I was making a speech to a huge audience in the Atlanta Stadium.

Four gentlemen sipping their drinks in comfortable armchairs in the Rittenhouse Club were going through the usual motions of damning

[1] The President to Frank Beaven, 9 March 1940, FDRL.
[2] Governor of Pennsylvania, 1935–39.

Roosevelt and all his works—the Vice-President of the Pennsylvania Railroad, the President of a Trust Company, a retired millionaire art collector and the head of a great oil company. The knocking party went on for sometime when one of the four finished his drink, rose, walked over to the mahogany encased radio and turned it on. Out came that well known voice—the voice that Wall Street uses to inculcate fear in the breasts of their little grandchildren—and the voice said, "I am thinking in connection with the care of our poor and hungry. I wonder what is being said by my rich friends in their over-stuffed armchairs in their well-stocked clubs."[3] All four men in the Rittenhouse recoiled—and one of them, finding his voice, exclaimed, "My God, do you suppose that blankety blank could have overheard us?"

[3] FDR's exact words in his Atlanta speech on 29 November 1935 were: "I can realize that gentlemen in well-warmed and well-stocked clubs will discourse on the expenses of Government and the suffering that they are going through because their Government is spending money for work relief. I wish I could take some of these men out on the battle-line of human necessity, and show them the facts that we in the Government are facing."

WHAT IS UNEMPLOYMENT?

18 April 1940

Story-telling was not always for fun or for imparting lessons. Roosevelt could use it to strike hard at critics and disable them—smiling all the while, of course. His comments on unemployment at a press conference for the American Society of Newspaper Editors offers a good illustration of his approach.

THE PRESIDENT: The gentlemen whom I referred to the other night, at the Gridiron,[1] as having a well-developed sense of rumor, the colum-

[1] The Gridiron Club is an organization of Washington correspondents. The annual dinners of the Club feature sarcastic portrayals of the President and other high dignitaries. Unlike many others, FDR participated enthusiastically in the festivities of the Club as well as those of the White House Correspondents' Association. At one of the Gridiron dinners, according to the noted columnist Raymond Clapper, "President Roosevelt saw himself transparently disguised, riding in a huge chariot drawn by captive slaves, preceded by trumpeters, centurions, Roman senators and soldiers bearing banners inscribed 'F.D.R. Imp.' He heard social security pensioners, in the old folks home in 1968, chatting about him, then in his 10th term at the age of 86, but 'still the same old Franklin. . . .'" *Columbus* (Ohio) *Citizen*, 22 December 1936, quoted in James E. Pollard, *The Presidents and the Press* (New York, 1947), p. 794.

nists, the interpreters, had a perfectly grand time this month as to unemployment figures, so I sent for one or two of the so-called economic advisers—oh, more than that, five or six of them—some of them in the employ of the Government, some of them in the employ of private business, and I said to them, "I notice that you have given a figure on unemployment in the United States. Who is an unemployed person?"

Well, they began to hum and haw and no one ever gave me a definition.

I used certain examples which, perhaps, were not fair. I said, "I have got a girl friend, a graduate of Vassar College, been out about three or four years. She was not very happy at home—stepmother—so she said to her father, 'I think I have got to go my way and live my own life.'

And father said, 'All right.'

'How much are you going to allow me?'

'Well, you know I am a poor man. I appreciate the living conditions at home are not so easy; I will give you ten thousand dollars a year.'

She said, 'Is that all?'

He said, 'That is all; I am a stern parent.'

So she went her own way on ten grand and she tried to get a job. She got a job with [the magazine] *Delineator*; she had no training—she thought she was good—and they fired her at the end of the month. Then she went to *Vogue* and *Vogue* fired her at the end of the month and now she is hanging around the night clubs saying, 'I belong to the great army of the unemployed and when the census taker comes around I am going to tell him about it. I am unemployed.'

All right.

"Up in a place, a certain place I know, there is a fellow making fifteen hundred dollars a year. He has a daughter, twenty-eight years old and, looking at her, I would say that she will probably never marry. However, she was brought up to be a musician and she knows how to play a piano and does know the technique of music. She lives at home and during December, January, February, and March she gives music lessons and makes enough out of those music lessons to go to Poughkeepsie and the movies and buy a few ice cream sodas and so on. She is a nice girl, perfectly happy at home with Mama and Papa, and makes $250 a year in the winter and that is all she wants to make. She has a happy home and she maintains herself as far as clothing and pin money go.

"A census taker went around the other day and said to Annabelle, 'Are you unemployed?'

'Sure I am unemployed.'

"All right; how about the carpenter back home? He gets twelve dollars a day and works an average of 125 days a year. Well, they are making about fifteen hundred dollars a year and these days, in the last few years, they have been making around an average of fifteen hundred dollars a year. They are not starving, not on relief, but during about—well, probably a majority of the total days in the year, they aren't holding down a job because a carpenter's job, in most cases, is on a job-to-job basis or it is seasonal.

"You will always catch on any given date, the eighteenth of April or the twenty-eighth of April, you and I know that we always catch a third of the carpenters of the United States out of work and yet that third of the carpenters are not on relief and they are making enough to keep them off relief, although it is not as much as they ought to make.

"How about the army of wives? They go into the department stores right after Thanksgiving and stay through, right after the first of January. That is the Christmas season. They have been doing it for years. They sell goods. It is part of their scheme of life. The family is helped by the couple of hundred dollars they earn in the Christmas season."

In other words, this violent controversy among the columnists is probably a good thing. They use the usual language of columnists—against each other this time—and it was rather choice. . . . Fine; it is all right; I am all for it!

Now, no human being knows or will know how many unemployed people are in the United States until we all get together and define "Unemployment." Nobody has had the wit yet in the newspaper world to bring that fact out. That is an absolute fact. . . . Nobody in the newspaper world has as yet demanded a definition of "unemployment." That is a very interesting and startling fact, so how the hell can I talk about unemployment until you fellows define it? Is that fair?

TAX REFORM

7 January 1941

Harold Smith, Director of the Budget, and John B. Blandford, Assistant Director, were present at the press conference. Roosevelt explained to reporters the important features of his budget message. At one point in his narration, he noted that he had included in the message his usual call for "a thorough investigation of the possibilities of a comprehensive tax reform."

THE PRESIDENT: Harold Smith and Jack Blandford and I had a talk about putting that in.

I had been putting that in—about a better relationship between the Federal Government taxes—ever since I went to Albany in January, 1929.

I didn't want to put it in again, but Harold says, "It's always been in; you ought to put it in again."

I said, "Hope springs eternal," and he said, "Yes."

So I said, "All right, we'll put it in again," I said, "I'll put it again, and you can consider it as sort of a piece of candy for you boys," and somebody said, "All-day sucker."

It's one of those things that we hope before we die we'll make some progress in.

THE POOR, POOR MILLIONAIRES
AND THEIR HIGH TAXES

7 January 1941

CORRESPONDENT: . . . do you agree with the statement made in 1939 that perhaps in the upper brackets the surtax rates are too high?

THE PRESIDENT: . . . Of course you know the joke about a great friend of mine, a lawyer in New York, who was talking about the taxes of some of his clients.

He said, "Take so and so; why, he's liable to pay in income taxes 80 per cent of his income, between the Federal and the State."

I said, "Yes, I've heard that before; *does* he?"

He said, "Hmmm—no."

So this rot that is written and printed about people being liable to pay these great high-bracket taxes—show me the man who *does!*

I will issue the challenge to any of you to show me the man who pays anything like the actual higher-bracket taxes, because he doesn't; he has all kinds of exemptions and exceptions—exempt bonds and so forth and so on—so it is just pure, unadulterated tripe—that is the only word I can use—to talk about people paying the percentages named in the brackets. They *don't.*

PURE MOLYBDENUM

15 April 1941

FDR was asked whether he had anything to do with bringing about a settlement of the dispute between the leaders of the Steel Workers' Organizing Committee (S.W.O.C.) and of the big steel companies.

CORRESPONDENT: Mr. President, now that the S.W.O.C. and Big Steel have reached an agreement on wages, can you tell us what went on last week in your conference with Mr. Murray, and Olds and Fairless?[1]

CORRESPONDENT: . . . Did you have something to do with bringing about that agreement?

THE PRESIDENT: Oh, no. I never have anything to do with that. . . . We talked about all kinds of technical things, as to the amount of molybdenum that was needed for a ton of steel, and things like that! Carborundum, for instance!

CORRESPONDENT: Talk about escalator clauses?

THE PRESIDENT: Only escalators where they are needed to get people one floor up!

[1] Philip Murray was President of the Congress of Industrial Organizations. Irving S. Olds and Benjamin F. Fairless were respectively Chairman of the Board and President of the United States Steel Corporation.

THE MISSISSIPPI RIVER BOAT

28 May 1941

FDR commented on a report that he had received from Gano Dunn Yano of the Office of Production Management on the adequacy of the steel industry. The report stated, among other things, that it would take four million tons of steel in order to increase steel production capacity by ten million tons.

THE PRESIDENT: He reminded me of the story in Mark Twain—I think it was in Huck Finn—and there was a great rivalry in the Mississippi River, in the old days, about which boat had the loudest whistle. And there was one boat that was built that took all the prizes, up and down the river, for the loudest whistle. The only trouble was that when the ship whistled she had to stop because the whistle took all the steam!

TACKLING THE BRASS PROBLEM

10 October 1941

FDR wanted to launch a vigorous campaign for the collection of scrap metals.

THE PRESIDENT: Er—charity begins at home. This morning, Mr. Crim, Head Usher of the White House, came to me and said that he had been rummaging around in the basement, and had turned up about half a ton of copper and brass waste. Now if that happens in the White House, isn't it reasonable to assume that an awful lot of Government-owned

metal which is not only usable but extremely useful, is lying around all
through Washington, and in other Government buildings, and other parts
of the country? . . . .

CORRESPONDENT: Sounds like Calvin Coolidge!

THE PRESIDENT: Sounds just like President Coolidge all right.

CORRESPONDENT: Do you plan to melt up any brass hats?

THE PRESIDENT: Well, we are doing that now, and we have a much
politer name for it. We call it "liquidating." Essentially the same thing!

WHAT WAR MEANS

17 December 1941

The nation was at war against the Axis Powers, following the Japanese attack on Pearl Harbor. America and Russia were now allies.

THE PRESIDENT: I always like a little story that one of my people
who came back from Russia told me the other day. When the Germans
were approaching not one city, but many cities where industrial plants
were turning out fighting munitions, the Russians, realizing that they
probably would lose the city or cities, began to move their factories. And
how did they move them? They ran a freight train—backed it into the
factory, and they loaded the tools into the freight cars. And with every
tool—into the same freight car—went the man who was operating that
tool. Their simple objective, when they moved 600 or a thousand miles
away was to reestablish the factory. They would have the people, the
workers, with their tools. They did not have to put new people—untrained
people—onto these tools.

And I wonder just a little bit what the average American would do
if our Government backed a freight train in and said to every worker:
"Five minutes notice. You can't say good-by to your family. Get into
that freight car with the tools you are working with. There is your suitcase—a hamper of food, a couple of bottles of water. We will let you
out when you get a thousand miles inland."

That is what war means.[1]

[1] Informal remarks to the Management-Labor Conference, 17 December 1941, *Public Papers and Addresses, 1941*, pp. 538–39.

SEARCH FOR AN ERG

6 January 1942

Roosevelt was discussing the question of increased production of
military equipment. He referred to a suggestion that it might be more

appropriate to view the effort in terms of "manhours" than of actual production figures of bombers, ships, and the like.

THE PRESIDENT: In other words, if we see that this country is every week increasing by manhours, we know we are going places. But it is a fantastic term when you talk of manhours. I don't get it. I still don't understand what 10 million manhours means. And I am open to suggestions.

There is an old—there is an old crossword puzzle word called an "erg,"—an E-R-G—a unit of work. I don't know what an erg is. If somebody could get that across in simpler terms than manhours, it would be an awfully good thing. It is something that we need to have invented. We might all be thinking about it. I think I might almost offer a prize.

Lloyd George, in '18, when I went over to the other side, said, "You Americans have got inventive genius. Invent me a term to take the place of the word 'cooperation.' "

Nobody has done it yet. It is an amazing thing. It is a horrible word, but we haven't got a substitute yet.

GO, SHARPEN YOUR PENCIL!

6 January 1942

THE PRESIDENT: I sent for the Maritime Commission, and I pointed out to them that one of the really vital things we have to get is more tonnage, and while on the relative sinkings and buildings at the present time we are holding even, we have got to make substantial gains of building over losses.

And I said to them, "What are you making now?"

"Well, we are making nearly 6 million tons this year."

I said, "What can you step it up to?"

"Well," they said, "We can step—step it up another million tons."

I said, "Not enough. Go back and sharpen your pencils!"

That is just illustrative of the method.

So they went back and sharpened their pencils, and they came back and they said, "It will hurt terribly, but we believe that if we are told to we can turn out 8 million tons of shipping this year."

I said, "Now you are talking."

And I said, "All right now, for '43 what can you do? Can you turn out 2 million more tons, to a total of 10 million tons of shipping?"

And they scratched their heads, and came back and said, "Aye, aye, sir!"

That's just an illustration.

Then it came to planes, tanks, anti-aircraft guns. And I have been telling them to go back and sharpen their pencils!

WORK FOR POUGHKEEPSIE CARPENTERS

6 January 1942

FDR had instructed the Office of Production Management to place contracts with firms that had traditionally been engaged in the manufacture of civilian items. He pointed out that unless such firms were helped to switch over to the production of articles needed by the Government, they might be forced to lay off many of their workers. Roosevelt described the problem to reporters in his own inimitable fashion.

THE PRESIDENT: I was home—oh—about four months ago, and a fellow named—well, never mind the name—from Poughkeepsie came to see me. He, and his father, and grandfather, ran a sash and blind works —made window sashes and blinds. The firm is a little over a hundred years old.

And he came to me, and he said, "I'm all out of orders. There is no more private building in Dutchess County. What will I do? We have got 30 first-class carpenters and cabinet makers that have been with me for years and years."

"Well," I said, "can't you do some war work?"

He said, "I don't know. Are they ordering any wood cabinet work for this war? I don't think so. We don't do steel."

I brought him down to Odlum's[1] office and explained the situation. And I got busy on this thing. I said—when I was getting my nose done— to [Rear-Admiral] Ross McIntire,[2] "You are just a little tiny cog in the Navy Department, are you still buying steel medicine cabinets to put up on the wall?"

And he said, "Yes."

"Couldn't you use a wooden medicine cabinet?"

He said, "Sure."

"Are you still buying steel book cases, and steel desks for your hospitals?"

He said, "Yes."

"Couldn't you use wooden ones just as well?"

"Sure."

Well, that's one—just one illustration.

Then I sent for the Maritime Commission. I said, "On your ships, do you—in the Officers' quarters or the Mess's or the First Mates', use— don't you have a certain amount of wainscotting?"

They said, "Yes."

"And where are you getting it?"

---

[1] Floyd Odlum, head of the Division of Contract Distribution, Office of Production Management.

[2] Ross T. McIntire, Surgeon General of the Navy and Physician to the President.

"I don't know."

The net result was that this man in Poughkeepsie came down here, and he was handed a list of wooden cabinet work that could be used for the Government—substitutes mostly.

And he was asked, "Aren't there any other woodworking companies like yours in Hudson Valley that are going out of business for lack of work?"

And he said, "Yes. One in Newburgh, one in Kingston, one in Hudson, and I think one in Peekskill that I know of. They are all in the same fix I am in."

And they said to him, "All right. How much can the five companies in the Hudson River Valley take?"

... And he went back, and they have got enough Government orders to keep 150 men steadily at work for at least a year on building wooden substitutes for the Government.

Now that sort of thing we are beginning to get into our stride, but ... as you know, it means going and searching out the places where that kind of a solution of the problem is needed.

CUT FEDERAL EXPENDITURE!

13 February 1942

THE PRESIDENT: Well, let us, for example, take the case of—oh—the bright boys who say you can curtail all of the Federal expenditure. Well, all right. When some bright boy who writes that and sobs over it that it hasn't been done, you ask him a question and say "Where?"

He says, "Oh, well —. That's a detail. That has nothing to do with me. I am a leader of public opinion on this thing. I am not supposed to know any details."

I had one of those chaps in the other day. You have read a lot of his stuff, and—and I said, "Where?"

And he couldn't tell me where, that was not his business, where to curtail.

So I said, "All right, let's take an example—meat inspection. It costs the Federal Government an awful lot each year for the inspection of meat and to see that it is decent meat for people to eat."

I said, "Do you want to curtail that? Perfectly possible in wartime to curtail that. Absolutely simple. All you have to do is to get the Congress to eliminate or greatly curtail meat inspection. It's a cinch. Why not? It's war time. Who cares whether we eat diseased meat in wartime? Save money! It will save—what?—a few million dollars."

Well, that's a pretty good example. ...

Your glib boys say, "Oh, cut them all out. Cut them all down!"

A SENSE OF PROPORTION

17 March 1942

Sentiment was mounting in Congress that strikes should not be permitted while the war was in progress. Anxious that restrictive legislation should not be hastily enacted, FDR emphasized that organized labor was supporting the war effort vigorously and that "little local strikes" did not represent any serious threat.

THE PRESIDENT: Practically speaking, there are no strikes today. . . . . . . you get 15 or 20 people who don't like the kind of tobacco that a foreman smokes. They don't like the smell of it. Well, they might go on strike to make him change his brand of smoking tobacco. Now things like that have happened. . . . Silly little things. They really don't affect the war effort nearly as much as lots of other things.

Just by way of illustration, . . . one of my professional economist friends the other day . . . told me that since the—our war effort began—I don't know what it was—beginning June, 1940, something terrible had happened. We had lost 30 million manhours of work through strikes in a year and three quarters, . . . that if we hadn't lost that 30 million man-hours of work in a year and three quarters, Japan would never have declared war on us. We never would have lost the Philippines, or the Dutch Indies, or Singapore. And the dear fellow wrote to me really honestly believing it.

And I wrote him back: I have got something almost more serious to tell you about. This is bad enough what you say, but do you realize that if it hadn't been for the common cold in America, we would be in Berlin? We would be in Berlin today if it hadn't been for the common cold, because there were 60 million man days lost in that same period through common colds!

In other words, why don't we in this country get a little sense of proportion and think things through? Well, headlines are responsible for it. Somebody has got to write a good lead. I know—I would like to myself, but let us keep a little sense of proportion!

THE BEER CAP EMERGENCY

3 April 1942

CORRESPONDENT: Mr. President, a very serious question was raised this morning—a report that the War Production Board is banning the use of tin plate for beer caps.

THE PRESIDENT: That is serious!

CORRESPONDENT: Have the brain-powers of the Government been saddled with the problem of finding a substitute for that?

THE PRESIDENT: No. But I guess we could work out something, of course, and get one which is a little easier, and cheaper, and *quicker* all right!

15 September 1942

A reporter informed Roosevelt that several organizations had protested against the allocation of what they regarded as an unduly large share of salvaged tin scrap to brewers and soft-drink bottlers.

THE PRESIDENT: Well, you know, there are lots of soft-drinks that are put up with caps. . . . Well, I suppose one of the simplest things to say is this: that we don't want to prevent people from drinking soft-drinks in the country. And I think it is part of our civilization to drink soft-drinks! . . . And if somebody would invent a bottle cap that was not made of metal, they would have the everlasting thanks of the soft-drink drinkers throughout the nation. Nobody has discovered it yet!

THE GREAT RUBBER SALVAGE CAMPAIGN
16 June 1942

Roosevelt had launched an intensive campaign "to bring in from homes, offices, factories and farms all articles of rubber which have been or can be discarded." He had urged the people to undertake an "active search of attics, closets, basements, and backyards for rubber articles no longer in use." These articles were to be delivered during a period of two weeks at any of the nation's 400,000 gas stations where they were to be weighed and paid for by gas dealers at one cent a pound.

As Roosevelt was about to open his press conference for the day, a correspondent placed before him a cartoon by Cliff Berryman that had appeared in the *Washington Evening Star*. It showed Senator Alben Barkley and Speaker Sam Rayburn bringing in a large basketful of rubber stamps, and saying: "Mr. President, we won't need these rubber stamps any more. They're all worn out!" Roosevelt was depicted as replying: "Thanks, boys. If you find you do need more, we'll find a way!"

THE PRESIDENT: Yes, yes, all right.

CORRESPONDENT: What about rubber checks?

CORRESPONDENT: What's that on his desk—something of rubber? . . . .

THE PRESIDENT: I don't think there is any news, except that the rubber campaign got off to a big start yesterday. Miss Diana Hopkins[1] turned in a basketful of rubber toys, and this afternoon Fala[2] turned in two rubber bones.

And I have been getting things. I have got a doll's hot-water bottle here that a lady sent me from Rocky Mount, North Carolina. And one of my ingenious naval officers is going around collecting rubber mats out of people's cars. Getting on pretty well, chiefly with real ingenuity.

[1] Diana was the ten year old daughter of Harry Hopkins. She had lost her mother in 1937 and since then the Roosevelts had taken a special interest in her.

[2] FDR's black Scotty dog.

STATUES

7 August 1942

Roosevelt had told reporters that the campaign to collect metallic scrap should be intensified.

CORRESPONDENT: Mr. President, . . . there comes to newspapers and radio people from all over the country the suggestion that possibly you could organize to pick up the cannon, and things of that sort, that are lying around on courthouse squares, plus some of the statues of bronze. . . . Would you care to say anything about that?

THE PRESIDENT: Taking the last point first, there are a great many statues in the country which would probably look better if they were turned into guns![1]

[1] A few weeks later FDR turned down a suggestion from an enthusiast that the statues in the District of Columbia should be relocated as part of a general program of beautification. He conceded that the District was "pock-marked with generals, statesmen, foreigners, visiting firemen etc., on horseback, standing and sitting—all without any particular reference to a plan." He was of the view, however, that "we should spend no money these days in redistributing heroes round the parks and squares of Washington" and that "we should let sleeping heroes lie." The President to Frederic A. Delano, 26 September 1941, in Basil Rauch, ed., *The Roosevelt Reader* (New York, 1957), p. 290.

THE REAL BUDGET EXPERTS

9 January 1943

It was the annual "budget seminar" and FDR, as usual, accused reporters of being ignorant about financial matters.

CORRESPONDENT: Good morning, teacher.

THE PRESIDENT: Good morning everybody. How are we?

STEVE EARLY: Mr. President, ready sir?

THE PRESIDENT: No, no, no!

EARLY: Aye, Aye, sir! . . . .

THE PRESIDENT: I see a great many people coming in who know nothing about budgets or taxes. Is it all right?

CORRESPONDENT: That's right. We hope to learn.

THE PRESIDENT: Probably the ladies know more about budgets than any of the men here. [Laughing and counting the ladies present] one, two, three, four, five—that's about all.

. . . I see that there are only, out of those in the room—I see only three budget experts. No four; and they are all ladies! The rest of you men, you don't know a thing about it! It's all right.[1]

[1] Roosevelt often acknowledged that his understanding of the intricate problems of monetary and fiscal policy was inadequate. In 1939, after listening to a radio debate between the economy-minded Senator Harry Byrd of Virginia and the Chairman of the Federal Reserve Board, Marriner Eccles, FDR told the latter over the telephone: "Well, I just called to condemn you and commend you. I condemn you because you kept me up last night. . . . But now I want to commend you. I think your address was excellent. You made the problem so simple that even I was able to understand it." Quoted in Marriner C. Eccles, *Beckoning Frontiers: Public and Personal Recollections* (New York, 1951), p. 417.

IF THE RUSSIANS CAN DO IT. . . .

19 February 1943

A correspondent told Roosevelt that the "farm bloc" was of the view that if he went ahead with his plan to raise the strength of the Army to about 10.8 million, spring planting would be seriously affected.

THE PRESIDENT: Let me tell you a nice story, and as an illustration. I was talking to one of the newspapermen in North Africa who had come back from Russia.

It was in the spring of 1942, after they had withstood the Germans all through the winter of 1941–42, the Russian line having been pushed back from twenty miles from the city to nearly a hundred miles from the city. Nevertheless, Moscow was in real danger, even in the spring of 1942; and they had gone through a very tough winter. They didn't have enough fuel, and they hadn't laid in enough food.

So the Russian authorities took—I think it was 300,000 school children, between the ages of twelve and eighteen; and they took them out to a radius of perhaps a hundred miles from the city, all the way out. And they planted every acre of fields as soon as the ice was out of the soil. And as soon as they had done that, they put them into the forests. And they took pretty good care of these children—it was war—not as well as they had taken care of them in time of peace. And they cut wood until harvest-time came, and then they put them back in the fields to harvest all the food that they possibly could. Then they put them back in the woods again.

And in that way Moscow was supplied, by autumn, with enough wood to keep people warm. I mean reasonably warm—not the way we heat our homes. And they had enough food to live on—men, women, and children— in this great city with millions of people in it.

They didn't have enough manpower to put grown-up people, either men or women, into this work. The men were fighting, or running the transportation—and the women were running the transportation, and fighting, and all the utilities, and they were in the munitions factories which still remained in Moscow.

And the result—this fellow said to me that during the winter of 1942– 43, this winter, there has been relatively less suffering, and fewer problems of food and heat than the previous winter. I use that as a little illustration.

. . . I said once that I thought that the younger people in the villages and towns of this country could help the farmers of this country very, very materially. We have sporadic examples, like the case of the town in California, where they had a crop all ripening inside of one week.

And they couldn't get labor.

The whole town turned out—the drugstore fellow, the soda-water fellow, the doctor, the lawyer, the newspaper men—the linotype man and the editor—and the women of the town. Not a large number. I think twelve hundred people in the town. But they all turned out and helped pick the crop. And the result was that at the end of the week the crop was in. Now we haven't done nearly enough of that.

A REPEAT PERFORMANCE

The best of story-tellers are probably likely to repeat their stories. But their skill is shown in the manner in which they tailor a story to fit a given occasion or situation. FDR possessed this happy faculty. Even a listener who could recognize the outlines of a story he had heard before remained attentive in order to find out how Roosevelt worked it out the second time. Presented below are two versions of a Roosevelt story told on two occasions thirteen months apart from each other.

9 April 1943

FDR was discoursing on the issue of the cost of living. He likened it to a four-legged stool. Holding the line on wages constituted one leg while holding the line on the cost of food was the second leg. The third leg was the development of the rationing system.

THE PRESIDENT: And the fourth leg of the stool is equally important with the other three, and that is the problem of preventing too much purchasing power in the form of cash. That means the development of taxation and savings—those two elements.

I always think of the fellow who came to see me about two weeks ago, . . . an old friend of mine, not far from Washington, but not in Washington. He came to complain about the cost of living. And I have known him a great many years. He is a very highly skilled mechanic, getting mighty good wages, and very thankful for it; but he was complaining about what his wife said to him every night when he got home.

And the previous night his wife had said, "This is terrible." And holding up in front of her a little bunch of asparagus, she said, "What do you think? A dollar and a half for this little bunch of asparagus!" It was about the middle of March.

Well, said this man to me, "It's terrible. A bunch of asparagus a dollar and a half!"

I said, "Look. I am just going to ask you a question—maybe I'm right, maybe I'm wrong. Did your wife ever buy a bunch of asparagus in March before?"

He said, "Why, what do you mean?"

I said, "You know where it came from? It came from Florida. Did you ever eat Florida asparagus in March before?"

He said, "You know, I never thought of that. I will have to talk to my wife about it."

And I said—just a shot in the dark, "Do you remember in the last couple of months, have you eaten any fresh strawberries?"

He said, "Yes, come to think about it. About the end of February we had an awful nice box of fresh strawberries."

I said, "Did you ever do that before?"

He said, "No, I guess not."

"Well, you know where they came from. Probably raised under glass, or something like that, down in the south of Florida."

There is a great deal of that in the country and it comes from the fact that so many people have a great deal more money in their pay envelopes on Saturday night than they ever had before, that they want to go into the luxury business of eating.

And therefore, taxation and savings are the answer, one of the legs— of the four legs of the stool!

30 May 1944

Reporters asked the President to comment on certain amendments approved by the Senate Committee on Banking and Currency to the Office of Price Administration Extension Act designed evidently to raise the prices of certain commodities. FDR responded by discussing the danger of an inflationary rise in prices. He said he himself raised lumber and that he got $29 for a thousand board feet. If he were to view the matter selfishly, he would like very much to see lumber selling at $79 per thousand board feet.

THE PRESIDENT: Well, we have all got that streak in us. If you pick out cotton, you will have somebody else on your neck, and then—then you will get inflation. . . .

Substantially, the price that asparagus and some other things bring is a pretty good price, and I know it has made the cost of buying asparagus in the White House awfully high. This is the asparagus season.

Which reminds me of a friend of mine, a foreman of one of the substantial trades, who came in last January, and said to me, "I have an awful time when I go home." He says, "My old lady is ready to hit me over the head with a dishpan."

I said, "What's the trouble?"

"The cost of living."

"Well," I said, "what, for instance?"

"Well, last night I went home and the old lady said, 'What's this? I went out to buy some asparagus, and do you see what I got? I got five sticks. There it is. A dollar and a quarter. It's an outrage.'"

Well, I looked at him, and I said, "Since when have you been buying asparagus in January—fresh asparagus?"

"Oh," he said, "I never thought of that."

"Well," I said, "tell that to the old lady, with my compliments." . . . .

CORRESPONDENT: Mr. President, is that . . . the same foreman who bought the strawberries in the winter?

THE PRESIDENT: It happened to be a different one, but it's all right! Still marks a true story!

CORRESPONDENT: I just wondered if it was the same man that came in then!

SHOW ME A BETTER 'OLE OR SHUT UP!

11 June 1943

A correspondent stated that some members of Congress who were opposed to subsidies as well as the loan programs of the Reconstruction

Finance Corporation appeared to be leading a drive against the Administration.

THE PRESIDENT: Well, didn't they have an expression in England in the last war called "The Better 'Ole"?

[FDR was probably referring to a well-known British cartoon character, Old Bill, who says to a complaining comrade crouching alongside in a shell hole, "If you know a better 'ole, go to it!"]

CORRESPONDENT: Yes.

THE PRESIDENT: I would very much like to have somebody say to me, . . . "I have found a better 'ole." And it's all—all very very well in life to adopt the attitude that you don't like this, you don't like that, or you don't like the other thing. Of course, the real answer is, what in blazes do you like?[1]

> [1] FDR frequently complained that few of his critics came forward with constructive suggestions. Some adopted a "yes, but" attitude and some were content merely to talk endlessly about the "problem." In an unusually sharp letter Roosevelt once charged a New York banker with failure to offer any concrete suggestions for remedying "the fundamental causes of economic and social ills." "I think," FDR continued, "your general attitude is a little like that of the doctor who was called into consultation in the case of an unfortunate man who was about to die of an exceedingly large tumor. The first and only expression made by the consultant was, 'What an amazing and wonderful tumor! I must write a paper about it.'" Roosevelt to Fred I. Kent, 11 February 1938, FDRL.

WHY DON'T YOU APPOINT A CZAR?

15 June 1943

FDR said that there was "a lot of loose thinking" in Washington and people tended to get so confused by the trees that they did not see the forest as a whole. Instead of thinking things through and coming up with workable suggestions they offered "happy thoughts" in profusion.[1]

THE PRESIDENT: . . . it has been suggested of course, by people who don't always think things through, that the mere fact of having some sort of glorified "czar" would cure the whole thing.

And one of the best illustrations of that is that when this suggestion was made to me, I said to the gentleman who suggested it, "Well now, what sort of things would the czar do?"

"Well," he said, "a friend of mine in a certain State had a carload of food that he wanted to send to the processor, or the distributor, and he knew that the carload of stuff would be about ripe for shipping the following Monday. So he put in his order for a freight car.

[1] *Public Papers and Addresses, 1943*, pp. 255–56.

"Now," he said, "the railroad people said he couldn't have a freight car, and what I want is a czar who will be able to say to Mr. Eastman [Director of the Office of Defense Transportation], 'I have got to have that freight car there next Monday.' "

Well, you see how perfectly absurd the whole thing is. Mr. Eastman would come back and say, "I am awfully sorry but I have got—just to take any old figure—I have got a million freight cars and I have got demands for a million and a half. So I have got to parcel them out in the fairest way I possibly can. I have got to try to make a million cars do the duty of one million and a half. That means that quite a lot of people are not going to be served when they want to be served. It's a condition and not a theory. I have only got a million cars."

So I said to this gentleman, I said, "In other words, you would have a czar with authority to say to Mr. Eastman, 'Whether you like it or not, Mr. Eastman, you have got to transport food ahead of anything else. I am the food czar.' "

Well, pretty soon I guess, Donald Nelson [Chairman, War Production Board] would say to Mr. Eastman, "I am moving some very much needed spare parts for airplanes from the Middle West to the seaboard, in order to ship them over to Africa, and I want a hurryup order."

Mr. Eastman would say, "I am awfully sorry but I have had to give those cars to the food fellow."

And somebody else would say—the Army or the Navy—in time of war —they have got to have a car to take this, that, and the other thing that is needed by the Army and Navy in Europe or the Southwest Pacific.

Mr. Eastman would have to say, "I am terribly sorry but the food czar won't let me."

You see what a perfectly impossible situation it is.

A LITTLE INFLATION

19 October 1943

Roosevelt told reporters that Edward O'Neal, President of the Farm Bureau Federation, had visited him and that among the subjects discussed was inflation. O'Neal had earlier testified before a House Committee that "a little inflation wouldn't hurt anybody."

THE PRESIDENT: So I told him the story about a friend of mine, who is a perfectly good citizen, quite strong-minded, had no vices.

Somebody went up to him one day and said "Did you ever try a little pill of cocaine?"

And he said, "No. I wouldn't touch cocaine: I might form a habit."

Well, this friend of his said, "Well, you know, it's the loveliest sensation in the world. It's perfectly grand. You just feel up in the skies. There isn't anything as wonderful as the sensation that cocaine gives you."

And he talked so enthusiastically that this fellow said, "All right, give me a pill."

And then he took it, and he felt just grand, just what his friend had said.

He came back the next day, and said, "That was the most wonderful sensation I have ever had. Slip me another."

Well, within a week he was taking two, and at the end of a month he was a cocaine addict—a drug addict.

And I said [to O'Neal], "You know, this inflation business is a little bit like that, Ed. You get a little inflation—you say you like a little inflation—and then you will want twice the amount, and then you will get the inflation habit."

. . . Don't take cocaine, or inflation!

STRIPPER

20 May 1944

Fred M. Vinson, Director of the Office of Economic Stabilization, sent the President a very long memorandum on the "Premium Price Plan for Stripper Oil Wells." Roosevelt forwarded it to James F. Byrnes with a note:[1]

THE PRESIDENT: I would not recognize a stripper well if I saw one on the stage! Apparently Fred knows all about the girls and has sent you a copy of this memorandum.

Educate me please.

[1] The President to James Byrnes, 20 May 1944, FDRL.

HOW ICELANDERS CAN MAKE AMERICANS HAPPY

24 August 1944

THE PRESIDENT: I was saying to . . . [Iceland's] Minister a few minutes ago there is an American habit of cocktails, but we haven't yet acquired the Scandinavian habit of the things that go before cocktails. Don't sell us cod liver oil. I don't like cod liver oil—but go into the things that pay more money. Send us some smoked salmon, and things of that kind that go well before the cocktails. In that way you can help, and we can help, by general trade between Iceland and the United States.

... It has been easier, because of the shorter distance, to send your hors d'oeuvres to England, but they don't know a good hors d'oeuvre when they see it. Please send us some, for we are very fond of them. And specialize in them, not the vulgar stuff, but the specials.[1]

[1] Toast at a State Dinner to the President of Iceland, 25 August 1944, *Public Papers and Addresses, 1944*, p. 239.

HOW I CO-OPERATED WITH THE ALMIGHTY
29 October 1944

The following excerpts bring out FDR's deep affection for trees and his commitment to conservation.[1]

THE PRESIDENT: I remember the line in the poem, "Only God can make a tree." . . . I don't see the trees I ought to see. That is something that we in this country have fallen down on. We have been using up natural resources that we ought to have replaced. I know we can't replace coal, . . . but trees constitute something we can replace.

I remember a story, and it is taken out of Germany. There was a town there, . . . this is back when I used to be in grade school in Germany —and I used to bicycle. And we came to a town, and outside of it there was a great forest. And the interesting thing to me, as a boy even, was that the people in that town didn't have to pay taxes. They were supported by their own forest.

Way back in the time of Louis something of France—the French king was approaching this town with a large army. And the prince of the time asked the townspeople to come out to defend their principality, and he promised them if they would keep the invader out of the town, out of the principality, he would give them the forest.

The burghers turned out. They repulsed the French king. And very soon the Prince made good. He gave the forest to the town. And for over two hundred years that town in Germany had to pay no taxes. Everybody made money, because they had no taxes. In other words, it was a forest on an annual-yield basis. They cut down perhaps seventy percent of what they could get out of that year's mature crop. And every year they planted new trees. And every year the proceeds from that forest paid the equivalent of taxes.

... while only God can make a tree, we have to do a little bit to help ourselves. . . . It doesn't amount to very much, this cost of planting trees.

[1] Extemporaneous remarks at Clarksburg, West Virginia, 29 October 1944, *Public Papers and Addresses, 1944*, pp. 379–81.

... When I was a small boy, I realized that there was waste going on; and when I went to the State Senate as a young man, somebody appointed me to the Conservation Committee. Some parts of upstate New York were being eroded, a lot of topsoil was running away, we were getting more floods than we ever had in the old days.

And just as an experiment, I started planting a few acres on run-down land. I tried to pasture some skinny cows on it. And at the same time, I went into the old woods and cleaned out no-account trees, trees that were undergrown or would never amount to anything, crooked trees, rotten trees.

Well, the answer was this. When the last war came on, the old woods had some perfectly splendid trees, because I had cleaned them out, cleaned out the poor stuff.

And during that war, I made four thousand dollars, just by cutting out the mature trees. And I kept on every year. And in the winter time, when the men weren't doing much, they cleaned them out. And the trees grew.

And a quarter of a century later, there came this war. I think I co-operated with the Almighty, because I think trees were made to grow. ... And in this war, back home, I cut last year—and this is not very Christian—over four thousand dollars' worth net of oak trees, to make into submarine chasers and landing craft and other implements of war. And I am doing it again this year.

... I hope that when I am able to cut some more trees, twenty or twenty-five years from now—it may not be I, it may be one of the boys— we will be able to use them at a profit, not for building mine chasers or landing craft, but for turning them into some humane use.

IV

THE POLITICAL CARNIVAL

IN THE HOSPITAL
2 August 1933

THE PRESIDENT: I've got a really good story, if you haven't heard it before. Irwin Steingut[1] dropped in the day before yesterday. He is the minority Leader, you know, in the Assembly. He told me that about three weeks ago he had been in the hospital. He had had a very serious operation and soon after his operation Mrs. Roosevelt and I sent some flowers from the White House to the hospital. Well, the flowers came and Irwin thought that he would thank me in person. So he lifts up the telephone receiver and he gets the telephone girl in the hospital and he says, "I want Washington." She says, "Who do you want?" He says, "I want to speak to the President." "Bang" goes the telephone receiver and five minutes later up come two doctors, an interne and an orderly from the psychopathic ward.

[1] New York Democrat. Minority Leader in the New York State Assembly.

HENRY WALLACE

29 November 1933. Warm Springs, Georgia.

CORRESPONDENT: Has Mr. Wallace[1] been behaving?
THE PRESIDENT: Well, I don't know; the only problem about Wallace and Ickes[2] is that neither of them took a bath while down here.
CORRESPONDENT: Throw them in the pool, Mr. President.
SECRETARY WALLACE: Good farmers wait until Saturday.

[1] Henry A. Wallace, Secretary of Agriculture.
[2] Harold L. Ickes, Secretary of the Interior.

THE INCENDIARY

15 December 1933

Roosevelt started to light a cigarette and some sparks dropped on his clothes.
CORRESPONDENT: Every President is used to playing with fire. You won't burn up!
THE PRESIDENT: When I was two years old I was discovered on the floor burning matches. Perhaps that was a prophecy!

THE VIEWERS-WITH-ALARM

28 June 1934

THE PRESIDENT: A few timid people, who fear progress, will try to give you new and strange names for what we are doing. Sometimes they will call it "Fascism," sometimes "Communism," sometimes "Regimentation," sometimes "Socialism." But, in so doing, they are trying to make very complex and theoretical something that is really very simple and very practical.

I believe in practical explanations and in practical policies. I believe that what we are doing today is a necessary fulfillment of what Americans have always been doing—a fulfillment of old and tested American ideals.

Let me give you a simple illustration:

While I am away from Washington this summer, a long-needed renovation of and addition to our White House office building is to be started. The architects have planned a few new rooms built into the present all too small one-story structure. We are going to include in this addition and in this renovation modern electric wiring and modern plumbing and modern means of keeping the offices cool in the hot Washington summer. But the structural lines of the old Executive office building will remain. The artistic lines of the White House buildings were the creation of master builders when our Republic was young. The simplicity and strength of the structure remain in the face of every modern test. But within this magnificent pattern, the necessities of modern government business require constant reorganization and rebuilding.

If I were to listen to the arguments of some prophets of calamity who are talking these days, I should hesitate to make these alterations. I should fear that while I am away for a few weeks the architects might build some strange new Gothic tower or a factory building or perhaps a replica of the Kremlin or of the Potsdam Palace. But I have no such fears. The architects and builders are men of common sense and of artistic American tastes. They know that the principles of harmony and of necessity itself require that the building of the new structure shall blend with the essential lines of the old. It is this combination of the old and the new that marks orderly peaceful progress, not only in building buildings but in building government itself.

Our new structure is a part of and a fulfillment of the old.[1]

[1] Fireside Chat, 28 June 1934, *Public Papers and Addresses, 1934,* pp. 317–18.

THEOLOGICAL APPRAISAL OF THE LIBERTY LEAGUE
24 August 1934

A group of prominent persons opposed to the New Deal had launched the American Liberty League. Four of the officers of the group were Democrats—Al Smith, John J. Raskob, Jouett Shouse, and Irenee du Pont. Shouse called on Roosevelt and sought to explain the objectives of the League. FDR was ready to accept the challenge.

CORRESPONDENT: Anything you can say on the formation of the American Liberty League?

THE PRESIDENT: . . . Jouett Shouse . . . came in here and pulled a piece of paper out of his pocket and read me the two objectives which I think all the papers have printed, and I told him that both of the objectives would be subscribed to by every American citizen; that they were what might be called axiomatic, unequivocally acceptable to all Americans, and when he asked me whether there were any objections to the formation of the private organization, I said of course not, it is none of my business and I wouldn't have any objections anyway to a private work which had as its principles working for axiomatic principles of American life. Well, that's about all that happened. He said, "Thank you very much" and went out. . . .

CORRESPONDENT: Then you are for the Constitution?

THE PRESIDENT: I won't say "still" because somebody will say that was too passive; I'll say "actively."

Of course, again talking just between us, . . . the thing to note about an organization of this kind . . . is this: that when you come down to the definition of American principles you want to go the whole hog; you want to go all the way instead of stopping short. An organization that advocates two or three out of the Ten Commandments, may be a perfectly good organization in the sense that you couldn't object to the two or three of the Ten Commandments, but that it would have certain shortcomings in having failed to advocate the other seven or eight Commandments.[1]

To put it again in a Biblical way, it has been said that there are two great Commandments—one is to love God, and the other is to love your neighbor. A gentleman with a rather ribald sense of humor suggested that the two particular tenets of the new organization say that you shall love God and then forget your neighbor, and he also raised the question as to whether the name of their God was not "property."

Now as a matter of fact these two things [in the Liberty League's statement] are worth reading. One is that the organization will designate officials that will teach the necessity of respect for the rights of persons and property as fundamental to every successful form of Government, and will teach that government to encourage enterprise.

Going back again, there isn't much said about your neighbor, and if you analyze the Declaration of Independence . . . there are quite a number of things that the average and more than average human gets out of Government besides these two things. There is no mention made here in these two things about the concern of the community, in other words, the Government, to try to make it possible for people who are willing to work, to find work to do. For people who want to keep themselves from starvation, keep a roof over their heads, lead decent lives, have proper educational standards—these are the concern of Government, besides these two

---

[1] FDR referred to the "Ten Commandments" in a similar fashion a few months later in a letter to Newton D. Baker, a prominent Democrat and Secretary of War during the Wilson Administration. Roosevelt wrote that a Senator with a sense of humor had told him that the Republican National Committee "in secret confab searched the woods for an issue; they discarded the constitutional issue and decided in a month or two to come out in favor of the Ten Commandments, proclaiming from the housetops that the Democratic Party wished, A. To amend the Ten Commandments. B. To add to the Ten Commandments. C. Scrap the Ten Commandments." The President to Baker, 26 September 1935, FDRL.

points. And another thing which isn't mentioned . . . is the protection of the life and liberty of the individual against elements in the community that seek to enrich or advance themselves at the expense of their fellow-citizens. They have just as much right to protection by Government as anybody else.

I don't believe that any further comment is necessary after this—what would you call it—a homily? Except that in *The Times* this morning —I lay in bed and laughed for ten minutes—if you will turn to the financial page of *The Times*, "Topics in Wall Street," that has a small paragraph—one that appealed to me. Darned good too, most of them because they give you a real highlight on what's going on—and there was one paragraph that started off like this—I forget the exact phraseology: "The speculative fraternity in Wall Street regards the new American Liberty League as a direct answer from Heaven to their prayer." . . . .

CORRESPONDENT: Did Mr. Shouse invite you to become a member?

THE PRESIDENT: I don't think he did. Must have been an oversight!

BE KIND TO TUGWELL

12 September 1934

CORRESPONDENT: By the way, Mr. Tugwell[1] was up here yesterday? . . . What did he want?

THE PRESIDENT: Just to say goodbye. . . . He was awfully worried. . . . He is going to the Rome conference. What time does the ship sail?

CORRESPONDENT: We don't know.

THE PRESIDENT: Then I might tell you boys what he is worried about. Don't for the love of Pete use it. Don't telephone it to New York. . . . On this Hawaiian sugar suit, with respect to the quota for Hawaii, attacking it on the grounds that it was unconstitutional, the suit apparently has been filed. Henry Wallace was going to Washington the other night from New York and when he passed through Baltimore at 4:30 A.M., a hand came into his berth and shook him roughly and said, "Here is a subpoena." Rex said that apparently it was the first time, since Henry Wallace is a perfectly mild man, the first time he completely lost his temper and he lost his temper all day.

Rex is scared perfectly pink that on the way to his boat somebody is going to slap a subpoena on him and he and his wife will have to give up the European trip. So be kind to him and don't flash it down because it may put ideas into their heads.

---

[1] Assistant Secretary of Agriculture, Rexford (Rex) Guy Tugwell.

GETTING "CACTUS" JACK OUT OF UVALDE, TEXAS

August-October 1934

Vice-President Jack Garner had retreated to his home in Uvalde, Texas, and resisted Roosevelt's efforts to bring him back to Washington. "There are hundreds of demands for your appearance all over the country but I am telling them all that you are on the trail of a bear or are hooked on to a big fish and cannot possibly be disturbed," he wrote to Garner. If Garner would only return, FDR offered to send a plane for him "air cooled and upholstered in any color you desire."[1] Garner craftily appealed to Roosevelt to "let your poor servant have as much rest as possible."[2]

THE PRESIDENT: You must be an awful trial to your wife! She must be tired of seeing you just "settin round." I feel reasonably certain that she would like to clean the house, get a little holiday and not see you for about a week!

However, I will leave it up to her. If she sweeps you out some morning, take a train or a plane or a boat or something and come and stay with me for a few days in Washington. If she cannot get you out of the house any other way, it would be nice if she would come with you.[3]

Garner replied to FDR that if he were to be court martialled and shot at sundown for disobeying orders, Postmaster General Jim Farley and Assistant Secretary of State Raymond Moley should at least be sentenced to hard labor for life since they had promised to "fix" his case or, as a last resort, to get a Presidential pardon. The Vice-President went on to advise Roosevelt to ensure economy in government and not to spend more than he collected. He said that FDR's earlier letter had brought some much-needed rain to Uvalde; he should write again and bring another rain.[4]

THE PRESIDENT: 1. The decision of the court, after long deliberation was as follows: The defendant Garner is acquitted because the Court was much impressed by his plea that he had glue on the seat of his pants and, therefore, could not in decency leave Uvalde.

2. The Court is in full accord with defendant's suggestions to use the pruning knife on expenditures.

3. The Court hopes that this letter will bring rain but that the defendant will not get too wet.[5]

[1] The President to John Garner, 11 August 1934, FDRL.
[2] Garner to the President, 21 August 1934, *ibid.*
[3] The President to Garner, 25 September 1934, *ibid.*
[4] Garner to the President, 1 October 1934, *ibid.*
[5] The President to Garner, 5 October 1934, *ibid.*

THE SOUTH WILL DOMINATE
THE UNITED STATES

23 November 1934. Warm Springs, Georgia.

REXFORD G. TUGWELL:[1] Do you want to tell them about the future population?

THE PRESIDENT: . . . The figures show that in the course of the next fifty years the majority of the people of the United States will be descended from Southern stock. That is an extraordinarily interesting fact. In other words, in the North and in the cities, the increase in population has stopped. It practically has stopped. Practically all the increase in population in this country today is in the South. Now a couple of generations of that means that the majority of people will have Southern blood. That is an interesting fact and we have got to consider what that population is going to be in fifty years.

We have got to raise the standards of education; they are perfectly terrible. The standards of living are low. Yet here is probably as fine a stock, human stock, as you can find anywhere in the United States. It is going to dominate the United States in the course of a couple of generations and what is it going to be like? That is looking at it from a national point of view.

. . . To give you a thought, what we are after primarily is to improve the standard of living for the country as a whole. . . . Better homes, slum clearance, better roads, they all tie together. Better education is very, very important.

I think I told you the story about the first year I was down here, when a young man came up to the porch with his cap in his hand and said, "Can I speak to you, Mr. Roosevelt?"

I said, "Yes, come up, son. What can I do for you?"

He said, "Will you do a great favor for us?"

I said, "What do you want?"

He said, "We are having our school commencement next week and we would be awfully glad if you would come over and give the prizes."

I said, "Delighted to. Are you the president of the graduating class?"

He said, "No, sir; I am the principal of the School."

I said, "My God, man, how old are you?"

He said, "I am nineteen."

"Have you been to college?"

"Oh, yes; I finished my Freshman year at Athens, Georgia."

There was a fine boy who got enough money to finish his Freshman year and then he had to go back to get money for the next term. It would take him eight years to get through college.

I said to him, "How much are you being paid?"

[1] Assistant Secretary of Agriculture.

He told me that he had 150 children and that he was getting paid, as principal, board and lodging and $400 a year. He told me that he had three people teaching with him and that they were just local girls, which meant that they had never had anything, probably, except a local high school education.

Think of the enormous population being brought up that way and yet, off the record, the Governor of Georgia is still in favor of the one-room teacher, the one-room school.

SNEAKING AWAY FROM CAMP

30 November 1934

Vice-President Garner, still vacationing in Uvalde, Texas, wrote to the President that he had gotten lost in the woods and had to climb a tree to get his bearings.[1]

THE PRESIDENT: That story about your falling out of the tree and killing a deer was garbled in transmission. As we get it now we are led to believe that you got tired of shooting deer and that you climbed a tree, fell out of it on top of the deer and choked it to death! You must have been reading about that Abernathy man who used to choke wolves to death with his bare hands.

I still don't believe you got lost. There must have been some darn good reason for staying away from camp!

[1] Jack Garner to the President, 17 November 1934; the President to Garner, 30 November 1934, FDRL.

A GRAND FELLOW

19 December 1934

CORRESPONDENT: Gene Black died this morning.[1]

THE PRESIDENT: I know. It is too bad. I am awfully sorry about that. . . . I always loved Gene Black because he would come in and I would say, "Don't you think we had better do this? I have made up my mind."

And he would answer, "Now, Boss, just let me present the other side of the case to you." And he would do it in five minutes and, at the end of that time, he would say, "Now listen: I have told you the other side of the case; I am a good soldier; I will do whatever you want."

[1] Eugene Black, Governor of the Federal Reserve Board.

OLD CURMUDGEON
8 March 1935

> CORRESPONDENT: Mr. President, is Secretary Ickes resigning?
> THE PRESIDENT: What did you say?
> CORRESPONDENT: Is the Secretary resigning?
> THE PRESIDENT: Does he look resigned?

THE LARGE BROWN ENVELOPE
20 March 1935

THE PRESIDENT: Harry Hopkins was in yesterday. He thought we would try a game on you people in the press room: have him go out with a large brown envelope and, if somebody asked, "What is in that envelope?" he would say, "It is my pardon from the President."

We were afraid somebody might take it seriously—didn't have the nerve.

FASHION TIPS FROM "CACTUS" JACK
19 July 1935

At the press conference held on 17 July 1935 some reporters, instigated by FDR, solemnly complimented Appointments Secretary Marvin McIntyre on his "snappy" new suit. Roosevelt thereupon announced that McIntyre had made his sartorial decisions after studying in a theatre program an advertisement entitled "What the well-dressed man will wear." FDR added that the suit was made of goat's hair. "It is recommended by the Vice-President."

At the next press conference Roosevelt spotted a reporter in a new suit.

CORRESPONDENT: Hello, Mr. President.
THE PRESIDENT: Don't you look perfectly lovely today!
CORRESPONDENT: The first summer sale, Mr. President, $15.75.
THE PRESIDENT: As much as that?
CORRESPONDENT: As much as that.
THE PRESIDENT: You go to Jack Garner and find out where he gets his suits. He buys his suits for $15.50. Why go and waste your money like that and pay $15.75 for a suit?
CORRESPONDENT: I thought I was getting a bargain.
THE PRESIDENT: I am going to have to appoint a committee to save money for these fellows.

THE CARE AND DISPOSAL OF ELEPHANTS

17 December 1935

Seizing on a seemingly innocent or innocuous question, Roosevelt could give a reply with a spontaneity and humor that a professional "gag" writer might well envy.

CORRESPONDENT: Are you disposed to explain your action of approving the allotment of $61,000 to build a new house for elephants at the Zoo in Washington?

THE PRESIDENT: Yes; in the first place, you are too low—it is $61,800. Don't forget the 800. And in the second place, the reason for approving that was it was brought to my attention by the Smithsonian and the Natural History Museum in New York and various scientific and political societies that the elephant is in grave danger of becoming extinct. [The elephant is the symbol of the Republican Party and the donkey of the Democratic Party]. The same thing happened in the case of the buffalo about thirty or forty years ago, and by the liberal expenditure of Federal funds the buffalo is still in existence as a rather rare and interesting animal. We hope to preserve the elephant in the same capacity for future generations, and therefore we are making this appropriation to be used, first, in the National Capital to which tourists resort from all over the nation, and, secondly, a large part of this money, I understand, will be used not only for an elephant house but also for digging a pit for the elephant!

CORRESPONDENT: Mr. President, you are sure you are not trying to make a donkey out of the elephant?

THE PRESIDENT: No danger of their becoming extinct!

GOOD OLD DING AND HIS BIRDS AND BEASTS

27 December 1935. Press conference for members of the American Association of Schools and Departments of Journalism and the American Association of Teachers of Journalism.

Roosevelt spoke at length on the state of the American press. He deprecated the tendency of some correspondents and columnists to base their stories on bits and pieces of information haphazardly gathered. Reporters should not swallow "scarehead stories" of some disgruntled official "who thinks there is nobody else in the world, and nothing else in the world as important as what he is doing."

THE PRESIDENT: Again, "just between us girls," there is good old Jay Darling. He has the greatest enthusiasm on the protection of wildlife in the United States—perfectly fine, a lifelong student of it—and we persuaded him to give up his cartoon work and come down here.[1]

Jay came down, and he couldn't see anything in the Government except birds and animals. It was fine. I loved his enthusiasm, and . . . he slipped over on me the only bill that I know of—I signed it without knowing what was in it.

He had a bill that started off as a perfectly fine, simple bill for the extension of wildlife refuges, and it created the machinery to set up wildlife refuges all over the country—but of course no money involved. He brought it over to me, and it looked like a good tie-in with field agencies that had to do with wildlife. I said, "That's fine."

He takes it up to the Hill, and he pushes it; and finally the bill passes and comes down to me. It is quite a long bill, with six or eight pages. I read the first page, and that is just the way it was before. I looked over the last page, and that was just the way it was before. I signed the bill. Then I discovered that Jay, up there on the Hill had tucked in the middle a paragraph appropriating $6,000,000![2]

Talk about an unbalanced budget!

Jay was horrified down here because of Government red tape. Oh, of course there is Government red tape. Here is the Comptroller General and all the other people that simply create delays of weeks and months sometimes before you can get things through, especially in a new thing like this wildlife conservation. So good old Jay got himself terribly upset. The one thing he cared about was birds and beasts. Of course, marvelous stories about Government red tape came out directly from Ding.

I am enthusiastic about wildlife preservation myself, but there is such a thing as a sense of proportion!

[1] J. N. Darling, familiarly known as "Ding," was a popular cartoonist.
[2] FDR told Ding that he was "the only man in history who got an appropriation through Congress, past the Budget and signed by the President without anybody realizing that the Treasury had been raided." "Nevertheless, more power to your arm!" the President added. The President to J. N. Darling, 29 July 1935, FDRL.

"I AM BEST!"

The election campaign was warming up. FDR staked his claim to be regarded as the champion prognosticator of election results.

15 September 1936

CORRESPONDENT: Have you any comments on the Maine election?
THE PRESIDENT: No, except that I am a damn good guesser. . . . I

have come to the conclusion that when I am through here I am going to syndicate myself. It is cheaper than taking a poll and more accurate than any poll. That is pretty good. I am best!

CORRESPONDENT: Let us see how good you were; how close were you?

THE PRESIDENT: I was pretty close. Let's see: There were five of them running. I was awfully close on three. I wasn't so badly off on one and I was away out on the other.

CORRESPONDENT: Which one were you out on?

THE PRESIDENT: Congressional district. . . .

CORRESPONDENT: In view of the fact that you are best as to your Party, what is your guess as to the November election?

THE PRESIDENT: I will put it down on paper beforehand and nobody else will see it.

CORRESPONDENT: Can we see it afterward?

THE PRESIDENT: All right.

CORRESPONDENT: Will you have it certified that it is the same one you wrote down?

THE PRESIDENT: Ruby,[1] do you remember in 1930 we had a pool? The boys up in Albany and I, we each put—I think it was quite a pool— we put $5 in the hat on what my majority would be. Mind you, they were all experts. . . . They were all experts and I won the pool. Jim Kierney[2] was next, but he was out 50,000. . . .

CORRESPONDENT: As an expert on these things, do you approve of the odds of 5 to 3 offered by Lloyds of London on your re-election?

THE PRESIDENT: Lloyds did that? I am afraid somebody might construe that to be British support!

27 October 1936

CORRESPONDENT: How do you feel about the results on November 3rd?

THE PRESIDENT: That is down here in an envelope.

CORRESPONDENT: Will you be listening to the Election returns at Hyde Park?

THE PRESIDENT: Yes. I made a very bad guess in 1932; you remember that. I made a very good guess in 1930 but a very poor guess in 1932.

CORRESPONDENT: How far off were you?

THE PRESIDENT: I think I gave myself only 310 electoral votes, as I remember it.[3]

[1] Correspondent Ruby Black.
[2] Probably James Kieran, a reporter for the *New York Times*.
[3] Actually in the election of 1932 FDR secured 472 Electoral College votes as against 59 for Herbert Hoover.

CORRESPONDENT: Are you a bit more optimistic this time?

THE PRESIDENT: Well, that is in the envelope.

CORRESPONDENT: In your campaigning, have you found any reason to revise your original figure?

THE PRESIDENT: That would be telling what is in the envelope. There are three dates in the envelope.

CORRESPONDENT: Three dates?

THE PRESIDENT: There is a guess made way back last winter, another made in the spring and another made about a month ago. They may be the same and they may be different.

CORRESPONDENT: Will you give us all three when it is over?

THE PRESIDENT: We may be able to get a pool up on that!

CORRESPONDENT: We had a very good one four years ago.

THE PRESIDENT: Count me in on it. It is all right. . . .

CORRESPONDENT: Are you getting bearish or bullish?

THE PRESIDENT: That would disclose what's in the envelope.

6 November 1936

THE PRESIDENT: I suppose I should start the Conference by saying that I haven't got any news but I do want to say this: that this reception this morning was perfectly thrilling and I appreciated it enormously. Perfectly grand. . . .

CORRESPONDENT: Mr. President, have you opened the envelope, sir?

THE PRESIDENT: I have; I did —; I wish you would not ask me the question because I am so far off.

CORRESPONDENT: There were a lot of us that were!

THE PRESIDENT: Here it is—there is the original. The first date was January 30, 1936, and I was very careful to put down no names at that time because nobody had been nominated. I figured out a Democratic vote in the Electoral College of 325 and a Republican vote of 206. The next time I wrote on it was June 5, which was about three weeks before the Convention, and again I did not put any names down. The Democratic vote in the Electoral College dropped to 315 and the Republican vote had gone up to 216. And then the next time I took it out was August 2, right after I got back from Canada. Then I put down the initials: "F. D. R. 340; A. M. L. 191." And then, here is the worst of all, on Sunday last, November 1: "F. D. R. 360, A. M. L. 171." I apologize![4]

CORRESPONDENT: What frightened you?

THE PRESIDENT: Oh, just my well known conservative tendencies!

[4] In the election of 1936 Roosevelt won 523 Electoral College votes, leaving a mere 8 votes for his Republican opponent, Alf Landon. Postmaster General Jim Farley proved to be a far more accurate forecaster than his chief. He correctly predicted that Roosevelt would carry every state except Maine and Vermont.

THE SUNFLOWER

25 September 1936

Governor Alf Landon of Kansas, the Sunflower State, was Roosevelt's Republican opponent in the Presidential contest of 1936. At the press conference Walter Trohan of the *Chicago Tribune* appeared with a sunflower.

TROHAN: I put this [sunflower] on. The campaign is on. Can you give us any news on that?

THE PRESIDENT: Only news I can give you on that is what one of my neighbors said: that it is yellow all through; that it has got a black beard and that it is only good for parrot food.

THE GENTLEMAN'S SILK HAT

29 September 1936

In the campaign of 1936 FDR described his Republican critics—especially wealthy businessmen—as forgetful men. They were unwilling to remember that the New Deal program had averted starvation, saved homes and farms, raised farm prices, and revived industry.[1]

THE PRESIDENT: In the summer of 1933, a nice old gentleman wearing a silk hat fell off the end of a pier. He was unable to swim. A friend ran down the pier, dived overboard and pulled him out; but the silk hat floated off with the tide. After the old gentleman had been revived, he was effusive in his thanks. He praised his friend for saving his life. Today, three years later, the old gentleman is berating his friend because the silk hat was lost.

[1] Opening speech of the 1936 campaign, Democratic State Convention, Syracuse, N.Y., 29 September 1936, *Public Papers and Addresses, 1936,* p. 385.

I HAVE THEIR FEVER CHARTS

14 October 1936

THE PRESIDENT: Today for the first time in seven years the banker, the storekeeper, the small factory owner, the industrialist, can all sit back and enjoy the company of their own ledgers. They are in the black.

That is where we want them to be; that is where our policies aim them to be; that is where we intend them to be in future.

Some of these people really forget how sick they were. But I know how sick they were. I have their fever charts. I know how the knees of all of our rugged individualists were trembling four years ago and how their hearts fluttered. They came to Washington in great numbers. Washington did not look like a dangerous bureaucracy to them then. Oh, no! It looked like an emergency hospital. All of the distinguished patients wanted two things—a quick hypodermic to end the pain and a course of treatment to cure the disease. They wanted them in a hurry; we gave them both. And now most of the patients seem to be doing very nicely. Some of them are even well enough to throw their crutches at the doctor.[1]

[1] Campaign address at Chicago, 14 October 1936, *Public Papers and Addresses, 1936*, pp. 487–88.

WHO WON THE BATTLE?

21 October 1936

THE PRESIDENT: Three and a half years ago we declared war on the depression. You and I know today that the war is being won.

But now comes that familiar figure—the well-upholstered hindsight critic. He tells us that our strategy was wrong, that the cost was too great, that something else won the war. That is an argument as old as the remorse of those who had their chance and muffed it. It is as recent as the claims of those who say that they could have done better.

You may remember the First Battle of the Marne in the World War. Almost everybody thought that it was Marshal Joffre who had won it. But some refused to agree. One day, a newspaperman appealed to Marshal Joffre: "Will you tell me who did win the Battle of the Marne?" "I can't answer that," said the Marshal. "But I can tell you that if the Battle of the Marne had been lost the blame would have been on me."[1]

[1] Campaign address at Worcester, Mass., 21 October 1936, *Public Papers and Addresses, 1936*, pp. 522–23.

THE FARMER MAKES AN ADDITION TO HIS BARN

11 January 1937

FDR attached great importance to the modernization of the Presidency and had appointed a high-level Committee on Administrative

Management to study the problem. The Committee was composed of Louis Brownlow, Charles Merriam and Luther Gulick. At a press conference attended by members of the Cabinet and of the Committee, Roosevelt explained the principal recommendations of the Committee.

THE PRESIDENT: Now this report. . . . The unthinking person says, "Aha! The first thing that this report suggests is creating two new departments." Sure.

Now, I will tell you a story about a farmer who lived near me. He was in trouble—inefficient. He went down to the county agent and the county agent went down and looked him up and talked it over with him. It appeared that he didn't know how to do things. The first thing the county agent found there was the fact that he [the farmer] had fourteen outbuildings. He had three separate henhouses; he had a couple of tool sheds, and a couple of wagon sheds and a number of other out-buildings. The first thing to do was to get rid of his overload.

What did he do in his own time? He built an addition to his barn. That looked wasteful, but, having built the addition to his barn, he took all the things that had been in all of the out-houses and put them all in the barn, or addition to his barn, and then he tore down all of his outhouses. He got rid of them and saved a tremendous figure in his overhead and besides an awful lot of steps. He didn't have to walk a mile a day between out-houses. All of the things that they contained were in the one addition to his barn.

. . . In other words, would it be worth our while in the Federal Government, where we have 105 departments of government, including the 10 regular departments—in other words, 95 outside and 10 regular departments—isn't it worth while to create two new departments and bring the 95 under them? Of course it is.

. . . Let me again suggest . . . that these are matters of commonsense management. The word "management" is a thoroughly clear American word. The housewife is a good "manager"—we all know what that means. If we say our wives are good managers, everybody understands what we mean. If a small gasoline station is working out well and making money, what do we say about the owner? We say, "He is a good manager." If it is a corporation, large or small, they have a "good management." What we are trying to do is to put a good management into the government in exactly the same sense of the term.

. . . Well, unfortunately from my point of view as far as personal comfort goes, the Constitution of the United States says that there is just one manager and nobody else. I am the manager, and if business does not go well—well, I've got trouble. I fail at re-election. I am the manager and I am responsible. I am responsible for the misdeeds, in the long run, of somewhere around 580,000 Federal employees. If the number of those misdeeds pile up and I could have prevented them, the population knows where to place the blame and so does Congress.

HERBERT HOOVER

16 January 1937

THE PRESIDENT: . . . a member of the family rushed in the other day and said, "We are all wrong about the Child Labor Amendment; we shall have to reverse our position—former President Hoover has endorsed it."[1]

[1] The President to Luther Gulick, Director, Institute of Public Administration, New York, 16 January 1937, FDRL.

THE JUDGE WHO WAS ALWAYS UP WITH HIS CALENDAR

15 April 1937

In February, 1937, Roosevelt submitted to Congress his proposals for judicial reorganization and soon ran into greater trouble than he had anticipated. He fought back vigorously for a while and, in a press conference for members of the American Society of Newspaper Editors, he came up with a story that packed a sharp punch.

THE PRESIDENT: For example, if you go back on the Supreme Court thing, there have been an awful lot of people in a great many papers who, ever since my Message of February fifth, have stated, baldly and bluntly, that one reason for adding judges to the Supreme Court . . . was that I had said that their calendar was crowded and they were behind in their work. Now, people who appear before the Senate Committee quote me that way. Of course I never said anything like that in my life. I never suggested it for a moment. They are absolutely up with their calendar! I will tell you a story that illustrates it.

When I was a practising lawyer in New York in 1907, I used to have occasional police court clients, people who had been disorderly at two o'clock in the morning in Times Square, and they generally would be taken by the police to the old Jefferson Market Court. There was an old fellow down there, an old Tammany magistrate, who was a law to himself—there was no supervision over magistrates in those days—and he had a rule that, by God, he was going to close his court at one P.M. every day.

Well, if I had a Harvard friend to defend on a Tuesday morning, that was all right. There would be only twenty cases before the old judge and he had from ten to one to dispose of his twenty cases. My client would get heard; he would get heard and he would get a fair deal from the court. But, if my client happened to have been picked up on a Satur-

day night or a Sunday night and had to appear in Monday morning court
before the same old judge, there would be 220 cases. But he had his rule
about one P.M. and he would run those 220 cases through his court
without hearing the defendant. It was ten dollars or ten days! And they
were all tried. His calendar was not crowded on Mondays any more than
it was on Tuesdays. He was always up with his work.

But what I did say and what is perfectly true—ask any lawyer who
has had any Supreme Court practice whether they are satisfied with the
fact that only twelve per cent of the applications and petitions for cer-
tiorari are granted and eighty-eight per cent are turned down. That is
all that I said, but it was plenty.

HOW FDR CARRIED KANSAS IN 1936
15 April 1937

Gathered in the Dining Room of the White House were the members
of the American Society of Newspaper Editors. Roosevelt noted that his
good friend, William Allen White, editor of the *Emporia* (Kansas)
Gazette, was absent.

THE PRESIDENT: Thank the Lord it is informal. Thank the Lord it
is off the record. It is more difficult for me than the Gridiron Dinner because, at the Gridiron Dinner,[1] I have the last word and nobody can talk
back. At this party you can and do talk back!

I am very sorry that the principal talker-backer is not here tonight,
Bill White. Somebody will have to substitute for him. You know, in the
Campaign, I got Bill White into a position that he has never been in before. I was sitting on top of a railroad train, on the back platform, and
he was down in the crowd. I had a loud speaker and he did not! So, when
we pulled into Emporia, honestly I did not know that Bill was out there.
I stood out on the back platform and after I had been duly introduced by
the Democratic Chairman or someone like that, I put up my hand like
that [indicating] and looked all around through the crowd and I said,
"Where is Bill White?"

Of course the crowd howled with glee. I had them at a disadvantage
right off. I said, "Bill is an old friend of mine. He goes back twenty-five
years. And the interesting thing is that Bill agrees with me three years
and a half out of every four." I said, "As for the other six months out of
the four years—" At that moment I caught sight of Bill. I said, "There

[1] A function organized by the Gridiron Club, an association of Washington correspondents, in which prominent political personalities including the President are lampooned.

you are!" I said, "You come right up here and tell me your story." And I said to the crowd, "Now, as long as he is here, I won't tell you about him during the other six months."

Of course that was extremely unfair political advantage to take over good old William Allen White. I apologized to him afterwards, but it did help me to carry Kansas.

DOC COPELAND'S PHILOSOPHY

27 April 1937

CORRESPONDENT: There seems to be almost universal approval of your economy movement until you get down to individual cases.

THE PRESIDENT: Yes, it depends on whose baby gets the measles.

CORRESPONDENT: Will Senator Copeland[1] prescribe for that?

THE PRESIDENT: Well, look—off the record, as V.P. [Vice-President John N. Garner] said to me a couple of days ago—this is really off the record—"When it comes to old Doc Copeland, he has two rules: One is to vote for every appropriation and the other is to vote against every tax."

[1] Democratic Senator Royal S. Copeland of New York was a doctor and author of *Dr. Copeland's Home Medical Book.*

THAT IS SOMETHING YOU DO NOT ASK

21 September 1937

In August 1937 FDR had named Senator Hugo L. Black of Alabama to fill the vacancy in the Supreme Court caused by the resignation of Justice Willis Van Devanter. Subsequently it was revealed that Black had once been a member of the Ku Klux Klan and the President found himself in a very delicate position. He denied charges that he had been aware of Black's association with the Klan.

CORRESPONDENT: Justice Black's nephew in Washington made a speech before the Alabama Club. . . . At that luncheon he said that Mr. Black had given a full account of his activities to those persons who were responsible for his appointment. Is there anything you want to say about that?

THE PRESIDENT: Not in answer to that. I can only tell you . . . exactly what I told you before. Somebody asked me, in the first conference, if I knew anything about it and I said, "No." A typical newspaper editorial like the Poughkeepsie paper said that I must have known. It is the same old thing and the same old story. . . .

CORRESPONDENT: In that connection there seem to be some interesting developments as to whether any effort was made to ask Justice Black . . . for any explanation before the appointment was made? Can you answer that?

THE PRESIDENT: The other answer covers it. In other words, . . . suppose I were to appoint Ernest[1] to the Interstate Commerce Commission. Do you suppose I would say, "Listen, Ernest, how many illegitimate children do you have running around the country?" That is something you do not ask.

MARVIN MCINTYRE: You might ask Ernest just out of curiosity.

THE PRESIDENT: Yes, I might have asked Black a lot of things out of curiosity!

. . . A man's private life is supposed to be his private life. He may have had certain marital troubles which, if they came out, might be pretty disagreeable. It is certainly not incumbent on the Department of Justice, the President or anybody else to look into that, so long as it does not come out and a fellow has led a perfectly good life. . . . You must assume that the man, if he has led a decent life up to the present time, is all right. You cannot go and ask him about it.

[1] Ernest K. Lindley, correspondent of the *New York Herald Tribune*.

EVERY SENATOR WANTS ONE

6 April 1938

THE PRESIDENT: We are having one very amusing thing: They put through an appropriation for these agricultural products laboratories, and I think every Senator is asking for one of them. How many are there of them? There are four. And of these four laboratories, all of them, the Senators, want one to be put in a state. Of course we cannot put four in forty-eight states very well, and the pressure on me is perfectly terrific, and the pressure on Henry [Wallace] is pretty bad. So we worked out a formula. We are going to auction them off! In other words, we are going to give the four of them to the four states that offer the highest bid and put in the most money themselves. . . .

CORRESPONDENT: You might put them on rollers, Mr. President.

THE PRESIDENT: Yes, put them on rollers and move them around. I think that is a happy solution. . . .

DILEMMA OF THE DAUGHTERS
OF THE AMERICAN REVOLUTION
21 April 1938

In a press conference for members of the American Society of Newspaper Editors, FDR gleefully recalled how he had handled the formidable Daughters of the American Revolution a few hours earlier.

THE PRESIDENT: I am not going to ask any questions but I am going to tell you what I said to the D.A.R. today. I am going to preach the same sermon to you that I presented to them. It is a perfectly good text.

I said that I probably had a more American ancestry than nine out of ten of the D.A.R. I had various ancestors who came over in the Mayflower and similar ships—one that carried the cargo of furniture—and furthermore that I did not have a single ancestor who came to this country after the Revolutionary War; they were all here before the Revolution. And, out of the whole thirty-two or sixty-four of them, whichever it was, there was only one Tory!

Well, they began to wonder if they ought to applaud that or not.

And . . . now I will come down to the text. It is just as good for you people as it was for the D.A.R. I am putting you in the same category!

I said; Here is the text. Keep it in front of your heads all of the time, dear ladies, first, that you are descendants of immigrants.

And they did not know whether to applaud that or not.

Secondly, that you are the descendants of revolutionaries.

They did not know whether to applaud that or not.

So there is the text and I won't expound on it any further. Now shoot!

AN EXERCISE IN LATIN
10 May 1938

Egged on by some of his advisors—"White House Janizaries," as they were described by a critic—FDR had initiated a campaign to "purge" the Democratic Party of certain vigorous opponents of his policies. The ardent New Dealer, Claude Pepper, won the Democratic Senatorial primary in Florida, but in Pennsylvania it was a different story. The "purge" subsequently ended in a fiasco and the only scalp that Roosevelt could claim was that of John O'Connor of New York City, chairman of the House Rules Committee.

CORRESPONDENT: Anything to say about the Florida election?

THE PRESIDENT: Oh, I think the little old Latin phrase.

CORRESPONDENT: What is it? What phrase?

THE PRESIDENT: I will put it in English: "The thing speaks for itself!"

CORRESPONDENT: Mr. President, any Latin phrase for the Pennsylvania situation?

THE PRESIDENT: No, but you might read Dante's Inferno!

THE BRITISH DO IT DIFFERENTLY
21 June 1938

Joseph Kennedy, American Ambassador to London, had called on Roosevelt and reporters sought to question the latter concerning the visit.

THE PRESIDENT: Joe, when he landed, . . . told this to the boys at the dock: . . . he had met in England exactly the same kind of people that he used to meet on Long Island, exactly the same kind of people, who said that the world was coming to an end, everything was terrible and how they would have to close their country houses and sell their Rolls Royces. They were exactly the same crowd and the only difference was that in England they did not blame it on their Government, which I think is a grand line, a brilliant line.

And he was enlarging on it this morning and he said, "You know, they have a problem come up and they talk it over for weeks. Certain elements in the community may not like it; they make their protest, sit around the table and talk it over and if the thing goes through that they do not like, they quit grousing. That is the real difference between Government in England and Government here."

THE CHINESE WAY
24 June 1938

In a fireside chat before the Democratic primary elections FDR asserted that he had every right to speak out where there might be a clear issue between candidates involving principles or a clear misuse of his own name. He expressed the hope that liberal candidates would confine themselves to arguments and not to resort to blows.

THE PRESIDENT: In nine cases out of ten the speaker or writer who, seeking to influence public opinion, descends from calm argument to unfair blows hurts himself more than his opponent.

The Chinese have a story on this—a story based on three or four thousand years of civilization: Two Chinese coolies were arguing heatedly in the midst of a crowd. A stranger expressed surprise that no blows were being struck. His Chinese friend replied: "The man who strikes first admits that his ideas have given out." [1]

[1] *Public Papers and Addresses, 1938,* p. 400.

RESTRICTING THE FRANCHISE TO GRADUATES
9 September 1938

Roosevelt referred to a New Jersey group that advocated the denial of voting rights to persons on relief.

THE PRESIDENT: . . . this organization of "ladies"—put "ladies" in quotes—in New Jersey . . . have organized a movement to keep anybody who unfortunately happens to be on the relief rolls, through no fault of their own, from voting because they are paupers.

CORRESPONDENT: The Women's Rebellion?

THE PRESIDENT: Yes. I think it is incorporated. I think it is called Women's Rebellion, Inc. Of course the logical conclusion to that would be for another women's revolution or men's revolution to start with the franchise to be confined to people with A.B. degrees or more.

I remember President Eliot,[1] twenty or twenty-five years ago, at the time the question of women's suffrage was coming up, somebody said to him, "President Eliot, are you in favor of women's suffrage?"

He said, "No."

They said, "Why? Do you think it would increase the ignorant vote in the country?"

He said, "Why, no, I am very much in favor of an ignorant vote in the country. It is because I do not think women know enough about Government affairs to be given a franchise."

President Eliot was then told that quite a number of college graduates have indicated that they favored giving it to holders of college degrees and, in response to that, he said, "When that happens in this country, we will have a republic for three years and no more!"

[1] Charles W. Eliot, President of Harvard University.

ROOSEVELT'S REVERENCE FOR THE HOLY BOOK
4 October 1938

CORRESPONDENT: Mr. President, the Federal Communication Commission took action last week which raised the question of radio censorship. They voted four to one . . . to cite a small station out in Minne-apolis for reasons to show cause why their license should not be taken away. That action would include the entire blue network of National Broadcasting on the ground that the broadcast of Eugene O'Neill's play "Beyond the Horizon," had been guilty of putting profane and indecent language on the air. The specific charges were that in O'Neill's play the words "Hell," "damn," and "for God's sake" had been used.

. . . Now, that raises the whole question of Government policy with respect to the question of morals, etc., so far as the air is concerned. I wonder if you would comment? . . . .

THE PRESIDENT: I would not dare comment on it because, off the record, it would get me into the most awful censorship of words which are used extensively in the Bible![1]

> [1] FDR went on to raise another issue: ". . . you remember the situation last spring or winter with Mae West? Now the script was all right—if you or I read it, all right—but Mae West—My God, what she put into it! How do you censor intonation? Now, that is a nice question. How can you censor intonation?"

BULLITT'S SEARCH

2 December 1938. Warm Springs, Georgia.

It was a lean day for reporters. Roosevelt simply would not be drawn out. When the newsmen made no secret of their disappointment, FDR mockingly suggested a theme for them to work upon.

CORRESPONDENT: How about a powerful speech this afternoon?

THE PRESIDENT: I think I will turn over the speechmaking to other people.

CORRESPONDENT: . . . Very splendid conference, thank you!

CORRESPONDENT: . . . My assignment sheet is sort of blank.

THE PRESIDENT: Can't you talk about the return of warm weather?

CORRESPONDENT: . . . We are enjoying it and letting it go at that.

THE PRESIDENT: You might write a piece about Bullitt[1] in search of a good climate.

CORRESPONDENT: Doesn't he like France?

THE PRESIDENT: When he arrived from the other side he decided he would want some nice warm weather and he went to Bermuda and froze to death. Then he came back, hit a snow storm and then he went down to the Bahamas where they rained him out. Finally he came to Warm Springs and now he is getting it.

> [1] William Bullitt, US Ambassador to France.

SHARING THE BASS DRUM

7 January 1939

Roosevelt warned Democrats that disunity and squabbling in their ranks would lead to disaster for the Party.

THE PRESIDENT: . . . we always bear in mind the story of the Orangemen's parade in North Ireland on the anniversary of the Battle of the Boyne.

The parade was set but the Orangemen had no bass drum. And what is a parade without a bass drum!

But the captain of the Orangemen had a good personal friend in the captain of the Fenians in the same town.

He explained his problem to his friend, the captain of the Fenians, and asked him to cooperate by lending the Fenian drum for the Orangemen's parade.

"Sure," said the captain of the Fenians. "I'll give you my fullest cooperation. I will lend you the drum; you couldn't have a decent parade without it."

"But," he added with a twinkle in his eye, "since I'm personally responsible for the safety of the drum you'll understand if I have to make one personal condition. You'll have to agree to take the drum out of the parade when you get to Queen Street.

"For that's the corner where we Fenians are going to be laying for you."

If we Democrats lay for each other now, we can be sure that 1940 will be the corner where the American people will be laying for all of us.[1]

[1] Address at Jackson Day Dinner, Washington, D.C., 7 January 1939, *Public Papers and Addresses, 1939*, pp. 60–61.

A CONFERENCE WITH THE SECRETARY OF COMMERCE

31 March 1939

CORRESPONDENT: Have you been discussing with the Secretary of Commerce, Mr. President?

THE PRESIDENT: Yes. Last night we discussed the relative merits of bridge and poker. We came to no conclusion.

TOMMY

25 July 1939

Thomas (Tommy the Cork) Corcoran, who had been brought to FDR's attention by Felix Frankfurter, had gained the confidence of the President and had become an influential figure at court. Many old-timers viewed with alarm and indignation the activities of Corcoran and his associates and among them was Post Master General James A. Farley. There were recurrent reports that Corcoran was trying to undermine Farley's position.

CORRESPONDENT: Mr. President, are you going to have any corroboration or denials or other comments on reports that Mr. Corcoran is trying to remove Mr. Farley as Chairman of the Democratic National Committee?

THE PRESIDENT: I do not know what you can call it. You can call it Tommyrot! . . . That refers to your story, you see, and not to Mr. Corcoran.

AMENDING THE SIMILE

8 August 1939

THE PRESIDENT: Last Winter, in speaking at the Jackson Day Dinner, I referred to the sad state the country would be in if it had to choose between a Democratic Tweedle Dum and a Republican Tweedle Dee. I want to amend that simile, so let me put it this way: The Democratic Party will not survive as an effective force in the nation if the voters have to choose between a Republican Tweedle Dum and a Democratic Tweedle Dummer.[1]

[1] The President to Pitty Tyson Maner, President, Young Democratic Clubs of America, 9 August 1939, *Public Papers and Addresses, 1939*, p. 437.

THE TALE OF TWO CONGRESSMEN

25 October 1939

THE PRESIDENT: About a week ago a certain member of the House of Congress came in and said, "Mr. President, it is a terrible situation down there in Alabama. People are starving. The livestock, they cannot feed it; they will have to kill it, they won't have anything to feed on over the winter and it means during the spring they will starve. It is very widespread."

I said, "How widespread?"

And he said, "Twenty-five counties in Alabama affected and nine in Mississippi."

He went out and an hour later a legislator from Mississippi came in and he said, "This is a terrible situation because people won't have enough feed for the winter and they won't be able to keep the livestock alive."

I said, "How widespread is it?"

And he said, "It is bad; twenty-five counties in Mississippi and nine in Alabama."

. . . It is all right as long as they stick to the same line of talk.

DEFINITIONS

26 October 1939

A Radical is a man with both feet firmly planted—in the air.

A Conservative is a man with two perfectly good legs who, however, has never learned to walk forward.

A Reactionary is a somnambulist walking backwards.

A Liberal is a man who uses his legs and his hands at the behest—at the command—of his head.[1]

[1] Radio Address to the *New York Herald Tribune* Forum, 26 October 1939, *Public Papers and Addresses, 1939*, p. 556.

AN OLD CHESTNUT

27 October 1939

The political future of Vice-President John N. Garner was the subject of discussion.

CORRESPONDENT: I was interested in a story in Fred Wile's column the other day about a poem to Jack Garner and one line is, "He is riding high and he is riding straight, and he is headed for the White House gate." I wanted to know which direction?

THE PRESIDENT: Well, off the record, you remind me of President Coolidge's remark about Senator Borah when he pointed him out riding in Rock Creek Park. He said, "That is the most interesting sight in Washington. He is going in the same direction as his horse!"

CORRESPONDENT: Do we have to keep that off the record?

THE PRESIDENT: Well, that is an old chestnut.

POWER FAILURE

28 June 1940

Wendell Willkie of Indiana had been nominated as its candidate for the Presidency by the Republican Party at its convention held in Philadelphia. Willkie had been connected with utility interests engaged in the production and distribution of electricity.

THE PRESIDENT: I am sorry to be late this morning but I tried to get downstairs and the elevator was not working. Somebody had turned the power off. I hope it is not a connotation of what happened in Philadelphia last night!

THE DUNCE CAP CLUB

12 July 1940

During the months before Roosevelt publicly announced his decision to accept the nomination of the Democratic Party for a third term, he solemnly called on every reporter who asked him "third term questions" to wear a dunce cap and to go and stand in the corner.[1]

CORRESPONDENT: The Dunce Cap Club which you formed a few years ago and which has a large membership of reporters who have asked third term questions will hold a meeting in Chicago to dissolve the organization and turn in their dunce caps.

Could we hope for from you, as the founder of the organization, some sort of communication formally dissolving it?

THE PRESIDENT: Well, I will tell you: I'd have to look at the list of the membership of the organization. . . . I will say this, that the progress that has been made on the whole has been pretty good. I should say that probably quite a percentage of the people who used to stand in the corner are now back, sitting at their desks in the schoolroom. They have removed their dunce caps but I don't say that the corner is empty.

CORRESPONDENT: Mr. President, he said to turn in their dunce caps. Where are they going to turn them in? Put them in your Library?

[1] The "Club" came into existence on 29 June 1937 when correspondent Bob Post asked FDR whether he would accept the nomination of the Democratic Party for a third term. "Oh, my God! This is hot weather," said Roosevelt. "Bob, go into the corner over there and put on the dunce cap and stand with your back to the crowd."

DEFINING A DEMOCRAT

15 April 1941

CORRESPONDENT: Mr. President, will Mr. Hopkins[1] be a dollar-a-year man?

THE PRESIDENT: [Laughing] No, he will not.

THE CORRESPONDENT: Will he be an Administrative Assistant then, sir?

THE PRESIDENT: No. I don't know what he will be, but he won't be a dollar-a-year man.

CORRESPONDENT: Will he get paid?

THE PRESIDENT: Yes, sure. He's a Democrat. What a foolish question!

[1] After resigning his position as Secretary of Commerce, Harry Hopkins had been living in the White House and performing important special missions for the President. In October, 1941, FDR set up the Office of Lend-Lease and named Hopkins Administrator.

UN-AMERICAN ACTIVITIES

16 September 1941

Critics of the Administration charged that interventionist sentiment was being propagated through motion pictures, and a Senate Committee launched an investigation. In commenting on the situation, FDR spoke of yet another threat to "Americanism" posed by the wide dissemination in the United States of a war-mongering book written by aliens. With tongue-in-cheek, of course!

CORRESPONDENT: Mr. President, you have been known for several years as a very enthusiastic motion picture fan. Have you been impressed with the dangers of war propaganda in motion pictures lately?

THE PRESIDENT: I have not. . . .

CORRESPONDENT: Do you care to comment on the hullabaloo about it?

THE PRESIDENT: No. I saw Berryman's cartoon in tonight's *Star*. I think it's worth reprinting. It's rather—rather good. Are you familiar with that? [He held up a copy of the *Washington Evening Star* and displayed a cartoon by Jim Berryman.]

. . . A Picture of Charlie Chaplin. And he is standing in very much the old Charlie Chaplin attitude, holding a subpoena to appear before the Senate Committee investigating motion picture propaganda. And Charlie is saying, "Now, I—now what could I possibly tell these past-masters about comedy?" . . . .

Well, I have got another one. . . . It is to a Senator. . . . The date is September 10. It is addressed to Senator So and So, Washington, D.C.:

Have just been reading a book called the Holy Bible. Has large circulation in this country. Written entirely by foreign-born, mostly Jews. First part is full of war-mongering propaganda. Second part condemns Isolationism, with faked story about Samaritan. Dangerous. Should be added to your list and suppressed.

PLEASE DON'T DIE!

10 October 1941

Roosevelt expressed concern over the fact that a large number of persons had been found unsuitable for induction into the armed forces and discussed the problem of improving the health of the American people.

THE PRESIDENT: I suppose, under the Constitution, a person has a right to die at an early age. Constitutional.

But I think . . . what we call government, local government, state government, has a right to say to that fellow, "Now, look, don't die. Why don't you get better? Why let this thing go on?"—and know more or less as to whether that individual insists on dying or not!

Constitutionally, he has the right to do it. But the Government ought to know what his attitude is!

TRYING IT ON THE DOG

3 November 1941

THE PRESIDENT: We like to do things, talk about them, fight about them among ourselves, say pretty awful things to each other, and finally work things out.

It always reminds me—this system of ours—of a remark that James Bryce, the famous historian, made in my presence in Washington, when Uncle Ted was President. We were talking about different forms of government, and Lord Bryce, who was the British Ambassador and had a twinkle in his eye—as is very essential for all people, not alone Ambassadors—said, "You know, you people in this country and in Canada, and other places where there are democracies, are singularly fortunate in having a Federal system." And we all said, "Why?"

"Well," he said, "you have many States in this country, and somebody comes along, and one of those States has a bright idea, something that sounds perfectly grand, something very novel, something that the people in that particular State grab ahold of on election day and put into effect. And sometimes it is an awfully good idea, and sometimes it is a pretty poor idea."

And as he said, "Perhaps I shouldn't refer to the States of the Union as dogs, but it is a little bit like the idea of trying it on the dog, and if it works, it will spread to other States, and if it doesn't work, it will stop right there, and some day be repealed."

If you look back into our history as a country for a hundred and fifty years, you will find that a great many things that today we are accepting as part of our lives and part of our system have been brought forward in just that way. First they have been tried on the dog, and they worked. Then they have been tried in several other places, and they worked. And gradually they extended to the body politic of the United States.[1]

> [1] Informal remarks to a conference of Dutchess County Teachers, Hyde Park, New York, 3 November 1941, *Public Papers and Addresses, 1941*, p. 456.

"NEGATIVE PREGNANT"

16 December 1941

America was at war with the Axis Powers. There was some speculation that FDR might offer some important position in the Administration to Wendell Willkie.

CORRESPONDENT: Mr. President, are you offering any job to Wendell Willkie?[1]

THE PRESIDENT: No. Not at the present time. I don't think I would say that I am not offering *any* job, because he told you yesterday that he hadn't been offered a job *yesterday*. So I don't think that the negative —what they call a "negative pregnant"—is now called for—if you remember your old Hill's Rhetoric![2] . . . I don't know whether you have studied that. You had better. It's good!

> [1] Unsuccessful Republican Presidential candidate in 1940.
> [2] Apparently FDR was referring to Adams Sherman Hill's *The Foundations of Rhetoric and Their Application* (New York, 1891) or *The Foundations of Rhetoric* (New York, 1893).

A CHINESE PRAYER

17 December 1941

THE PRESIDENT: . . . I was thinking of an old idea of self-discipline —an old Chinese proverb—of a Chinese Christian. He prayed every day—

he had been told to pray to our kind of God—and his prayer was: "Lord, reform Thy world, beginning with me." It is rather a nice line for us all to keep in the back of our minds.[1]

[1] Informal remarks to the Management-Labor Conference, 17 December 1941, *Public Papers and Addresses, 1941,* p. 561.

ALGEBRA

30 December 1941

THE PRESIDENT: [Indicating a nearly empty work basket] Isn't that basket rather good for these days? Right up to date!

. . . I asked Steve if we had any news. He said, "Yes";—a remarkable Message I sent up to the Hill today on parity for peanuts!

. . . Up to the 7th of December we had a thing which was labeled by some people an "All-out Program" and other people called it a "Victory Program." I have discarded both those names. I'm calling it today the *War Program.*

. . . Now that Program on the 7th of December—I have got to go back to my Algebra—let us call it "x." And "x" looked awfully big to the people who brought it to me, with, I might also say, fear and trembling that I would knock them over because it was so big.

And I took a look at it, on the night of the 7th December, and I said that was made before the attack. And I sent it back to them to make it bigger. In other words, I added "y" to it.

And I got back a combined program of "x" and "y."

And as a result of our talks during the past week among ourselves and with the British, and with the Canadians, I have come—not reluctantly but very gladly—to the decision that the "x" plus "y" program does not represent the productive capacity of the United States, and in order to bring it to that total productive capacity, I am adding "z" to it.

. . . I think you get the point! . . .

CORRESPONDENT: What about taxes, Mr. President? . . .

THE PRESIDENT: You shouldn't have such a vulgar mind as to think about taxes! . . . He is frightfully vulgar, isn't he?

PARASITES

30 January 1942

Roosevelt said that he had received a memorandum to the effect that the saturation point of construction of housing had been reached in

Washington and that persons living in the city for social reasons or simply because their children were studying in local schools should be asked to move out.

THE PRESIDENT: Well, . . . somebody was going to ask me a question about moving non-defense people out of Washington. And it is a question of inherent powers. And I suppose if we were to make it uncomfortable for the—what shall I call them?—parasites in Washington, the parasites will leave. There are a good many parasites in Washington today. We all know that. I don't know whether that is an exercise of inherent power or not, but I am inclined to think they would get out.

CORRESPONDENT: . . . this town is considerably upset about it.

THE PRESIDENT: Well, I know what I would do. I would write a story with a headline—large headline—in the Washington papers. The headline—very simple—go right in a box—right across the front page: ARE YOU A PARASITE?

Now a lot of people in this town are going to say, "I wonder if I am a parasite or not!"

CORRESPONDENT: Well, you . . . ought to appoint a "Parasite Commission." We could clean house. We could run them out.

THE PRESIDENT: We went into it in the World War. Lots of people were personal friends of mine who came down to Washington and just had a good time—didn't do a lick of work—men and women. . . . I never counted them, but there were an awful lot around and they clogged up the actual work—war work of the Government. . . . they were having a good time!

SOMETHING FOR THE SPORTS PAGE
10 April 1942

Washington buzzed with colorful accounts of a "fistic encounter" that had taken place the previous night at the Hotel Willard between Jesse Jones, Secretary of Commerce, and Eugene Meyer, Publisher of the *Washington Post*. The incident had lent a touch of drama to the annual dinner of the Alfafa Club. The two men had apparently grown to dislike each other during the Hoover years when Meyer was Chairman of the Reconstruction Finance Corporation and Jones a Director.

CORRESPONDENT: Anything from Jesse Jones or Eugene Meyer since their fight?

THE PRESIDENT: I have no news.

CORRESPONDENT: Mr. President, are you in a neutral corner on that? . . .

THE PRESIDENT: I hope they don't make me the umpire—or the referee. That would be bad.

CORRESPONDENT: Are you counting time . . . .

THE PRESIDENT: . . . I can say this, but not for quotation: I hope that there won't be a second round! . . . .

CORRESPONDENT: Do you think we ought to put it on the sports page?

THE PRESIDENT: Yes!

WHO'S RUNNING THE SHOW?

6 November 1942

At a press conference held specially for editors of business journals, Roosevelt sought to make the point that the War Production Board headed by William Knudsen was composed of responsible businessmen, most of whom were Republicans. He told them of a conversation that he had with Knudsen and brought into play a bit of mimicry.[1]

THE PRESIDENT: I think you know the story about Knudsen, who came in one day. He was submitting lists to me from time to time, and he brought in a list of twenty names of big businessmen.

And I looked it over; I knew pretty well who they were.

And I said, "Bill!"

I said, "Look! Something got by you. There is a Democrat there!"

And he said, "Oh, no, Mr. President. There's no Democrat there. He was nominally."

I said, "Well, what about that fellow there? He comes from Atlanta, Georgia."

"Oh," says Bill, "he galls himself a Demograt but—he voted for Villkie!"

So you—you business people, you are running the show now!

[1] FDR could dress up an old chestnut in a brand-new outfit to suit the occasion. He had given a somewhat different version of the story to reporters at a press conference on 15 April 1941: "That was what I said to Bill Knudsen the other day. In about the fourth or fifth list of these dollar-a-year men, they were all listed as Republicans except a boy who had graduated from Yale last June and never voted; and I said, "Bill, couldn't you find a Democrat to go on this dollar-a-year list anywhere in the country?" He said, "I have searched the whole country over. There is no Democrat rich enough to take a job at a dollar a year!"

HOME ON THE RANGE

1 December 1942

There was a story widely believed in the United States that Roosevelt's favorite song was "Home on the Range." This created a problem

for the President because too many of his admirers tended to sing it on
the slightest provocation, hoping to gladden Roosevelt's heart.

THE PRESIDENT: Steve says that there is nothing ready to serve.
Quite a lot—quite a lot of food that's on the—on the range, but it isn't
cooked for you yet.

CORRESPONDENT: Mr. President, do you plan to name Ickes Secretary
of Labor? . . .

THE PRESIDENT: Oh, nothing—nothing on the fire.

CORRESPONDENT: Nothing on the *fire*, Mr. President? . . . .

CORRESPONDENT: Maybe it has been cooked, Mr. President?

THE PRESIDENT: It isn't cooked. . . . I think you could say it's not on
the range.

CORRESPONDENT: What do you mean by that, Mr. President?

THE PRESIDENT: What? The first thing I know somebody will start
singing "Home on the Range!"

THE SOLUTION TO THE "MANPOWER" PROBLEM AND ITS SOCIAL CONSEQUENCES

11 June 1943

THE PRESIDENT: Oh, we have all talked—I have too—and printed—
I have too—columns and columns, for example, about the question of
manpower. Well, a lot of people got completely panicky about—about
manpower.

. . . I went out through the country, I came back to Washington, and
said—and I said to a lot of friends, "Don't talk to me about manpower
any more, because the manpower question has been solved by woman-
power." Now that is a simple fact.

. . . And some of the . . . impressions of a neophyte like I was, going
around, are interesting.

I said to one of the old West Pointers in one of the places where they
had a lot of WAACs, "How are you getting on with these 'gals' around
here?"

And he said, "We have put in 750 more. We not only need them, we
can use them very usefully to release manpower as opposed to woman-
power for the various fronts."

And he said, "Incidentally, we old West Pointers, they have taught
us something. We were sloppy. They salute better than we do. They are
snappier in every way. They have improved the morale of the place fifty
per cent."

. . . I went into one of the plane factories, I think it was in Omaha,
and I said to one of the old—the old type of foremen—machinist foremen,

and I said, "How do you like—you have been in this business for a long time—how do you like having all these 'gals' around here, in places fifty per cent of them?"

"Well," he said, "it has done something to us." "I don't know what it is," he says, patting his chin. "Look at my face."

I said, "What's the matter?"

He said, "I used to shave twice or three times a week, but I have to shave every day now!"

He says, "My wife is kicking about it."——

He said, "No, not that, but I wear a clean shirt every day, and it means more wash back home!"

THE MOON AND POLITICS

30 August 1943

CORRESPONDENT: Mr. President, regarding your report to the nation the other night, there has been some speculation in some quarters as to its political portent, and some of your loyal opposition have released statements on it. Is there any comment that you would like to make, sir?

THE PRESIDENT: It reminds me of what a member of the family said this morning. He said, "Why, in your next speech, don't you try it on— a different way? Suppose a paragraph or two saying, 'The moon is beautiful'? Probably you will be accused of playing politics, because there are a lot of young people that like to sit out under the moon!"

ON "LAYING"

14 September 1943

Reporters questioned FDR on certain aspects of the draft.

CORRESPONDENT: Mr. President, did you discuss the draft of fathers with your Congressional leaders?

THE PRESIDENT: Oh, I think you are a little premature on that.

Yes. I did. I think they are going to ask General Marshall and Admiral King[1] to go before them—talk about the necessities of the case.

CORRESPONDENT: Have you any views of your own that you could give us on that question?

THE PRESIDENT: I think there's only one thing that you might make

[1] General George C. Marshall, Chief of Staff, and Admiral Ernest J. King, Chief of Naval Operations.

clear, that . . . if a married man with a child is in an essential industry in this war, he would not be drafted, but there are a good many fathers laying around who are—a good way of putting it—who are neither in the army nor performing any essential service. We all know that type of father!

CORRESPONDENT: Grammar, Mr. President? [It sounded like "Grand ma."]

THE PRESIDENT: What? . . . .

CORRESPONDENT: The *grammar*?

THE PRESIDENT: The grammar?

CORRESPONDENT: "Laying" around.

THE PRESIDENT: Oh! Oh! That's all right. I prefer the ungrammatical way of doing it!

CORRESPONDENT: Mr. President, would you call them "chronic layers?" . . . .

CORRESPONDENT: Do you think men that fit into that category sir, could well go into the Army?

THE PRESIDENT: I know a great many right here in Washington!

LONG PANTS

12 October 1943

Roosevelt was discussing critical comments in the British press on observations made by certain Senators concerning British troops.

CORRESPONDENT: Mr. President, there is another conflict of testimony that you might clear up. One of the Senators said that the British . . . officers wore American uniforms to avoid being shot by the French. Another report is that they wore the American uniform because they—the pants are long-legged and protected them against mosquitoes. Could you tell us about that?

THE PRESIDENT: . . . I think that's a matter that is very properly for Senatorial debate! But as long as I was talking about trousers, it had better be a closed debate!

DR. NEW DEAL AND DR. WIN-THE-WAR

28 December 1943

Dilworth Lupton, columnist of the *Cleveland Press*, had attended the previous press conference and had stayed on for a talk with FDR. He wrote subsequently that the President was of the view that the "New

Deal" label for his program had become outmoded and that it would be appropriate to replace it with the slogan "Win the War." The report had evoked widespread interest.

DOUGLAS CORNELL OF A.P.: Mr. President, after our last meeting with you, it appears that someone stayed behind and received word that you no longer liked the term "New Deal." Do you care to express any opinion to the rest of us?

THE PRESIDENT: Oh, I supposed somebody would ask that. In the future—I will have to be terribly careful in the future how I talk to people after the press conferences. However, what he reported was accurate reporting, and—well, I hesitated a bit as to whether I would say anything. It all comes down, really, to a rather puerile and political side of things. I think the two go very well together—puerile and political!

However, of course some people have to be told how to spell "cat"— lots of people have to be told how to spell "cat," even people with a normally good education. And so I—I got to thinking the thing over, and I jotted down some things that—oh—a lot of people who can't spell "cat" had forgotten entirely.

And of course, the net of it is that—how did the New Deal come into existence? It was because there was an awfully sick patient called the United States of America, and it was suffering from a grave internal disorder—awfully sick—all kinds of things that happened to this patient, all internal things. And they sent for the doctor. And it was a long, long process—took several years before those ills, in that particular illness of ten years ago, were remedied. But after a while they got remedied. And on all those ills of 1933, things had to be done internally. And it was done—took a number of years.

And there were certain specific remedies that the old doctor gave the patient, and I jotted down a few of those remedies. The people who are peddling all this talk about "New Deal" today, they are not telling about why the patient had to have remedies. I am inclined to think that the country ought to be asked too, as to whether all these inexpensive critics shouldn't be asked directly just which of the remedies should be taken away from the patient, if you should come down with a similar illness in the future. It's all right now—it's all right internally now—if they just leave him alone.

But since then, two years ago, he had a very bad accident—not an internal trouble. Two years ago, on the seventh of December, he was in a pretty bad smash up—broke his hip, broke his leg in two or three places, broke a wrist and an arm, and some ribs, and they didn't think he would live, for a while. And then he began to "come to"; and he has been in charge of a partner of the old doctor. Old Doctor New Deal didn't know "nothing" about legs and arms. He knew a great deal about internal medicine, but nothing about surgery. So he got his partner, who was an orthopedic surgeon, Dr. Win-The-War, to take care of this fellow who had been in this bad accident. And the result is that the patient is back on his feet. He isn't wholly well yet, and he won't be until he wins the war.

And I think that is almost as simple, that allegory, as learning again to spell "cat."[1]

[1] FDR listed about thirty major legislative measures enacted during the "New Deal" years. In view of changed circumstances, he emphasized, "the overwhelming first emphasis should be on winning the war." "And when victory comes," he added, "the program of the past, of course, has to be carried on." Plans must be worked out to "bring about an expanded economy which will result in more security, in more employment, in more recreation, in more education, in more health, in better housing for all of our citizens. . . ."

It might be recalled that FDR had begun his story with a reference to the "puerile and political side of things. After he had completed his narrative Bert Andrews of the *New York Herald Tribune* asked him whether his allegory added up to a fourth term declaration. "You are getting picayune," FDR responded. "That's a grand word to use—another word beginning with a P—picayune!"

ROOSEVELT UNDER THE KNIFE

4 February 1944

As it appeared increasingly probable that FDR might seek a fourth term, some critics became interested in raising questions concerning his health.

THE PRESIDENT: Oh, I—I will save Steve's life, because—Steve came in yesterday morning with blood in his eye.

I said, "What's the trouble?"

"Oh," he said, "they woke me up three times during the night, after midnight, to ask if you had been under the knife."

That was the headline desired.

And I said, "Sure, I was under the knife. I am under the knife whenever I cut my fingernails."

But actually, I don't know why I should talk about this, it is merely— it might be called a—a preventive—and that is very often necessary, to use a preventible. I had a pain for . . . twenty years or less; . . . what you call a wen on the back of my head. And it had grown a bit lately, so I went out to the Naval Hospital, and two very good surgeons and knives, and God knows what, removed it under a local anaesthetic. I think I was in the hospital half an hour. So now she's out.

CORRESPONDENT: Did those—Mr. President, did those Naval "gims" permit you to smoke while they did their hacking—to relieve—

THE PRESIDENT: No, but I yelled for a cigarette right after it!

INTERNATIONAL MONETARY CONFERENCE
26 May 1944

A correspondent's question on whether Congressmen would be included in the American delegation to the United Nations Monetary Conference scheduled to begin at Bretton Woods on 1 July 1944 got caught in the cross-fire of banter.

CORRESPONDENT: Mr. President, will the press be admitted to that meeting?

THE PRESIDENT: Yes, but you can't sleep with the delegates.

CORRESPONDENT: Why? . . .

THE PRESIDENT: Enough said.

CORRESPONDENT: Does that hold both ways, Mr. President?

THE PRESIDENT: Yes, yes. No more questions. You will get me embarrassed!

EARL GODWIN: I was going to ask—

CORRESPONDENT: [Interposing] How about Congressmen, Mr. President?

GODWIN: [Continuing]—who wants to sleep with the delegates?

STEVE EARLY: There may be some ladies.

CORRESPONDENT: How about Congressmen?

THE PRESIDENT: Well, you sleep with them all the time, so what's the difference?

HOW TO RUN A SUCCESSFUL CONFERENCE
23 August 1944

The President received delegates to the Dumbarton Oaks Conference who were discussing the framework of a new world organization.[1]

THE PRESIDENT: A conference of this kind always reminds me of an old saying of a gentleman called Alfred E. Smith, who used to be Governor of New York. He was very, very successful in settling any problem between capital and labor, or anything that had to do with the State Government in which there was a controversy.

He said if you can get the parties into one room with a big table and make them take their coats off and put their feet up on the table, and give each one of them a good cigar, you can always make them agree. Well, there was something in that idea.

[1] Informal remarks before the delegates to the Dumbarton Oaks Conference, 23 August 1944, *Public Papers and Addresses, 1944*, p. 232. The delegates represented the governments of the United Kingdom, the United States, the Soviet Union, and China.

DON'T LIBEL MY DOG

23 September 1944

Speaking at a dinner sponsored by the International Brotherhood of Teamsters, Roosevelt launched a spirited attack on Republican "campaign falsifications."[1]

THE PRESIDENT: . . . The whole purpose of Republican oratory these days seems to be to switch labels. The object is to persuade the American people that the Democratic Party was responsible for the 1929 crash and the depression, and that the Republican Party was responsible for all social progress under the New Deal.

. . . Now there is an old and somewhat lugubrious adage which says: "Never speak of rope in the house of a man who has been hanged." In the same way, if I were a Republican leader speaking to a mixed audience, the last word in the whole dictionary that I think I would use is that word "depression."

. . . These Republican leaders have not been content with attacks on me, or my wife, or on my sons. No, not content with that, they now include my little dog, Fala. Well, of course, I don't resent attacks, and my family doesn't resent attacks, but Fala *does* resent them. You know, Fala is Scotch, and being a Scottie, as soon as he learned that the Republican fiction writers in Congress and out had concocted a story that I had left him behind on the Aleutian Islands and had sent a destroyer back to find him—at a cost to the taxpayers of two or three, or eight or twenty million dollars—his Scotch soul was furious. He has not been the same dog since. I am accustomed to hearing malicious falsehoods about myself—such as that old, worm-eaten chestnut that I have represented myself as indispensable. But I think I have a right to resent, to object to libelous statements about my dog.

[1] *Public Papers and Addresses, 1944*, pp. 285, 289–90.

THE PRESIDENT'S HEALTH

24 October 1944

The election campaign was in full swing. Certain hostile newspaper commentators asserted that FDR was in very poor health and was too worn-out to be able to shoulder the burdens of a fourth term as President. Such comments apparently needled Roosevelt. On 21 October, braving heavy rains, he rode through New York streets in an open car and, as he greeted a huge crowd in Ebbets Field, he even threw off his Navy cape and stood bareheaded in the rain.

At the next press conference FDR greeted reporters cheerfully but directed a barbed comment at his critics.

THE PRESIDENT: I don't think I have got anything today, except an admission that just a few of you—very small percentage—are going to be disappointed in the answer—I will put it that way—the answer to the question is: "Yes, I haven't even got the sniffles!"

ADVICE TO POLITICIANS WHO WANT TO GO TO HEAVEN

4 November 1944

THE PRESIDENT: Some of us are trying to get excited about politics. Some of us become even rather agitated. You ought to know. Yes, there are a few politicians, even—men and women—who work themselves into such an emotional state that they say things I hope they will be sorry for before they die.

... I get tremendously amused by some of this—not all of it—because I wish in a way I were back in 1910, when I was running for the State Senate in the State of New York, and I had a particularly disagreeable opponent, and he called me names. Well, I wasn't anything in those days —I wasn't President—and I answered him in kind. And the names that I called him were worse than the names that he called me. So we had a joyous campaign.

In this campaign, of course, all things taken together, I can't talk about my opponents the way I would like to sometimes, because I try to think that I am a Christian. I try to think that some day I will go to Heaven. . . .[1]

[1] Informal remarks at Bridgeport, Connecticut, 4 November 1944, *Public Papers and Addresses, 1944*, pp. 390–91. FDR's reference to "women" was actually to Congresswoman Clare Boothe Luce who had criticized him in sharp language.

FOURTH TERM FROLICS

10 November 1944

FDR had been triumphantly re-elected to a fourth term as President of the United States, defeating the Republican candidate, Thomas E. Dewey of New York.

CORRESPONDENT: Happy Fourth Term!

THE PRESIDENT: The strange thing is I haven't any news.

CORRESPONDENT: That is fine, sir.

THE PRESIDENT: It is?

CORRESPONDENT: Keep it that way. We'll stop right now. . . .

THE PRESIDENT: I just said to the front row that I didn't have any news, and there was a chorus of "Thank God!" . . . .

CORRESPONDENT: Time for a change.

CORRESPONDENT: What a bedlam. . . .

CORRESPONDENT: Mr. President, we understand that one third of the firm of "Martin Barton" is like a fish out of water.[1]

THE PRESIDENT: That's a good line too.

CORRESPONDENT: Did you win your election bet, sir?

THE PRESIDENT: No, I called it off. I got scared! . . . .

CORRESPONDENT: May I be the first to ask you, Mr. President, whether you are going to run in '48?

THE PRESIDENT: That's a question I was asked in 1940, isn't it? It's hoary—absolutely hoary!

[1] In a campaign speech at New York City's Madison Square Garden in 1940 FDR spoke derisively of the opposition to his policies from "Martin, Barton and Fish." The chant "Martin, Barton and Fish" was an instant success and was used effectively against the Republicans and their Presidential candidate, Wendell Willkie. Roosevelt probably sought to convey the impression that the forces behind Willkie were reactionary opponents of New Deal reforms (House Minority Leader Joseph Martin of Massachusetts), publicity agents of vested interests, (Rep. Bruce Barton of New York), and blind enemies of collective security (Rep. Hamilton Fish of New York). Fish was defeated in the elections of 1944.

FDR: HOUSEKEEPER

14 November 1944

CORRESPONDENT: Can you tell us about your inauguration plans?

THE PRESIDENT: I saw it on the ticker. . . .

CORRESPONDENT: Can you confirm it?

THE PRESIDENT: Yes, it's all right. I had Ed Halsey and Dave—what's his name, the Architect of the Capitol?—Dave Lynn down Saturday, and I said, "You know, I am terribly concerned about dollars and cents because I am afraid a lot of people in the Senate—Senator Byrd is the Chairman of this Committee[1]—and what are *you* laughing at—and they

[1] Senator Harry Byrd of Virginia was a fiscal conservative and a persistent critic of Roosevelt's "spending policies." The wealthy Senator was one of the biggest apple-growers in the United States. "I know what's the matter with Harry Byrd," Roosevelt told Rexford Tugwell once when

have appropriated twenty-five thousand dollars for the inauguration. But, you know, I think I can save an awful lot of money."

And with that desire to save money, I said, "I think I can do it for less than ten per cent of that cost. I think I can do it for less than two thousand dollars. Give them a light buffet luncheon, that will be the only expense.

The ladies here will be fascinated over what a good housekeeper I am.

MAY CRAIG: That's not what fascinates me!

THE PRESIDENT: So they were quite interested. They said, "How can you do it for less than two thousand dollars?"

A lot of that can go to consommé and chicken-a-la-king, and a few sandwiches and coffee. "Well," I said, "I think I can do it."

---

the latter headed the Resettlement Administration. "He's afraid you'll force him to pay more than ten cents an hour for his apple pickers." Rexford G. Tugwell. *The Democratic Roosevelt* (New York, 1957), p. 444n.

DID HE OR DIDN'T HE?

21 November 1944

In its story on the Presidential election, *Time* magazine had reported an incident in the polling booth at Hyde Park:

From the green-curtained booth came a clank of gears as the main control lever jerked irritably back and forth. Then a voice, familiar to all of the U.S. and to most of the world spoke distinctly from behind the curtain: "The goddamned thing won't work."[1]

CORRESPONDENT: Do you remember anything sinister in the polling booth, at Hyde Park, Mr. President?

THE PRESIDENT: I don't know. I don't know who the fellow was that wrote that story for *Time*, but I am going to withdraw his card from these conferences—if he comes to these conferences—I don't know who he was—on the ground of deafness.

Part—part of what he said was true—perfectly true, but just . . . for the sake of the record, so that I won't get any more letters from ministerial associations! . . . as I—I went into the booth, an old friend of mine, Tom Leonard, who is one of the inspectors—a captain at the election booth—or whatever they call it was standing right outside. And I got hold of this handle that you have to pull round back of your neck, and it didn't click. So I started another go at it, and that locked it. And I couldn't do anything about it. The time was locked—the curtain was locked.

So I said to Tom, over the top of the . . . curtain—I said, "Tom, the damn thing won't work."

Now, the trouble is that some person—whoever he was I don't know—but he must have been awfully deaf, because he added another short word before the word "damn" which I didn't use! Well, I suppose that is his—his privilege. However, he is too deaf to suit me—especially because I didn't, on that occasion, take the name of the Deity in vain. I said "damn."[2]

So that's all there is to it. Now, I am not going to ask the White House Correspondents' Association to expel him for being "deef," because that is pretty severe punishment. But the Association ought to know what to do with him. I suppose probably the best thing to do is to pay his expenses and have him go to a good ear doctor!

[1] *Time*, XLIV (13 November 1944), p. 19.

[2] FDR's version is corroborated by a diary entry of William Hassett on 7 November 1944. "A very familiar voice was heard to say: 'The damned thing won't work!'" William D. Hassett, *Off the Record with F.D.R.* (New Brunswick, 1958), pp. 292–93.

LEFT, RIGHT, CENTER: FDR'S POLITICAL PHILOSOPHY

19 December 1944

MAY CRAIG: There's a good deal of question as to whether you are going right or left, and I would like your opinion on which way you are going.

THE PRESIDENT: I am going down the whole line a little left of center. I think that was answered, that question, eleven and a half years ago, and still holds.

CORRESPONDENT: But you told us a little while ago that you were going to have Dr. Win-The-War and not Dr. New Deal.

THE PRESIDENT: That's right.

CORRESPONDENT: The question is whether you are going back to be Dr. New Deal after the war—

THE PRESIDENT: No, no. No. Keep right along a little to the left of center, which includes winning the war. . . .

EARL GODWIN: Mr. President, in being a little left of center, you have noticed in your life that many a progressive or liberal stays where he is and becomes hopelessly conservative as time goes on.

THE PRESIDENT: And you are exactly the same age as I am.

GODWIN: Yes.

THE PRESIDENT: Now, do you feel that you are getting more conservative?

GODWIN: I think I am.

THE PRESIDENT: Do you?

GODWIN: That's in contrast to some of the things I see.

THE PRESIDENT: Well, that's—that's bad. You must be older than I am! Old age hasn't crept up on me yet. You ought to be careful. You ought to watch that; it's a serious thing when it happens!

V

FOREIGN POLICY FROLICS

A "TICKLISH" ISSUE
10 May 1933

A world economic conference was scheduled to be held in London. Roosevelt had invited eleven nations with whom the United States had significant commercial relations to depute representatives to Washington for preliminary discussions. In a radio address on 7 May 1933, FDR had listed the four objectives of the discussions but carefully avoided any reference to a "solution" for the vexed problem of war debts.

CORRESPONDENT: Mr. President, do you or do you not consider the solution of the war debt vital to the success of the Economic Conference?

THE PRESIDENT: Have I stopped tickling the soles of my mother-in-law? Yes or no?

I don't know—it is too difficult a question to answer. Are my mother-in-law's feet ticklish? In other words, of course some clearing up of the debt issue would be a fine thing, but it is not necessarily tied in with the success of the Economic Conference. The two are not necessarily wired together. They may be, what shall I say, "platonic" friends.

GROUSE

5 August 1933

Roosevelt could not resist having fun with puns even if there was a visiting fuddyduddy in the audience.

Secretary of State Cordell Hull was present at the press conference. Reporters asked the President when he expected the London Monetary Conference to reconvene. Hull intervened to say that the agencies interested in the Conference would have their meetings early in September. By that time most of the European statesmen would have returned home from their August vacations, Hull added.

CORRESPONDENT: Do they all take the whole month of August off for their vacations?

HULL: President Roosevelt first called my attention to the fact that they leave promptly on the 12th of August and shoot grouse—for how many days?

THE PRESIDENT: About a month.

CORRESPONDENT: I think we ought to get some grouse over here.

THE PRESIDENT: We have enough grousing in this country.

JUST AS SURE AS GOD MADE LITTLE APPLES

14 March 1934

FDR was of the view that the United States should, in cooperation with Canada, build a St. Lawrence Seaway. Many Senators were, however, opposed to the St. Lawrence Treaty.

CORRESPONDENT: Mr. President, they are about to vote today on the St. Lawrence Treaty, and it looks like the vote is against you. I was wondering if you would care to offer any comment on that.

THE PRESIDENT: The first phase of it is that whether this thing goes through this afternoon or not makes no difference at all because the St. Lawrence Seaway will be built. That is perfectly obvious.

. . . It would be a perfectly proper thing and a possible thing for Canada to enlarge the International Rapids Canal on the Canadian side of the River without ever building a dam. . . . That seaway would be one hundred per cent under the control of Canada. And if Canada wanted to be mean—and lots of governments and peoples are mean to their neighbors—so far as treaties go, Canada has an absolute right, not a moral right but a legal right, to let British and Canadian ships use the Canadian seaway free of charge and to charge a toll to American ships.

. . . That is a distinct and definite legal right that Canada would have if we do not go along with her and do it jointly.

Now, one other phase of it—and I will tell you a story. A certain Senator said that he was going to vote against the treaty because of the Mississippi and the taking of water out of Lake Michigan. I asked him if he thought we had any right to divert water over and above the need for drinking and health purposes from one watershed into another. Then I told him a story about a case in up-state New York.

A fellow had a piece of property on a river but, at that point, there was practically no drop in the river—it was practically a flat river. He was most anxious to put up a grist mill and he didn't have any water power. People down in the stream below him had grist mills.

Suddenly he had a bright thought one night. He said to himself: "By cutting a little ditch through a little hill on my property I can run this water into the watershed of another little river and I can get a 50-foot drop. I can take the water out of this river and carry it through the ditch, drop it down over the wheel and put it into another river."

Of course, it was a grand idea. But, unfortunately, he ran up against what is known in the common law as riparian right of the man further down the stream. Well, the mills down the stream at once brought suit and said that ever since 1450 when the first case came up in England the rule has been on a watershed, on a river, that you have a right to use the water but you have to put it back into the river. You cannot divert it into some other watershed.

Well, this Senator, who is a good lawyer, admitted all that and finally said that international law is different. I said, "There aren't any cases of international law that are different from the old rule based on common sense."

He said, "Never mind whether international law is different or not. We are going to try to take all the water we want out of Lake Michigan and put it into the Mississippi, no matter what anybody else says."

So that is a perfectly clear-cut issue. The Government of the United States believes in the common law and believes that we have no right to injure our neighbor, Canada, by diverting water out of the Great Lakes into another watershed, any more than the fellow upstream a hundred years ago in New York had a right to divert water from one creek into another.

And so, the thing is going through, perhaps not today but the St. Lawrence Seaway is going to be built just as sure as God made little apples. The only difference is that I would like to see it done by joint action of two neighboring nations.

INSIDE NAZI GERMANY

7 September 1934

FDR had come to recognize by this time that the course that Adolf Hitler had embarked on was likely to culminate in German aggression and world war.

THE PRESIDENT: I had Monsieur Flandin, [French] Minister of Public Works . . . in to lunch, and . . . we spent most of the lunch hour talking about Germany.

CORRESPONDENT: What is the situation there?

THE PRESIDENT: Off the record, the French are not very happy. . . . What they are afraid of—we will have to keep this entirely off the record; you know I cannot talk foreign affairs about so-called friendly nations. . . . The situation,—all these fellows that have been coming back—really what they are afraid of in Germany is that the German economic situation is breaking down. . . . He [Flandin] says that a thing like that cannot go on. . . . The question, when?

They, they are afraid in France that when the thing does get to the point of closing down their factories, with already a very large unemployment list, then one of two things will happen: Either they will have chaos inside of Germany, with all of those fellows fighting among themselves—we got one report the other day from [Ambassador William E.] Dodd describing how Hitler's Secret Service was being followed by Goebbels' Secret Service, which was being followed by Reichswehr's Secret Service, which was being followed by the Gestapo, all of them following each other around; or else that the leaders over there, to retain their power, will start to march on something, to walk across the border. I suppose the easiest way would be toss a coin to see which border they will have to walk across to retain the present regime in power and the whole of Europe is scared pink of something like that.

CORRESPONDENT: How can they get the money to buy the bullets to shoot at people?

THE PRESIDENT: Of course the French say they have an awful lot of it on hand. The French are convinced. They say big guns are the easiest thing in the world. When you are casting a stern tubing for a ship, for the shaft tubing, it is almost exactly the same process as casting the tube of a gun, of a 14-inch gun. It is exactly the same thing. You cast two and you put one over in the corner! The French are convinced that they [the Germans] have all the small artillery, the 75's and the 155's . . . and that the Germans have more machine guns than the French Army. And they are also perfectly sure that they have as many airplanes available as France has.

Another lovely story is that the [German] school children—this is one of the silly ones, but it may be true; we do know that every factory worker in Germany works with a gas mask in a bag above his bench and every once in a while a whistle blows twice and everybody puts on his mask. I tell you the silly things because we get them all the time and only a few get printed.

The school children in Germany are going through an educational process. They have a box of matches and the head of the match is impregnated with the particular smell of the poison gases used in the World War. They gather around in the classroom and the children light a match and that is gas No. 3. They train them in knowing those different smells. It sounds crazy but we know there is a lot of that stuff going on. There are seven different smells and you have on the gas mask seven different slides —each one against a different type of gas.

Then there is the story of the professor of foreign languages at Bryn Mawr, who went over there last fall and visited a German professor in Stuttgart. She went to his house—she had stayed with him before. His family and workmen were working down in the basement.

She said, "What is all this work that is going on?"

"I am carrying out the orders of the Government. I am putting a bombproof in the cellar. We are all doing it."

She said, "What are you doing it for?"

"We get a remission of half year's taxes if we prepare against airplane attack. They are doing it in France."

She said, "They are doing it in France?"

"Oh yes, the papers say so. The English are doing it and they are doing it in the United States along the whole Atlantic Seaboard."

She said, "I have not been home for two months but I am sure I have not seen it."

"You do not know. We know. Our Government tells us."

Now there is a [German] professor who swallows the whole thing, hook, line and sinker.

And then the little boy came down at night to say his prayers, his age eight or nine years, and he kneeled at his mother's knee and said his prayers and ended up in good German, like a good German boy, and he said, "Dear God, please permit it that I shall die with a French bullet in my heart."

You get that sort of thing and that is what has got the French scared when ninety per cent of the German people are thinking and talking that way. If I were a Frenchman, I would be scared too!

THE NINE-POWER PACT

2 November 1934

Extremely cautious in discussing foreign policy issues with reporters, FDR used banter as a device to distract the questioners.

CORRESPONDENT: Mr. President, what if any recourse is left to us if any one of the signatories to the nine-power pact[1] completely disregards the obligations under it? . . . .

THE PRESIDENT: I will get out my library on that subject. I think there have been twelve volumes written on it so far.

[1] At an international conference held in Washington during November, 1921-February, 1922, nine nations entered into agreements relating to naval disarmament. They pledged to respect the independence and integrity of China and to uphold the Open Door principle.

MORE WORD PLAY

22 March 1935

CORRESPONDENT: Going back to foreign affairs, can you tell us whether you discussed the German situation specifically with Senator Borah?[1]

THE PRESIDENT: No, not specifically. We did discuss the European situation pacifically.

[1] William E. Borah, Senator from Idaho.

DOLLAR DIPLOMACY REDEFINED

4 September 1935

CORRESPONDENT: Is there anything you want to say further on this Ethiopian situation, that is, the cancellation of the oil leases?[1]

[1] FDR spoke lightheartedly, but the episode marked one of the developments that eventually culminated in the Second World War. In a desperate bid to fend off the aggressive designs of Fascist Italy, the Emperor of Ethiopia had signed an agreement with a subsidiary of the Standard Oil Company, granting it oil and mineral rights over nearly half of his Kingdom. When the grant of the lease became public, the controlled press of Italy reacted with anger and indignation. The United States Government was unwilling to offend the Italian dictator and Secretary of State Cordell Hull brought heavy pressure to bear on Standard Oil Company to surrender the lease. "President is Delighted Oil Grant is

THE PRESIDENT: No, I think it has got pretty full stories from Washington.

CORRESPONDENT: It was a good piece of diplomacy.

THE PRESIDENT: A good job. Of course you can—if I were writing the story, I would put it this way: . . . Since the 4th of March 1933, dollar diplomacy is no longer recognized by the United States Government.

CORRESPONDENT: Are you sure that it was dollar diplomacy and that there were no other currencies involved?

THE PRESIDENT: Off the record, I would say that would depend on the rate of exchange!

Abandoned," ran the headline in the *New York Times* (4 September 1935, p. 1).

TEMPTATION

30 October 1935

Fascist Italy had launched its aggressive attack on Ethiopia. Roosevelt declared, in a statement, that the United States Government "is determined not to become involved in the controversy." He referred to "tempting trade opportunities" that might be offered to Americans to supply materials that would prolong the war and declared that the American Government "is keeping informed as to all shipments assigned for export to both belligerents."

THE PRESIDENT: I said that anything going to belligerent governments would be checked up on. Of course, in the case of proscribed articles— arms, implements of war, munitions—it prohibits their shipment either to belligerent countries or to a neutral country for trans-shipment.

CORRESPONDENT: Can you tell us anything about some of the temptations that have been presented so far?

THE PRESIDENT: Well, yes. I will tell you a story on that and it is a rather interesting one. . . . When I was at Hyde Park a very splendid old gentleman came to see me, Mr. Johnson of Endicott-Johnson Shoe Company. It was about the 19th or 20th of September. Mr. Johnson said to me at length, "I would like to ask your advice. I have had an order from the Italian Government for a very large number of pairs of shoes."

I said, "What are they, ladies' slippers?"

He said, "No, they were heavy shoes."

I said, "Shoes that could have been worn by soldiers?"

He said, "Yes, I'd say so."

I said, "Well, what is your question?"

He said, "Would you fill the order if you were the Endicott-Johnson Company?"

I said, "No, I would not."[1]

He said, "All right. I won't."

[1] FDR's comment provides an indication of his distaste for Fascist Italy and its dictator, Mussolini. A few years later, in a letter to William Phillips, US Ambassador in Rome, Roosevelt wrote: "Isn't it curious that while the veneer in Italy is so highly polished, it peels off at the first opportunity? By the way, my Italian is somewhat rusty, Is there a word for 'gentleman' in that language?" The President to William Phillips, 4 February 1939, FDRL.

TRUE ACCOUNT OF A MEETING WITH LORD RUNCIMAN

26 January 1937

CORRESPONDENT: Regarding your conversation with Runciman,[1] you mentioned the trade subject. Did you mention any other subject that came up?

THE PRESIDENT: With whom?

CORRESPONDENT: Runciman.

THE PRESIDENT: No, that is all I mentioned. I might say we started in our private conversations, on the North Pole and went clear to the South Pole and then started at longitude zero and went clear around the world until we came into longitude zero, which is Greenwich.

CORRESPONDENT: Did they take in Fort Knox at any time?

THE PRESIDENT: Yes, and it took in not only gold but every known metal.

CORRESPONDENT: Were war debts encountered anywhere?

THE PRESIDENT: No, that was one topic that was not discussed because I understand when he landed in Boston somebody said "War debts" and he said, "God forbid." So I did not mention it.

[1] Lord Runciman, President of the British Board of Trade, had been a week-end guest at the White House.

CONSTITUTIONAL PROPRIETY

31 March 1937

Reporters asked Roosevelt about his discussions with Lord Tweedsmuir, Governor-General of Canada. His Lordship was present at the press conference.

THE PRESIDENT: You see—well, the Governor-General cannot officially say anything about Government affairs in Canada. If we both sit on the sofa, we can soliloquize to ourselves and [one] might overhear what the other fellow was saying.

DEALING WITH OUR BRITISH FRIENDS

6 October 1937

On 5 October FDR, in an important speech in Chicago, asserted that if aggression triumphed elsewhere in the world, America's own safety would eventually be in jeopardy. He called for a "quarantine" of those who engaged in aggression. The speech attracted world-wide attention.

CORRESPONDENT: Foreign papers put it as an attitude without a program.

THE PRESIDENT: That was the London *Times*. . . . We will get one or two stories from London which say, "Why doesn't the United States suggest something?" Why should we suggest something? Can't somebody else make a suggestion? We have done an awful lot of suggesting. Every time we enter into some kind of an effort to settle something with our British friends, when we make the suggestion they get 90 per cent and we get 10 per cent. When they make the suggestion it comes out nearer 50-50. Why should we be doing the suggesting?

A STATE OF MIND

19 October 1937

Newspapers like the *Chicago Tribune* and "isolationist" politicians like Senator Hiram Johnson of California strongly criticized the "Quarantine" speech.

CORRESPONDENT: Your old friend Hiram Johnson has delivered quite a statement. He said that America is on the road to war and he wants you to tell the people what you will do and what you will not do and wants to know what you mean by "quarantine." He said the people should know when you approach war . . . as to who is going to furnish the men and money for war. Also, suppose the President assumes leadership of the League of Nations and it decides on sanctions against Japan, whose Navy will enforce it. Those are the highlights.

THE PRESIDENT: I would like to make a very simple comment. . . . Do you remember . . . Bob Chanler—used to be sheriff of Dutchess

County—and he had a brother by the name of Armstrong who had been declared insane in the State of New York. Armstrong moved to Virginia and lived there. Bob, up here, divorced his wife and married Lina Cavalieri whereupon Armstrong Chanler of Virginia sent him the famous telegram, "Who is loony now?"

THE PARABLE OF CHINA'S IOWA

20 April 1938

Despite the aggressive posture of Germany and Italy in Europe and of Japan in Asia, a strong body of opinion in the United States was opposed to any action that might endanger American neutrality. In January, 1938, the anti-interventionists came within twenty one votes of getting the House of Representatives to approve the so-called Ludlow amendment. Sponsored by Congressman Louis Ludlow, the resolution sought a Constitutional amendment to provide that, barring an actual invasion, the United States could declare war only if such a course was approved by a majority of voters in a national referendum. This was the harsh reality that Roosevelt confronted. While continuing to reiterate his determination to maintain American neutrality, FDR took advantage of every possible opportunity to bring home to his visitors his conviction that developments in Europe and Asia might eventually endanger American security. He emphasized that complacency in America on the ground that "nothing could possibly happen to Iowa" might prove to be dangerous and costly. Such was the theme of the story that he told members of the Associated Church Press at a special press conference.

THE PRESIDENT: Let me tell you about Iowa.

I have a Chinese friend who was in college with me. He is a merchant in Canton but I hear from him once a year. I got a letter from him the other day. "Do you remember me telling you about my brother away in the interior, about three hundred miles southwest of Hankow? He was very prosperous, with an awfully nice home and a fine family. He had always been a pacifist. He has opposed a Chinese Army to protect the Nation of China. He said, 'We are so big, there is nobody that would dare to trouble us.' I never agreed with my brother."

It is a Christian family.

And the other day he [the Chinese friend] said, "I am very sorry to tell you that my brother and his wife and four children were killed."

They lived in the Iowa of China, the Iowa of China. Those planes came over and dropped a bomb on the house where they were cooling off. They killed three hundred people in the nearby village and two minutes later they were gone. They had wiped out one of the rural communities of the Iowa of China. He never thought it could happen, I never thought it would happen and his brother in Canton never thought it would happen.[1]

We know today—it was in the papers—that in 1918, before the War ended, the Germans were building a Zeppelin with the perfectly definite objective of sending her out in the spring of 1919 by way of Great Circle Route, over Iceland, Greenland, and down to New York, to drop a cargo of bombs on New York City. We have known that from the documents that we picked up afterwards.

CORRESPONDENT: How can we ever defend a territory going from Maine, through the Virgin Islands, and all the territory embraced by the Monroe Doctrine and around the Philippine Islands and coming back to the United States?

THE PRESIDENT: Well, of course if you have one enemy, we are all right. But suppose you have the two enemies in two different places, then you have to be a bit shifty on your feet. You have to lick one of them first and then bring them around and then lick the other. That is about the only chance.

---

[1] It is interesting to note that FDR gave a slightly different version of the parable of "China's Iowa" in a letter to a Dutchess County acquaintance, Rhoda Hinkley, in December, 1937. Hinkley had informed the President that a prominent commentator had criticized the Administration for its "meddling" activities in the Orient that might involve the United States in a war with Japan. Roosevelt replied that the American people and the Administration wanted peace, but not "the kind of peace which means definite danger to us at home in the days to come." He went on to add: "I happen to know a very nice Chinese family which lives quite far in the interior. For years they have said that China wanted peace at any price and that they felt no possible harm could come to them back from the sea coast. The other day most of the family was wiped out by some Japanese bombing planes which wrecked their community and killed one thousand people. I got a message from one of the survivors which read 'we are no longer for peace at any price.'" The President to Rhoda Hinkley, 16 December 1937, FDRL.

THE SENATOR'S QUERY

17 January 1939

With Europe edging towards war and with a substantial body of American opinion strongly opposed to any involvement in war, Roosevelt had to move with great caution. Humor was his ally as he tackled questions from correspondents who wanted him to spell out his plans.

RAYMOND P. BRANDT of the *St. Louis Post-Dispatch*: In your message on the State of the Nation you said there were means other than war to let the aggressor nations know our sentiments. My editor would like to know if you are willing to amplify that, and whether it would be loans to China, or lifting the Spanish embargo, economic blockades, cooperation with Latin America—

THE PRESIDENT: (interposing) Pete, your editor reminds me of old Senator Hale, of Maine, who, way back around 1880 or something like that, when they were talking about building up a Navy for the United States—they had not built any ships since 1865 and the Navy was practically non-existent—and he kept insisting, when they authorized the first ships for the new Navy, he wanted to know which ship or ships would be stationed off Portland Harbor [Maine] in case of war.

THE ARMCHAIR EXPERT AND HIS "UNIMPEACHABLE SOURCES"

17 February 1939

CORRESPONDENT: There was an article in the *Saturday Evening Post* of this week by the editor of *Aviation*, who was a guest of the German Government and who visited the various airplane factories, and he quotes the Air Minister as saying that they were willing to sell—

THE PRESIDENT: Now Fred [Storm], do you think that any official of any responsible government could comment on an article by a civilian in a popular magazine purporting to say what somebody else had said in some other country? That is the trouble with the American people today, that they are being fed that sort of thing and expected to believe it. Now, you can put that down: That is the kind of bunk—repeat the word, bunk —that is being handed out.

And in the same way, we have people who set themselves up with quasi-military or quasi-naval title as experts. They write attractively and sell their wares to a magazine or newspaper syndicate and they are thereupon accepted as experts by members of the House, the Senate and the general reading public.

We have lots of examples of that kind. I will tell you . . . [of] one fellow . . . at the present time. . . . His name is Eliot[1]—

CORRESPONDENT: George Fielding Eliot?

THE PRESIDENT: You know who he is. He has been connected with U.P., I believe, and somebody took him up. He wrote a very interesting book on the Service. He gave the real low-down!

[1] Five years later FDR was to appraise George Fielding Eliot, military commentator of the *New York Herald Tribune*, in a wholly different fashion. At a press conference on 15 August 1944 he described Eliot as the best writer on war developments. "I think he is the best writer on the war," Roosevelt said. "He is way ahead of Walter Lippmann, who has not thought about these things as Eliot has."

Brother Eliot is very simple. I believe he was born in this country ...
and taken to Australia when, I think, he was two or three years old. He
was brought up in Australia and, sometime during the world war—I
think he went as a private in the Australian forces, the Anzac Corps—he
went over to France and served in France in two or three engagements,
I think very well, as a private or corporal or maybe as second lieutenant.
All right; no kick on that. At the end of the war he drifted around for
a while and tried to sell some articles but he could not do it; he could
not make a living. He came back to this country and in 1921 or 1922 he
decides that he wants to go into our Army Reserve Corps. He goes through
an R.O.T.C. course. All right; fine. I think he went to two of them and
then was made, I think, a major in the Reserves.

About 1926 or 1927, along there, he got his usual annual post card
or letter from the War Department as a Reserve Officer. If he had not
received the post card or letter the thing would have come back, "Not
known at this address." At the end of a couple of years of this he was
dropped for complete failure to reply. He was dropped from the Army
Reserves.

Now, I ask you, is that a man with any pretense of being an expert
on military affairs?

He kept on trying to sell stories to the papers and magazines and
nothing happened; nothing doing.

This past fall he happened to get out a book which he just happened
to time right and it had a popular sale—it is well written—whereupon,
today, he is taken to be by everybody a great military expert.

Now, that is the kind of stuff that is handed out to the American
people. . . .

CORRESPONDENT: His premises are wrong?

THE PRESIDENT: The book does not mean anything at all. Then, if
you will remember, in one of those articles, there were some solemn as-
surances that he had from unimpeachable sources as to the number of
planes that Germany had. . . . Well, of course, if you state that solemnly
enough, people will believe it. "I have it from unimpeachable sources."
Well, his facts do not jibe with the facts the American Government believes to be true. On the other hand, if anybody with a "Major" in front
of his name, who has written for books and who has written for a newspaper syndicate and who has been widely heralded goes out and says "I
have it from unimpeachable sources," my God, what does one do about
it? You see the difficulty? . . . And then somebody in the House who wants
to talk pacifism or play up to his own district or something like that, or
somebody in the Senate, they pick it up and say, "See what this man says.
That's my authority." . . .

CORRESPONDENT: As you pointed out before, every male over sixteen
is an amateur strategist at heart and just eats that stuff up.

THE PRESIDENT: Yes, very much.

DR. SCHACHT'S GLOOMY PREDICTION

20 April 1939

CORRESPONDENT: Mr. President, how much longer do you think Japan can last out, . . . from the point of financial affairs?

THE PRESIDENT: I do not think anybody can answer a question like that, for this reason: We have had so many instances of nations . . . [about which] every human being that has our point of view has said: "My God, they are on the rocks; they won't last more than three months or six months," and then they have gone gaily ahead and never busted. There are a lot of nations that, from the point of view of the average American, are busted today and yet they go ahead day after day.

Schacht[1] told me in the spring of 1933, when he was trying to borrow money here, that Germany would last one year the way she was going. The summer of 1934 a friend of mine, an American businessman who knew him, went over to Germany and asked him how long Germany would last. Schacht almost wept: "My poor Germany will only last one year." I never see the same people twice! Another man went over in 1935 and Schacht said, "Germany at this rate, it cannot last more than one year." And in 1936 and 1937 the same thing. Finally Schacht got out in 1938 and Germany is still going on. Well, how do they do it? You don't know!

[1] Hjalmar Schacht was the German Finance Minister. Apparently FDR was fond of this story. He told it to Treasury Secretary Henry Morgenthau, Jr. on 11 April 1945. Morgenthau wrote in his diary: "Then he went on and told me the story about how Dr. Schacht came over here and wept on his desk about his poor country. He said that Schacht came over three or four times saying that the Germans were going broke and they never did. This is a story that I have heard the President tell about three different times, but he seems to enjoy telling it." John Morton Blum, *From the Morgenthau Diaries: Years of War 1941–1945* (Boston, 1967), p. 418.

WOULD WAR BREAK OUT?
FDR ON THE BETTING ODDS

23 June 1939. Annual press conference for editors of trade publications.

QUESTIONER: What is the latest international picture as you see it? How much can you tell us?

THE PRESIDENT: . . . Well, I will tell you. I will just give you two illustrations. What is the name of the U.P. man? . . . Webb Miller. Of course he is one of the best men we have in Europe. I said to him, "You know, I think the simple thing to do is to put things in terms of betting odds. The chances are that there won't be a war during the winter—after the fifteenth of October— that is, an European war." I said, "What are the betting odds on war between now and the fifteenth of October?"

"Well," he said, "I would say 3 to 2 against it."

That is damn close.

... Four days before, I had Bill Bullitt[1] down. He had just come over to get his shoulder fixed up and is going back to Paris.

I said, "Bill, what are your betting odds?"

He said, "2 to 3 there will be war. You can put your money on either horse."

My odds are even money and you can pick either side and I will take the other. That is the fairest and simplest way of putting it.

[1] William Bullitt, United States Ambassador in Paris.

THEY ARE NOT "SPIGOTEES!"

12 January 1940

Here is an excellent example of how Roosevelt employed his skill as a story-teller to drive home points of view that he regarded as important.

FDR was speaking at a press conference arranged for members of the National Conference of Business Paper Editors at the White House.

THE PRESIDENT: We Americans in time we are going to learn more about South America. We have altogether too much of the attitude that "Oh, well, they are spigotees."[1] We are frightfully dumb.

Well, I will tell you a story that illustrates why we have got to remember that they are human beings and consider themselves just as good as we are.

I told this story to a certain very large power executive who was talking of having his company—he already has quite a lot of South American electrical utilities—he was going down and he asked me if it would be a good idea to expand their electric properties in South America.

I said, "Perfectly grand, but I want to tell you a story":

When I was driving through the streets of Rio de Janeiro in 1936, at the end of November, with President Vargas,[2] with this great parade of

[1] "Spiggoty" is a slang term applied to any one of Latin stock. In the transcript the plural of the word, as used by FDR, appears as "spigotees."

[2] Getulio Vargas, President of Brazil.

troops, et cetera and so on, and they had cleared off the streets, over in the corner were a whole lot of very fine new busses, in this little park, that had been shunted off from the main street. They were fine looking transportation busses.

I said to Vargas, "Those are very good-looking busses."

He said, "Oh, yes; we have a very excellent traction company here, as far as the service goes."

I said, "Why do you say, as far as the service goes?"

"Well," he said, "there is a great deal of feeling in Rio and the whole of Brazil that we would like to own our own traction company."

I said, "Who owns this?"

He said, "This is owned in Toronto and Montreal."

I said, "In other words, you do not like foreign ownership of your main utilities."

He looked at me and said, "What would the people of New York City do if the subways were all owned in Canada?"

"Oh," I said, "why, there would be a revolution."

He said, "Well, perhaps you can understand our feelings a little bit."

Then he pointed to one of the big, high mountains and said, "Do you see that electric light line, that big transmission line?"

I said, "Yes."

He said, "Well, we have excellent electrical service. It comes from some waterfalls about forty miles back in the country. We have no complaint at all. But . . . we don't like it because that is owned in London. How would you like it if the Consolidated Gas Company of New York and the New York Edison Company were owned in London?"

I said, "There would be a revolution."

. . . we, as Americans, would demand . . . that the ownership should be in this country and not somewhere else.

That is a new approach that I am talking about to these South American things. Give them a share. They think they are just as good as we are and many of them are.

JOHN BULL CAN'T FOOL THE PRESIDENT

18 April 1940

The story-teller in the White House faced the task of arousing his people to an awareness of the importance of aiding Britain. At the same time, he had to convince them that he would not succumb to Britain's wiles, but would zealously safeguard America's interests.

Roosevelt's comments were made at a press conference for members of the American Society of Newspaper Editors. He told them of a cabinet meeting "about three or four years ago" when he had tried to discuss the implications of the expansionist activities of an unnamed European country and an Asian country.

THE PRESIDENT: Now then, I went on in this meeting . . . and I said, "We believe that the British Empire, to a certain extent, has stood more nearly for the democratic way of life and has been less trouble to us than some of these newfangled countries that believe in Nazism and Bolshevism, et cetera and, on the whole, Canada has been a pretty good neighbor to us and we have never had any threat against us by Bermuda or Jamaica or by any of the Windward or Leeward Islands. Ever since we got our freedom we have not had any trouble."

"Oh," this fellow said, "you are pro-British."

I said, "No; I am not. I know they have never caused me any trouble as a neighbor and I have a hunch that one of these newfangled countries, with different kinds of government, might cause me trouble in my old age if they were my neighbors."

"Oh," said this fellow, "you are pro-British."

"No," I said, "I have known the British ever since I was a small boy. I am onto their tricks; I know them every one of them. I know them when they are trying to slip something over on me. One reason they like me is that when I catch them, I tell them. And they have got to the point now where they say, 'I guess I can't fool the President; he is onto us.' "

Well, it is a good thing to be in that position.

FLYING BATTLESHIPS

28 June 1940

CORRESPONDENT: Is there any news of the Fleet movement yet?

THE PRESIDENT: . . . No, no news at all.

CORRESPONDENT: Have you any idea where it is?

THE PRESIDENT: Well, if you mean by latitude and longitude, no.

CORRESPONDENT: Would you go so far as to say, Mr. President, that it is still in the Pacific Ocean?

THE PRESIDENT: Well, you know we have been working on—we have been working to see if we could not develop lots of wings and put them on battleships so that they would be able to fly across the Continent just the same way we have been working on the beautiful suggestion that came from out of Colorado that we dig a tunnel through the Rocky Mountains so that we could ship the Fleet from ocean to ocean!

LEARNING GEOGRAPHY

8 October 1940

CORRESPONDENT: Can you tell us anything, Mr. President, about your conference this afternoon with Admiral Richardson and Admiral Leahy?

THE PRESIDENT: Oh, we are just studying maps.

CORRESPONDENT: Did the conference touch upon frontiers in the Far East?

THE PRESIDENT: We studied maps.

CORRESPONDENT: Pacific maps?

THE PRESIDENT: We studied maps and are learning geography.

CORRESPONDENT: Were they mostly in the Eastern Hemisphere?

THE PRESIDENT: All three hemispheres!

LENDING YOUR GARDEN HOSE

17 December 1940

Here, in its entirety and in Roosevelt's own words, is the greatest story that he ever told. It is an extraordinary example of a statesman and a leader trying to educate and persuade a whole nation by extraordinary means. A hundred speeches and a dozen messages to Congress might possibly not have had the same kind of impact as this homely anecdote about lending one's garden hose to a neighbor whose house was on fire. It was one of Roosevelt's most potent weapons in his fight for the lend-lease legislation.

THE PRESIDENT: Now, what I am trying to do is to eliminate the dollar sign and that is something brand new in the thoughts of practically everybody in this room, I think—get rid of the silly, foolish old dollar sign. All right!

Well, let me give you an illustration. Suppose my neighbor's home catches fire and I have got a length of garden hose four or five hundred feet away; but, by Heaven, if he can take my garden hose and connect it up with his hydrant, I may help him to put out his fire.

Now, what do I do? I don't say to him before that operation, "Neighbor, my garden hose cost me $15; you have got to pay me $15 for it."

What is the transaction that goes on? I don't want $15—I want my garden hose back after the fire is over. All right. If it goes through the fire all right, intact, without any damage to it, he gives it back to me and thanks me very much for the use of it.

But suppose it gets smashed up—holes in it—during the fire; we don't have to have too much formality about it, but I say to him, "I was glad to lend you that hose; I see I can't use it any more, it's all smashed up."

He says, "How many feet of it were there?"

I tell him, "There were 150 feet of it."

He says, "All right, I will replace it."

Now, if I get a nice garden hose back, I am in pretty good shape. In other words, if you lend certain munitions and get the munitions back at the end of the war, if they are intact—haven't been hurt—you are all right; if they have been damaged or deteriorated or lost completely, it seems to me you come out pretty well if you have them replaced by the fellow that you have lent them to.

CAN THE PRESIDENT STAND ON HIS HEAD

7 January 1941

Conscious of the vital importance of building up public support for the lend-lease program, Roosevelt made his moves carefully and cautiously. Reluctant to spell out how he intended to implement the legislation, FDR turned away reporters' questions with quips—as can be seen in the following two examples.

CORRESPONDENT: Mr. President, would you care to comment on the story that the lend-lease bill is written so that if it seemed necessary the British Navy could be purchased by the United States?

THE PRESIDENT: . . . there is nothing in the bill—not a thing in the bill to prohibit what might be a very dangerous situation—it doesn't prevent the President of the United States from standing on his head; but the President of the United States doesn't expect to stand on his head and has no desire to stand on his head. The same way, the President of the United States, being somewhat fond of the American Navy, doesn't expect to get rid of the American Navy. Give me another one.

CORRESPONDENT: This, sir, was the other way around—that you could acquire the British Navy under the terms of the bill.

THE PRESIDENT: Oh, that's a new one. That's today's. Well, I suppose that Congress might authorize me to acquire the German Navy too. Don't you think this is awfully, *awfully* cow-jumped-over-the-moon business? I do.

CORRESPONDENT: Mr. President can you tell us anything about your conference with the Apostolic Delegate?

THE PRESIDENT: . . . This is entirely off the record, of course. I suppose I should have, but I didn't—I should have discussed with him the possibility of acquiring the Vatican Navy!

4 February 1941

CORRESPONDENT: Mr. President, when, as, and if the lend-lease bill is adopted approximately as it is now written, what is the first thing you can do under that bill that you can't do, or what is the first aid that the democracies can get or will get that they could not get now?

THE PRESIDENT: Go out in the middle of Pennsylvania Avenue and stand on my head; because that is not yet prohibited.

CORRESPONDENT: How will that aid these democracies?

THE PRESIDENT: It might get favorable publicity.

CORRESPONDENT: If you find a nice, rainy day, the boys would like to go with you!

HUDSON BAY

10 January 1941

CORRESPONDENT: Mr. President, there's a book called *Sea of Destiny*, which tells how vulnerable we are through the Hudson Bay; have you given attention to that?

THE PRESIDENT: Never heard of it. In the winter time that's all "friz" and in the summer time it's full of mosquitoes.

A PRESENT FROM HITLER

31 January 1941

CORRESPONDENT: Mr. President, did Hitler's speech make any particular impression?

THE PRESIDENT: Must I tell you the truth?

CORRESPONDENT: Yes.

THE PRESIDENT: I didn't read it; I was too busy having a birthday.

CORRESPONDENT: It was meant for your birthday, sir!

THE PRESIDENT: . . . Well, I haven't opened all my presents yet!

SUMMING UP THE ST. LAWRENCE SITUATION

11 March 1941

CORRESPONDENT: Anything on the St. Lawrence, Mr. President?

THE PRESIDENT: No—all frozen up!

CAN A COW BECOME A HORSE?

25 April 1941

On 16 April 1941 columnist John O'Donnell, a vigorous critic of Roosevelt's course of aiding Britain, asserted that the United States was providing armed escort to British ships laden with munitions leaving Atlantic ports. A controversy ensued on whether the President had ordered "convoying" of British ships by the American Navy. Roosevelt contended that what was in operation was a policy of "patrolling" that had been initiated in September, 1939, and that the patrol zone was not restricted to 300 miles of off-shore as was believed.

THE PRESIDENT: It was maintained as a patrol for such distances as seemed advisable, in view of the conditions at the time.

. . . I think some of you know what a horse looks like. I think you also know what a cow looks like. If, by calling a cow a horse for a year and a half you think that makes the cow a horse, *I* don't think so. Now that's pretty plain language.

You can't turn a cow into a horse by calling it something else; calling it a horse, it is still a cow.

Now this is a patrol, and has been a patrol for a year and a half, still is, and from time to time it has been extended, and is being extended, and will be extended—the patrol—for the safety of the western hemisphere.

CORRESPONDENT: Could you tell us, sir, how far it may possibly go?

THE PRESIDENT: That is exactly the question I hoped you would ask! As far on the waters of the seven seas as may be necessary for the defense of the American hemisphere. . . .

JIM WRIGHT of the *Buffalo Evening News*: Mr. President, can you tell us the difference between a patrol and a convoy?

THE PRESIDENT: You know the difference between a cow and a horse? . . . All right, there is just as much difference, Jim.

. . . A patrol is a reconnaissance—I think that is the word—of certain areas of ocean to find out whether there is any possibly aggressive ship within that area, or areas, or the whole of the oceans, which might be coming toward the western hemisphere. . . .

It's a little bit like I was talking to one of the Senators over the telephone today. He happened to come from the West, and it's rather a good —rather a good simile. In the old days a wagon train across the plains—of course it had its immediate guard around it, that was perfectly true—but it didn't go—it didn't move across the plains unless it got reports from a long ways—200 to 300 miles off. It was not felt safe to wait until the Indians got two miles away before you saw them. It was advisable to find out if the Indians were 200 miles away.

I'M THE LEADER OF AMERICA FIRST
23 May 1941

THE PRESIDENT: . . . we know in the country—we know that there is a very great lack of understanding at the present time of the seriousness of the world situation as it affects us. . . . a great deal of this perfectly well-intended publicity [advocating aid to Britain] has been stupid. I begged them when they started the so-called Aid to Britain movement— I said, "You know there are an awful lot of people in this country that don't 'give a Continental' about Aid to Britain," but if you tell the whole sentence you get people to understand.

What is the whole sentence? "America First Through Aid to Britain." Now that's a very different thing that tells the truth. . . . Now the real sentence is, "Let us keep America going by giving aid to Britain while we are arming ourselves," and that is the thought to get across. And I think you can help tremendously to make people realize the seriousness of the situation and eliminate a lot of the perfectly silly prejudices that exist today because of wrong slogans—literally the wrong slogans.

I suppose, for example, that if there is any person in the United States who happens to be the leader of the America First movement,[1] it is the unfortunate fellow who happens to have the responsibility—who happens to be President of the United States. He is the leader of the America First movement. Now these other fellows jumped, and nobody's pointed the fact that they have grabbed off something that does not belong to them. There's a whole lot in that. I am just talking ordinary, old-fashioned common sense!

[1] The America First Committee which had come into existence in September, 1940, bitterly criticized Roosevelt's policy of aiding Britain and asserted that his course would involve the United States in a needless war. The Committee succeeded in mobilizing a substantial volume of opinion against the Administration.

YOU SAID IT!
3 June 1941

CORRESPONDENT: Could you tell us how the Atlantic patrol is coming along?

THE PRESIDENT: Coming along!

HAM FISH'S POLL

1 July 1941

THE PRESIDENT: Well, it's a grand day. Why the hell did you want to come up today. This is a day to wear asbestos!

I haven't got a blessed thing. I won't say a word. You can ask all the questions, and I will say, "No" or "Don't know." . . . I haven't even got an off-the-record hunch! . . .

CORRESPONDENT: Mr. President, your Congressman, Mr. Fish,[1] is conducting a poll now, on whether his constituents agree that the United States should enter the war or not. Have you received——

THE PRESIDENT: I didn't get one. . . . You remember President Coolidge's story. . . . His wife came back from church—he hadn't gone, he had a cold. No—his wife didn't go to church. He went to the church. And he came back. She said, "Did you get a good sermon?" "What did he preach about?" "Sin," said Coolidge. "What did he say about it?" "He was against it."

That's very much like this poll which Fish is conducting. . . . Sure— we are all against war!

[1] Republican Congressman Hamilton Fish, Jr., of New York whose Congressional district included Dutchess County. FDR disliked the isolationist Congressman and had privately referred to him as "Honorable Ham." "I wish this great Pooh-bah would go back to Harvard and play tackle on the football team. He qualifies for the job," Roosevelt wrote to Bernard M. Baruch on 1 November 1939. Elliott Roosevelt, ed., *F.D.R. His Personal Letters 1928–1945* (New York, 1950), II, p. 951.

YOUR PET GEOGRAPHER

8 July 1941

On 7 July American marines landed in Iceland. Roosevelt informed Congress, in a message, that he had ordered the Navy to take all steps "to insure the safety of communications in the approaches between Iceland and the United States, as well as on the seas between the United States and all other strategic points."

THE PRESIDENT: You take the case of Iceland. . . . In the first place you will ask the question, is it or isn't it in the Western Hemisphere?

CORRESPONDENT: What do you think?

THE PRESIDENT: It depends on which geographer I consulted last!

CORRESPONDENT: Well, as I understand the statement—the State Department has it straddling.

THE PRESIDENT: It depends on your geographer. . . . I remember a great many years ago, I was going up the north cape of Norway, in one of those cruise boats. We were standing at the rail up there and somebody said, "By Jove, we have just crossed the Arctic Circle." And she said, "Where? I don't see it!"

CORRESPONDENT: Mr. President, the last time you gave us the imaginary line, it ran between Iceland and Greenland. Has there been a shift in that location?

THE PRESIDENT: That is, as I say, depending on the geographer I had seen the previous night!

WHOSE "CULPA"?

16 August 1941

The press conference was held on board the USS "Potomac," off Rockland, Maine. Roosevelt had just returned from the historic Atlantic Ocean meeting with British Prime Minister Winston Churchill. The correspondents were sore because they had learned Churchill had some of his newsmen with him at the Atlantic meeting while Roosevelt had not taken along any American reporters.

THE PRESIDENT: . . . the Ministry of Information in England, at the last minute, had sent two gentlemen who they insisted were not newspapermen—they were people who wrote books!

I said, "Good God, I've got a whole lot of people who are not only newspapermen, but have written books too." If I had known, I would have done it too.

So they are two gentlemen who were literary gentlemen. They were told very definitely by me, and they acceded to it, [that if] the two literary gentlemen ever wrote anything over there inside of a year about this conference, that they were to give it to the three American press associations, in London, free of charge. That was about the best I could do. . . . I couldn't think of any better way to cover it.

I can't say, "Mea culpa," because it was the other fellow's "culpa."

THE ALLEGORY OF POPPA AND THE SCHOOL TEACHER

5 September 1941

This Rooseveltian story marked a development of immense significance in international politics. It heralded the adoption by the United

States of a policy of "active defense" against Axis submarines and the initiation of a *de facto* naval war against them.

On 4 September 1941 the American destroyer, the "Greer," proceeding to Iceland, had tracked a German submarine and begun to broadcast its position. A British aircraft attacked the submarine with depth charges and the German vessel fired a torpedo at the "Greer." The destroyer, which was not hit, dropped depth charges and the submarine fired a second torpedo that failed to find its mark. News of the attack on the American destroyer aroused widespread indignation in the United States. Anti-interventionists, however, loudly criticized what they characterized as provocative courses of action authorized by Roosevelt. They emphasized that no precipitate action should be taken by the United States that might lead to involvement in war in view of the fact that the "Greer" had not been hit.

Roosevelt reacted to the incident with a "shoot-to-kill" order to the American Navy. He declared that "when you see a rattlesnake poised to strike you, do not wait until he has struck before you crush him." This momentous course was indicated, characteristically enough, in Roosevelt's story to the correspondents a day following the attack on the "Greer."

THE PRESIDENT: Well, Judge, how are you this morning?

CORRESPONDENT: Very good, Squire!

THE PRESIDENT: You will all be asking about the attack of yesterday, so we might as well clear that up first.

There is nothing to add, except that there was more than one attack, and that it occurred in daylight, and it occurred on the American side of the ocean. . . . I heard one or two broadcasters this morning, and I read a few things that have been said by people in Washington, which reminded me of a—perhaps we might call it an allegory.

Once upon a time, at a place I was living at, there were some school children living out in the country who were on their way to school, and somebody undisclosed fired a number of shots at them from the bushes.

The father of the children took the position that there wasn't anything to do about it—search the bushes, and take any other steps— because the children hadn't been hit.

I don't think that's a bad illustration in regard to the position of some people this morning. . . .

CORRESPONDENT: Mr. President, is any search of bushes being made out there?

THE PRESIDENT: Yes, yes. . . . I don't go along with the father of those children. . . . You might almost say that the school teacher is searching the bushes.

CORRESPONDENT: Who is he?

THE PRESIDENT: Even where a father wouldn't.

CORRESPONDENT: Mr. President, what is the school teacher going to do if they find the marauder? What can be done? Seriously, can you discuss that?

THE PRESIDENT: I suppose eliminate him. Try to.

CORRESPONDENT: That's the idea. . . .

THE PRESIDENT: "Eliminate" is a reasonably good word!

CORRESPONDENT: I am confused as to who is the school teacher.

THE PRESIDENT: I am the school teacher. Call "poppa" some of these people that are saying, "Forget it. The children were not hit."

HE FLOATS!

17 October 1941

News had been received before the press conference began that the American destroyer, the "Kearny," had been torpedoed by a German submarine a few hundred miles off Iceland. FDR was not willing to make any hasty comment on the incident. Ten days later, in his Navy Day address, he referred to the "attack" on the destroyer and declared that the United States was "pledged to pull our own oar in the destruction of Hitlerism." He also announced that American merchant ships were to be armed "to defend themselves against the rattlesnakes of the sea." In view of the far-reaching importance of this decision, his reluctance to discuss the issue immediately after receiving news of the attack is understandable. When correspondent Tom Reynolds pressed him hard on the issue, FDR fended off questions by making sly references to Reynolds having, on some previous occasion, fallen from a boat into shallow waters in the Pacific Ocean.

THE PRESIDENT: . . . I have just said I am not commenting on it at all, until the Navy Department has established all the facts.

TOM REYNOLDS: Superficially, Mr. President, . . . the most remarkable thing seemed to be that the destroyer could be hit by a torpedo and still remain afloat.

THE PRESIDENT: What?

REYNOLDS: Doesn't one of those torpedoes have a pretty devastating effect on a lightly-armed destroyer?

THE PRESIDENT: I will have to put you in the Navy, Tom!

There is one thing about, . . . [Tom] he floats, doesn't he? We know that. At least we know he floats in the Pacific. The question is whether he will float in the Atlantic. It's a different density of water. This is all off the record, of course. He's taking it down, though!

CORRESPONDENT: Well, he's not ninety-nine per cent pure, Mr. President.[1] . . .

[1] Probably a reference to an advertisement claim that a certain brand of soap could float in water because it was ninety-nine per cent pure.

REYNOLDS: Er—still on the same question, Mr. President. May we assume that the instructions you issued in the case of the "Greer"—to hunt down the marauder—apply in this case?

THE PRESIDENT: Regular Navy orders. I don't know that I would say to hunt down the marauders. You ought to go into the Navy, Tom—really —honestly. Sea-faring—sea-faring. . . . Why, Lord—we'll get you to Annapolis and put you on the football team. You will be all right. . . . It's a short course. You get paid for the taking of it, and graduate as an Ensign and—

CORRESPONDENT: Let's throw him over the side!

HITLER SEEKS LESSON FROM JEW

24 October 1941

CORRESPONDENT: Mr. President, we have a story that one or two papers issued about a seaman in Honolulu who said he passed through the Red Sea. His ship, he said, was subjected to a very severe Nazi bombing. He said that they couldn't hit a bull with a bass fiddle, but indicated that [there was] a great deal of that in that area. Are you aware of that, or have you had anything on that line?

THE PRESIDENT: No. The only thing I heard on that was that Hitler had been going to one of the few prominent Jews left in Germany, and told him that he could stay, if he would explain to him how Moses managed to get the waters to stand aside and get the Children of Israel across!

THREE FATEFUL WEEKS
BEFORE PEARL HARBOR

One of the most portentous developments in modern history was taking shape and all signs pointed to the clear possibility of an early American involvement in global war. The eyes of America and of the world were focussed on Franklin Delano Roosevelt. The pressures on him at that time must have been truly enormous.

How did the great captains and kings of history bear themselves during periods of extreme tension? One wonders.

In the following excerpts from transcripts of several press conferences we find the resolute and masterful leader of a nation poised on the brink of war playfully teasing reporters about a projected trip to **Warm** Springs, Georgia. Included among the excerpts is an important briefing, "for background only," that FDR gave reporters on 25 November 1941. It is an example of the simple yet effective manner in which Roosevelt could present his views to his chosen audience on even issues of the utmost importance. Reporters could be in little doubt about the import of his briefing and their response took the form of a gift to their puckish President.

There was certainly no moratorium on mirth when Roosevelt was around, even during the three fateful weeks before Pearl Harbor.

14 November 1941

CORRESPONDENT: Does it look like Warm Springs tomorrow?
THE PRESIDENT: Unpack!
CORRESPONDENT: You are packed.
THE PRESIDENT: I said unpack.
CORRESPONDENT: Unpack? Not at all? . . . .
THE PRESIDENT: Oh yes. I hope so, later. As soon as I can.
DOORKEEPER DONALDSON: All in!
THE PRESIDENT: You who are headed for a certain famous cottage in Warm Springs tomorrow night, I think you might unpack for a few days because I will not be able to get off, partly because of a lot of things happening, and number two, because my nose is not quite settled yet! It's a bit blocked. . . .
CORRESPONDENT: Mr. President, in that connection, have you any plans to confer with the new Japanese envoy [Saburo Kurusu] when he comes?
THE PRESIDENT: No. Not yet. He gets here tomorrow. . . .
CORRESPONDENT: There is going to be war? . . . .
THE PRESIDENT: I sincerely trust not.

18 November 1941

THE PRESIDENT: It's a shame to be in on a day like this. If I didn't have you fellows today, I would probably have gone out and taken a drive.
CORRESPONDENT: Good driving!
THE PRESIDENT: It's all your fault.
CORRESPONDENT: We would rather be out riding too.
CORRESPONDENT: Let's go down to Warm Springs. You can ride down there.
THE PRESIDENT: Yes. It's out in the woods.
CORRESPONDENT: Still hope to get away?

THE PRESIDENT: Mmm—at the end of the week, but I don't know. I have no idea.

CORRESPONDENT: Mr. President, do you expect to see the Japanese again soon—Mr. Nomura and Mr. Kurusu?

THE PRESIDENT: I suppose so.

21 November 1941

THE PRESIDENT: . . . Warm Springs! Oh my!

CORRESPONDENT: What are the prospects for Warm Springs?

THE PRESIDENT: Just hoping—hoping. . . . .

CORRESPONDENT: No departure this week?

THE PRESIDENT: No. . . .

CORRESPONDENT: Mr. President, have you any reason to feel optimistic about the Japanese talks? . . . .

THE PRESIDENT: Oh well, that's one of those "Are you beating your wife?" questions.

CORRESPONDENT: Is there anything you could tell us about them?

THE PRESIDENT: No. No, no.

25 November 1941

CORRESPONDENT: Any Warm Springs?

THE PRESIDENT: What?

CORRESPONDENT: Any Warm Springs prospects?

THE PRESIDENT: I think you may!

CORRESPONDENT: This week, Mr. President?

THE PRESIDENT: It looks a little that way. I am not dead sure yet. You can get your suitcase out. . . . .

CORRESPONDENT: Just get it out?

THE PRESIDENT: Get it out and dust it off!

CORRESPONDENT: We have had it half-packed for ten days, Mr. President.

THE PRESIDENT: I don't think I ever gave the "unpack" signal this time, did I?

. . . I hope I will be able to go to Warm Springs on Friday afternoon, to stay a few days. And I have asked the President of the [Warm Springs] Foundation if he can postpone the dinner once more, and start the custom of a third Thanksgiving on Saturday night!

28 November 1941

The President and the correspondents were finally to get away from Washington to Warm Springs on this day. In the course of a press conference before their departure, Roosevelt almost casually gave them a very important briefing that culminated in his assertion that there was no chance of a compromise with Japan.

THE PRESIDENT: [to rotund Earl Godwin] Why, hello little stranger!

GODWIN: Thank you for the "little."

THE PRESIDENT: Are you packed?

CORRESPONDENT: All ready.

CORRESPONDENT: Mr. President, it looks like you are going into competition with the apple people.

THE PRESIDENT: That's right. An apple a day.

CORRESPONDENT: When do you think we will be back? . . .

THE PRESIDENT: Why—still hope to get off this afternoon at three o'clock. I was asked in the front row when I would come back. I can't answer the question because I don't know. I hope to stay until Tuesday, but I am not sure that I can.

If somebody will ask me what the reason is, the reason is the Japanese situation. . . .

CORRESPONDENT: Is there anything you can tell us sir, about these Japanese . . . negotiations?

THE PRESIDENT: I think it's better not.

GODWIN: If you have read newspapers carefully, I think you would come to the conclusion that we have been getting news based on Tokyo to a large extent. . . .

THE PRESIDENT: I think that probably is true, Earl, and it has been based on an American policy of infinite patience. . . . I think I could tell you—for background—but only for background—that the situation seems serious because our one desire has been peace in the Pacific, and the taking of no steps to alter the prospects of peace, which of course has meant non-aggression. Really boils down to that.

And also—as background—I was, last spring, talking along the line of general peace for the Pacific, based on a settlement of the war between China and Japan—the restoration of peace there, plus a permanent arrangement for non-aggression in the Pacific, and the restoration of normal economic relations, access to raw materials.

And as you know, the Secretary of State, with even more patience than I have—which is saying a whole lot—had been holding conversations from, I think it was April. And in the middle of them came the Japanese expedition to Indo-China, which is very far afield and caused us very grave concern, because it seemed to be a reasonable—to show a reasonable parallel with the Hitler methods in Europe. As for example, the infiltration, over a period of several months, of the German armies into Roumania and Hungary, placing themselves in the position where strategically they were set to attack Yugoslavia and Greece.

And of course—the drawing of the parallel made peacefully inclined people over here to wonder whether this occupation, with a limited number of troops in Indo-China, was the beginning of a similar action in the Far East, placing obvious American interests in great jeopardy if the drawing of such a parallel was justified.

The American flag, of course, does fly from the Philippines. And even before the Japanese went into Indo-China, one might almost say that the Philippines was located in a horseshoe, with the Japanese military control over the coasts of China, all the way down to the southern border of China, and Japanese military control of the opposite side—the east—over the mandated islands, so-called.

You look at the map closely, that is a sort of horseshoe, open at the southern end, and the Philippines in the middle of it. I think a study of the map would be advisable for all of us, because the Hitler method has always been aimed at a little move here and a little move there, by which complete encirclement, or the obtaining of essential military points was merely—that was a prelude to the extension of aggression to other places. It's a perfectly obvious historical fact today.

And we are of course thinking not only about the American flag in the Philippines, not only about certain vital defense needs which come from that open end of the horseshoe, but we are thinking about the— something even more important, and that is the possible extension of control by aggression into the whole Pacific area.

I don't think that anything more can be said at this time.

We are—we are waiting.

STEVE EARLY: Mr. President, it has been a long time since you defined "background." For the benefit of the newcomers will you do it again?

THE PRESIDENT: Well, Steve suggests I define "background." "Background," as I remember it, is that it is not to be attributed to me in any way, or to the White House in any way. But it is just so it will help you to write your stories. . . . And I don't think I would attribute it to "high sources in the Administration," but you call it "best information obtainable in Washington" or something like that.

CORRESPONDENT: I don't know any better. . . . .

THE PRESIDENT: It's the Government. In other words, it's the Government of the United States. It isn't—it isn't the President, and it isn't the Administration. It's your Government. That's the point of it.

CORRESPONDENT: Against further aggression?

THE PRESIDENT: Against further aggression. We are working to remove the present aggression. . . . .

CORRESPONDENT: The Chinese situation is absolutely solid and set, is it not?

THE PRESIDENT: Absolutely.

CORRESPONDENT: No chance of compromise?

THE PRESIDENT: No. . . . That is off the record altogether.

2 December 1941

From Roosevelt's briefing reporters realized that the die was almost cast. When this press conference was in progress, reporter Charles Hamilton arose, brandishing a substantial ash cane.

HAMILTON: Never since Mr. Theodore Roosevelt have we needed a big stick as much as we do today, so I am giving this to you.

THE PRESIDENT: I think, By Jove—

HAMILTON: I got it in Wales.

THE PRESIDENT: Charlie, thanks ever so much. That's one thing I have longed for. Only, Charlie, for your own safety, don't stand in the front row! That's all right. That's a good hefty one. You know, it has got an awfully nice balance.

CORRESPONDENT: Yes. I think we might get something out of that.

THE PRESIDENT: I do too. I think it's all right.

What was it we were talking about?

CORRESPONDENT: The nature of the inquiries made of Japan. . . . that already, in Indo-China, there were large additional bodies of Japanese forces . . . and that the forces that were on the way would still more greatly exceed the original number.

And the question was asked this morning of the Japanese Government at my request, very politely, as to what the purpose of this was— what the intention of the Japanese Government in doing this was, as to the future; and eliminating, of course, the possibility that it was for the policing of Indo-China, which was an exceedingly peaceful spot beforehand.

And we hope to get a reply to that very simple question shortly.

CORRESPONDENT: Was there any time limit put on it?

THE PRESIDENT: No, no. . . . One doesn't put a time limit on things any more. That's the last century. We are at peace with Japan. We are asking a perfectly polite question. I think that's all!

CORRESPONDENT: I remember Theodore Roosevelt put it—

THE PRESIDENT: [Laughing] Oh, yes. But that's the last generation!

9 December 1941

On 7 December 1941 Japan attacked Pearl Harbor and on the following day Roosevelt delivered his War Message before Congress. The United States was at war with the Axis Powers. At the first press conference held after those momentous developments it was fun as usual with Franklin Roosevelt. Security arrangements were tight and secret service personnel carefully examined the identity cards of correspondents.

STEVE EARLY: Tremendous conference.

THE PRESIDENT: They will get damn little!

CORRESPONDENT: How are you, Mr. President?

THE PRESIDENT: Well, fine. There's darn little news, except that I haven't finished my speech.

CORRESPONDENT MAY CRAIG: You've got a new system out there.

THE PRESIDENT: What?

CRAIG: A new system out there. It's going to take a long time to get [in].

THE PRESIDENT: What's that? What do you have to do? Have they frisked you?

CRAIG: Practically!

THE PRESIDENT: Now May, I don't think that's nice. . . . I will have to hire a female Secret Service agent here to do the frisking!

FDR, 1942 A.D.—LUCIUS AEMILIUS, 168 B. C.

17 March 1942

Roosevelt said that the only things burdening his shoulders—"I being popularly supposed to be overburdened"—were numerous unsolicited communications on military matters. These were usually based on the discourses of "some of the dear 'happy thought' people, commentators, and editors." What was a mere President and Commander-in-Chief to do in the face of the unceasing onslaughts of the kibitzers? FDR turned to history in search of companions in suffering.

THE PRESIDENT: Well, it has been a perfect headache. . . . well, I figured it out, being of an historical frame of mind, that probably some poor devil had gone through this process of annoyance in past years, some previous time in history, so I went quite far back and I found a very nice thing.

I think this comes from Book 44, Chapter 22, of a great historian by the name of Livy, who wrote about Lucius Aemilius, a Roman Consul who had been selected to conduct the war with the Macedonians, B.C. 168.

He went out from the Senate House into the Assembly of the People and addressed them as follows—it sounds as if it were written in 1942!:

> In all public places where people congregate and actually . . . in private parties—

Doesn't that sound just like Washington?

> there are men—

Of course today could be added women.

> who know who are leading the armies into Macedonia, where their camps ought to be placed, what strategical positions ought to be occupied, when and by what pass Macedonia ought to be en-

tered, where the magazines ought to be formed, by what mode of land and sea transport—

And to that we might today add air.

supplies are to be conveyed, when actions are to be fought and when it is better to remain inactive. And they not only lay down what ought to be done, but when anything is done contrary to their opinion they arraign the Consul as though he were being impeached before the Assembly.

This greatly interferes with the successful prosecution of a war. . . . I am not one of those who think that generals are not to be advised; on the contrary, the man who always acts on his own initiative shows, in my judgment, more arrogance than wisdom. How then does the case stand? Commanders ought first of all to get the advice of thoughtful and far-seeing men who have special experience of military affairs; then from those who are taking part in the operations, who know the country and recognize a favourable opportunity when it comes, who, like comrades on a voyage, share the same dangers.

If then, there is any man who in the interests of the commonwealth feels confident that he can give me good advice in the war which I am to conduct, let him not refuse to help his country, but go with me to Macedonia. I will supply him with a ship, a horse, a tent, and with his travelling expenses as well. If anyone thinks this is too much trouble, let him not act as a sea pilot whilst he is on land.

Isn't that a classic?

The city itself affords plenty of subjects for conversation; let him confine his loquacity to these; he may rest assured that the discussions in our councils of war will satisfy us.

I think it is rather nice. I think that ought to be printed. Be sure you make it B.C., not A.D.—168![1]

[1] FDR had received the Livy material from Bernard Baruch. "That quotation from Livy is a pure gem," the President wrote to Baruch. "I must use it at a press conference but I am not sure that the press would understand the delicate connotation." Elliott Roosevelt, ed., *F.D.R. His Personal Letters 1928–1945* (New York, 1950), II, p. 1292.

TRUE STORY OF GENERAL M ᴀᴄARTHUR'S ESCAPE TO AUSTRALIA!

20 March 1942

The United States was on the verge of a grave military disaster in the Philippines. A capitulation without parallel in American history since Appomattox lay ahead. FDR had ordered General Douglas MacArthur to leave the Philippines and to reestablish his headquarters in Australia. In the midst of these developments Roosevelt remained a serene and self-assured prankster.

THE PRESIDENT: I thought you were going to ask me about how he [MacArthur] got out.

Well, we had a few people in for supper the other night, and one charming lady—this was the day that it had been announced that Douglas MacArthur had got there—and she said, "Oh, Mr. President, tell me how he got there."

So I told her just how he got there, and she really believed it!

I told her that he had taken a rowboat, which was the only safe way, had disguised himself as a Filipino fisherman, and had passed right by— almost right alongside a lot of Jap warships, and destroyers, and submarines, and everything else, and they had not suspected that it was Douglas MacArthur at all. He had rowed all the way down there—right past the Japs! Perfectly simple. It was only a matter of twenty-five hundred miles.

And I think that several people at the table believed it!

HOW TO HANDLE SWEET YOUNG THINGS

21 April 1942

CORRESPONDENT: Mr. President, is there any comment you can make on the . . . recent developments in the Southwest Pacific? . . .

THE PRESIDENT: . . . you know, occasionally I have a few people in to dinner, and generally in the middle of dinner some "sweet young thing" says, "Mr. President, couldn't you tell us about so and so?"[1]

[1] The "sweet young thing" continued to figure actively in FDR's imagination. And he could use her for a variety of purposes—massaging the ego of his Chief of Naval Staff, for instance. On 12 August 1942 Roosevelt sent the following letter to Admiral Ernest J. King:

Dear Ernie:

You will remember "the sweet young thing" whom I told about Douglas MacArthur rowing his family from Corregidor to Australia

Well, the other night this "sweet young thing" in the middle of supper said, "Mr. President, couldn't you tell us about that bombing? Where did those planes start from and go to?"

And I said, "Yes. I think the time has now come to tell you. They came from our new secret base at Shangri-La!"

And she believed it!

CORRESPONDENT: Mr. President, is this the same young lady you talked about—

THE PRESIDENT: No. This is a generic term. It happens to be a woman.

CORRESPONDENT MAY CRAIG: Is it always feminine? . . . .

THE PRESIDENT: Now May, why did you ask me that?

CRAIG: I wondered.

THE PRESIDENT: I call it a "sweet young thing." Now when I talk about manpower that includes the women, and when I talk about a "sweet young thing" that includes young men.

CORRESPONDENT: Do you have those kinds of men . . . in the [White] House?

THE PRESIDENT: Yes, and the Senate too!

—and later told about Shangri-La as the take-off place for the Tokio bombers.

Well, she came in to dinner last night and this time she told me something.

She said, "We are going to win this war. The Navy is tough. And the toughest man in the Navy—Admiral King—proves it. He shaves every morning with a blowtorch."

Glad to know you!

As ever yours,

P.S. I am trying to verify another rumor—that you cut your toenails with a torpedo net cutter.

Elliott Roosevelt, ed., *F.D.R. His Personal Letters 1928–1945* (New York, 1950), II, p. 1339.

SHANGRI-LA

26 May 1942

When reporters asked him questions about the location of ships and of places involved in military operations, Roosevelt affected a most solemn manner and specified "Shangri-La" as the exact spot. He thus treated them with the same friendly consideration that he extended to "sweet young things" who asked him similar questions at supper parties.

THE PRESIDENT: . . . there is only one thing I have, in regard to our old lesson in geography, which we get twice a week. This comes from Louisiana.

A Southern newspaper editor was asked in a letter to the editor where Shangri-La was, and he said that he had examined carefully the maps of every parish in the State of Louisiana and been unable to find Shangri, La! . . . .

CORRESPONDENT: When is the ambassador of Shangri-La going to present his credentials?

THE PRESIDENT: That's right too. Will look into that.

CORRESPONDENT: Mr. President, I understood that was an American possession.

CORRESPONDENT: Have you any Shangri-La stamps for cancellation?

THE PRESIDENT: Yes. I have a special album sent me by the Lama!

A BUNDLE FOR WINSTON

9 July 1942

The British Prime Minister suggested to FDR that in view of the imperative need to cut down shipping space taken up by non-military items, the American project of sending "Bundles for Britain" should be wound up.

THE PRESIDENT: . . . I hate like blazes cutting off or diminishing the flow of "Bundles for Britain"—but it has to be done.

However, if you personally long for a seven-to-one Martini, I will send it across pronto.[1]

[1] Winston Churchill to the President, 14 June 1942; the President to Churchill, 9 July 1942, FDRL.

FDR AND THE DEVIL

17 November 1942

During the night of 7-8 November 1942 American forces landed in French Northern and Western Africa. After a brief struggle, the Vichyite French administration agreed to a cease-fire on 11 November. Many Americans, principally "liberals," sharply criticized certain political arrangements that General Dwight Eisenhower worked out with the French leader, Admiral Darlan.

Roosevelt told reporters that he had approved Eisenhower's course and emphasized that it was "only a temporary expedient, justified solely by the stress of battle."

THE PRESIDENT: I thought of putting in there, but I didn't, an old Balkan proverb, which I cannot have even attributed to me, because at the present time I don't like to call names any more than one has to. It's rather a nice old proverb of the Balkans that has—as I understand it—has the full sanction of the Orthodox Church. . . . look it up in an encyclopedia of Balkan proverbs if you want to; . . . mind you, this is okayed by the Church!

It says, "My children, you are permitted, in time of great danger, to walk with the Devil until you have crossed the bridge."

Rather nice!

THE PHILOSOPHY AND
ECONOMICS OF "FOREIGN AID"

24 November 1942

The extraordinary faculty that FDR had for presenting very complex and controversial issues in homely terms is brought out in this exposition of what came to be known in subsequent years as "foreign aid."

Referring to the appointment of Herbert Lehman as Director of Foreign Relief and Rehabilitation Operations in the State Department, Roosevelt told reporters that he expected misguided opposition to develop against the idea of American assistance to less fortunate countries. He asserted that a program could be worked out by which the standard of living of the people of those countries could be raised "without hurting our economy or the economy of the larger or richer nations as they exist at the present."

THE PRESIDENT: I can give you an illustration right here at home. Back in the old days, when I went South—the deep South—Oh, what—15, 20 years ago—the whole standard of earnings was so low that those people down there . . . couldn't buy anything at the store. And a great many Northern people . . . failed to realize that if their purchasing power down there in the South was higher, those people down there would . . . purchase . . . things that were made in the North, and therefore would put a whole lot of people to work in the North, and thereby increase the purchasing power of the North too.

Well, it sounds awfully simple the way you say it, but . . . nobody ever acted on it until we began to go up by leaps and bounds.

In rural Georgia, for example, back there, there was hardly a local store that was solvent, quite aside from the banks. They didn't turn their stock over. . . . there were no buyers on Saturday afternoons in the country districts in the South and there the stock remained.

Well, ... maybe one or two are still here that accompanied me down to Georgia in those days. But if you remember the local stores down there, if you went in to buy a hat, you would find it was an 8-year-old vintage— there was no turn-over. This meant that the fellow was losing so much interest on ... the money he had borrowed to buy his stock with, and each year he was going deeper into the red.

Now since then, in the whole of the agricultural South, they have had a greater turn-over, because they have had more buying power. Now it certainly hasn't hurt the North. It has given the North, and the manufacturing districts, the opportunity to make things and sell in the South that they have never done before.

... Now the same thing can be worked out in those of other nations— we are working at it—which today have got practically no purchasing power. It is going to help them enormously, but it is going to help us too. It's a perfectly obvious thing; and yet there are a lot of people in this country—they can't see the value of putting other people onto their feet.

Now you will begin to find in the United States quite a group of people that will say, in regard to the appointment of Governor Lehman the other day, "Is the United States going to shell out our food and our clothing? Are we going to spend our good money to—to rehabilitate other nations? What's the big idea?" Now you will find that an increasing—from now on—slogan. It will be put all over the United States.

CORRESPONDENT: *Are* we going to, Mr. President?

THE PRESIDENT: What? Sure, we are going to rehabilitate them. Why? All right. Not only from the humanitarian point of view—you needn't stress that unless you want to—there's something in it—but from the point of view of our own pocketbooks, and our own safety from future attack—future war!

FDR AND THE WAACS WITHOUT ANY CLOTHES
2 February 1943

Roosevelt had returned to Washington after holding discussions with Winston Churchill in Casablanca in North Africa. Reporters were eager to hear from him about what went on in Casablanca.

THE PRESIDENT: Oh, yes, I must tell you about the WAACs.[1] We found five WAACs—I think the only ones in Africa. And there they were, doing the telephone work, and the stenographic work for the staff meeting.

And I had them in to dine—all five—had a nice little party for them.

They had had a perfectly amazing experience. They had all been in the same ship ... in December, and the ship was torpedoed. And two of

[1] Members of the Women's Auxiliary Army Corps.

them were taken off in boats. The other three couldn't get into the boats, and they were taken in by a British destroyer, I think.

And finally all five of them were safely landed in Africa without any clothes whatsoever.——They had nothing except what they had on their backs!

AFTER THE QUEBEC CONFERENCE
31 August 1943

The Italian dictator, Benito Mussolini, had been overthrown on 25 July 1943 and a new government under Marshal Badoglio initiated steps that eventually led to Italy's surrender. Around the middle of August, Allied forces had overrun Sicily. On 17 August Roosevelt and Churchill began an important conference at Quebec, Canada.

Reporters who accompanied FDR to Quebec stayed at the Clarendon Hotel. To gather his colleagues for press briefings, Merriman Smith of the United Press usually sounded a gong. Newsmen who professed to be disappointed over not getting much news about the decisions arrived at in the course of the conference presented a citation to FDR at the first press conference held after their return to Washington.

Douglas B. Cornell of A.P.: Mr. President, . . . before the press conference starts, we would like to have a bit of an off-the-record executive session and transact a little business that was left over from the Quebec conference.

The President: Good.

Cornell: As the senior officer of the White House Correspondents' Association who was at the Quebec conference, Merriman Smith has a resolution to read:

Merriman Smith: [Holds up a very long sheet of paper] Don't be frightened by this Mr. President.

The President: I was a little worried.

Smith: It runs right down!

The President: I hope this is apologetic!

Smith: [Reads]

WHITE HOUSE CORRESPONDENTS' ASSOCIATION
August 31, 1943
KNOW ALL MEN BY THESE PRESENTS:
THAT
WHEREAS: It is WELL KNOWN that the recent QUEBEC CONFERENCE nearly was ushered into HISTORY with a ringing SALVO OF SILENCE; and
WHEREAS: It is WELL KNOWN that Monsieur F. ROOSEVELT and Monsieur S. EARLY by EXTRAORDINARY EN-

DEAVORS AVERTED that CATASTROPHE which would have been conducive to subsequent LEAKAGE and MOREOVER have made JUSTIFICATION of QUEBEC EXPENSE ACCOUNTS EXTREMELY DIFFICULT; now therefore be it

RESOLVED: That the UNDERSIGNED, survivors of the BATTLE OF QUEBEC and members of the WHITE HOUSE CORRESPONDENTS' ASSOCIATION, do hereby express their APPRECIATION of the CONSPICUOUS SERVICES of the aforesaid M. ROOSEVELT and M. EARLY; and do hereby CITE them for GALLANTRY IN ACTION ABOVE and BEYOND the CALL OF DUTY and be it further

RESOLVED: That these RESOLUTIONS be SPREAD upon the record of a WHITE HOUSE PRESS CONFERENCE and the CONTENTS thereof be COMMUNICATED to ALL PARTIES in INTEREST

Signed and sealed by a large number of veterans of Quebec.

THE PRESIDENT: Well, I am very glad to have that. Nothing is said, though, about a certain episode. Who was it that woke not only the White House correspondents but all the other correspondents, several hundreds of them, by ringing a dinner bell in the middle of the night?

Well, if you all only knew to what lengths I had to go to prevent the bell-ringer from being arrested under the old French Law, you would be even more appreciative. Steve and I worked on it for—for two whole days! The Mayor of Quebec—he got waked up too! And no jury would have exonerated them. So I had to use all the diplomatic methods possible. I had the State Department at work on it!

And finally everything was resolved all right, and we got them across the border. I had to get the Treasury Department to state they wouldn't be searched when they went across the border!

SMITH: For the bell?

THE PRESIDENT: Well, I am very grateful for that. It worked out very happily. . . . everybody had a good time, and it was what they call an enjoyable time. I think it's all right.

TELLING A LADY TO PACK UP IN A HURRY
30 March 1943

FDR spoke of the importance of working out plans well in advance to meet the problems that were bound to emerge immediately after the end of hostilities. He said he had discussed some matters relating to postwar arrangements with an important visitor, British Foreign Secretary Anthony Eden.

THE PRESIDENT: If some of you go back—some of you can, like my-self—go back to 1918, the war came to a rather sudden end in November, 1918. And actually it's a fact that there had been very little work done on the post-war problems before Armistice Day. Well, during Armistice Day and the time that the nations met in Paris early in 1919, everybody was rushing around trying to dig up things.

And the simile I used to Mr. Eden that day was that . . . the tempo seemed to be that of the lady who is told at Noon that she is to accom-pany her husband on a month's trip on the three o'clock train that after-noon. Well, I have seen ladies trying to pack for a month's trip in three hours, and that was a little bit the situation over here, and everywhere else, in making preparations for the Versailles conference. Everybody was rushing around grabbing things out of closets and throwing them into suitcases. Some of the . . . large portions of things out of the cup-boards were not needed at all.

I have forgotten how many experts we took to Versailles at that time, but everybody who had a "happy thought" or who thought he was an expert got a free ride!

APRES VOUS, GASTON!

12 February 1943

Roosevelt gave members of the American Society of Newspaper Edi-tors his version of the big social event of the Casablanca conference—the meeting between General Charles de Gaulle and General Henri Giraud. The two rival French generals had a frigid attitude towards each other.

THE PRESIDENT: Mr. Churchill and I decided it would be a great chance to see if we could bring De Gaulle and Giraud together.

I said jokingly—I said, "Now, we'll call Giraud the bridegroom, and I'll produce him from Algiers next Saturday afternoon. And you get the bride, De Gaulle, from London, and we will get them down here, and we'll have a shot-gun wedding.

Well, Saturday afternoon came, and I—I had my man there, but Winston couldn't produce the bride. And it took, Oh—until the following Friday morning before we could get De Gaulle there.

And then came the two days of conversations between them. And Churchill and I kept discreetly out of it, except that they had said, "Après vous, Gaston"—"Après vous, Alphonse"—and got nowhere!

VODKA WITH STALIN

17 December 1943

FDR had returned to Washington after conferring with Churchill and Stalin at Teheran. Reporters were eager to have Roosevelt's impressions of the Soviet leader.

CORRESPONDENT: Sir, could you tell us any of your personal impressions of Stalin?

THE PRESIDENT: Except that the actual fact of meeting him lived up to my highest expectations. We had many excellent talks. . . .

EARL GODWIN: Mr. President, would you care to tell us how those talks were conducted? Was it an easy matter?

THE PRESIDENT: Through an interpreter, which of course is not as easy as if I spoke Russian, . . . but still we got on all right. . . .

GODWIN: Was it stodgy, or anything of that sort?

THE PRESIDENT: Not stodgy at all, except the answer sometimes came before the translation was finished!

GODWIN: Did you find him—all we know about him is that picture with a handle-bar moustache, which evidently is out of date.

THE PRESIDENT: Yes, that is rather out of date.

GODWIN: What type would you call it? Was—is he—is he dour?

THE PRESIDENT: I would call him something like me—he is a realist.

GODWIN: Yes, he seems to be. . . .

MAY CRAIG: Tell us about it.

THE PRESIDENT: May, I don't write no social column.

GODWIN: . . . did you attend one of those dinners where they had forty-five toasts?

THE PRESIDENT: Well, I can tell you this, off the record . . . because that is a subject that—liquor—you don't talk about loud, you know that!

We had one banquet where we had dinner in the Russian style. Very good dinner, too. Russian style means a number of toasts, and I counted up to three hundred and sixty-five toasts. And we all went away sober. It is a remarkable thing, what you can do, if you try!

CORRESPONDENT: How, Mr. President? . . . .

THE PRESIDENT: When you go up to those places like Teheran, you learn!

CORRESPONDENT: We would like the opportunity.

THE PRESIDENT: I made one glass of vodka that big [indicating a two-inch width with his fingers] last for about twenty toasts—just about.

FDR, CHURCHILL, AND COLONIALISM

4 February 1944

At a press conference for the Negro Newspaper Publishers' Association, Roosevelt recalled his brief visit to Gambia in Africa and discussed the concept of international inspection teams under the auspices of a world organization to report on the progress made by colonial territories.

THE PRESIDENT: Last year I went to a place called Gambia in Africa, at the mouth of the Gambia river. Bathurst is the capital. I think there are about three million inhabitants of whom one hundred and fifty are white. And it is the most horrible thing I have ever seen in my life. I was there twice. The natives are five thousand years back of us. Disease is rampant, absolutely.

. . . And I looked up, with a little study, and I got to the point of view that for every—the British have been there for two hundred years—for every dollar that the British have put into Gambia, they have taken out ten. It is just plain exploitation of those people. There is no education whatsoever. A few missionaries. With all due deference to the missionaries, if they wouldn't try to live in the best houses in town, they would be better off!

. . . I am taking up with Churchill at the present time—he doesn't see the point yet—I think he will—the general thought that the United Nations ought to have an inspection committee of all the colonies that way, way down the line, that are not ready to have anything to say yet because the owning country has given them no facilities.

And if we sent—sent a committee from the United Nations, and I used the example of Gambia, to go down to Gambia: "If you Britishers don't come up to scratch—toe the mark—then we will let all the world know."

Well, Churchill doesn't like the idea. And his comeback was, "All right, the United Nations will send an inspection committee to your own South in America."

He thought he had me.

I said, "Winston, that's all right with me. Go ahead and do it. Tell the world. . . . you can right a lot of wrongs with pitiless publicity."

It would be a grand thing. I wouldn't mind if we had a committee of the United Nations come here and make a report on us. Why not?

A BEAUTIFUL LETTER FROM AN HONEST MAN

8 March 1944

FDR told a meeting of the Advertising War Council that peace was by no means around the corner and that the road to victory was bound to be long and difficult. Any group advocating "peace now" was simply working in the opposite direction.[1]

THE PRESIDENT: Well, just for example. I got a letter yesterday from a very prominent man who has been retired for some years, a five-page letter, making a plea to me to appoint a "secretary of peace" and send him over to Germany—it's a beautiful letter, and he meant it; it's an honest thing, from his heart—to see if we couldn't work out some means with Germany of ending this terrible slaughter, and the busting up of civilization. Not a word about some of the things we are hoping to get, such as the end of German aggression, and a change in the philosophy of the German Government. Oh no, not a word about that! But appoint a peace secretary to go over there—sort of a roving commission—to bring peace to the world.

Now there are a lot of people in this country that are doing things of that kind honestly. I don't believe in this "ulterior motive" stuff, but they just don't know.

[1] *Public Papers and Addresses, 1944,* p. 100.

D-DAY

6 June 1944

The long-awaited day had at last arrived. Allied forces had landed on the beaches of Normandy.

THE PRESIDENT: My Lord!—all smiles—all smiles. . . . .

AIDE JONATHAN DANIELS: You don't look like you're so solemn yourself, Mr. President!

THE PRESIDENT: No, I'm not so solemn, I suppose. . . . Well, I think this is a very happy conference today. . . . .

CORRESPONDENT: Mr. President, how do you feel about the progress of the invasion?

THE PRESIDENT: Up to schedule. And, as the Prime Minister said, "That's a mouthful."

. . . you will increasingly see the reasons why, at the behest of politicians and others, we didn't institute a second front a year ago when they began clamoring for it; because their plea for an immediate second front last year reminds me a good deal of that famous editor and statesman who said years ago, before most of you were born, about—during the Wilson administration: "I am not worried about the defense of America. If we are threatened, a million men will spring to arms overnight." And, of course, somebody said, "What kind of arms? If you can't arm them, then what's the good of their springing to something that 'ain't' there?"

PROFESSOR ROOSEVELT ON THE ITALIAN CONSTITUTIONAL SITUATION

9 June 1944

THE PRESIDENT: . . . the situation, I think is a—almost a new one in the history of kings. The King of Italy is still the King of Italy, but he isn't the King of Italy. In other words, he's in but he's out.

. . . And the . . . Crown Prince has been made . . . Lieutenant General of the Realm. Now, I never heard of one before—and apparently it means under their system that the cabinet resigns to him instead of to the King, and then he recalls somebody to be Prime Minister. . . . I haven't got the exact terms, but the King of Italy, as I say, is King of Italy, but he isn't King of Italy. He hasn't got any powers!

BASIC ENGLISH

June 1944

Winston Churchill forwarded to the President the report of a British Cabinet Committee on the possibilities of promoting Basic English. He pleaded for American support for acceptance of Basic English as a means of international intercourse. "My conviction is that Basic English will then prove to be a great boon to mankind in the future and a powerful support to the influence of the Anglo-Saxon peoples in world affairs," he wrote.

Roosevelt requested Secretary of State Cordell Hull for his comments on the suggestion. All that Hull could suggest was that the views of "competent Government specialists and private linguistic experts" should be ascertained. The President thought that any such move would "certainly sound the death knell of Basic English or anything like it." "I never know of any group of such people to agree to anything really different from the existing system—or, for that matter, anything new," he said: After instructing Hull to sound out Congressional opinion on the subject, FDR prepared a reply in his usual humorous vein to the Prime Minister.[1]

THE PRESIDENT: Incidentally, I wonder what the course of history would have been if in May, 1940, you had been able to offer the British

---

[1] Winston Churchill to the President, 20 April 1944; Cordell Hull to the President, 31 May 1944; the President to Hull, 5 June 1944; the President to Churchill, n.d., June, 1944?, FDRL.

people only "blood, work, eye water and face water," which I understand is the best that Basic English can do with five famous words.[2]

Seriously, however, we are interested and will look into the matter thoroughly.

[2] Churchill had spoken of blood, toil, tears and sweat.

SUFFERING AND ACHIEVEMENT

9 June 1944

FDR informed reporters that the invasion of France was proceeding satisfactorily.

THE PRESIDENT: Things are going pretty well on the other side. The chief trouble is the weather. The English Channel is not a pleasant place to cross. It's rough a great deal. As somebody remarked the other day, probably there has been more suffering—human suffering on the English Channel than any other place in the world!

And on the whole, things are going along very well. We have been doing awfully well north of Rome. We are about 40 miles north of Rome. . . . the whole operation—the English Channel, and the Mediterranean, Italy—all tie in together, as we have come to understand.

I think the greatest contribution—there is always a silver lining in every cloud that a war makes—is teaching people geography. A lot of people in this country now know where Italy is. Now, that's quite an achievement!

KEEP YOUR EYE ON THE GREAT OBJECT

29 August 1944

Reporters questioned the President concerning the decisions taken at the Dumbarton Oaks Conference. He warned them that if at that preliminary stage people got unduly involved in emphasizing details, they were apt to forget "the great object" of launching a new world organization.

THE PRESIDENT: And a very good illustration is this. In 1920 I was addressing a very big meeting out of doors up in Michigan, . . . and I got to talking about the League [of Nations].

And some woman got up and said, "I can't be for the League of Nations, it legalizes white slavery."

I said, "Where?"

So she trotted out article something, which authorized the League to set up machinery—the objective was perfectly clear—to put down white slavery by international agreement. And she construed, because it did not say "put down," . . . that it meant to regulate white slavery, and therefore to approve white slavery.

Well, I had a violent discussion with her, and we both left the meeting thoroughly angry.

Now that's what comes of bringing politics or partisanship, or—well, the old word I had used before: picayune—by the way, I found George Washington used that word—of bringing carping discussions into the details of a thing. . . .

THE GOOD NEIGHBOR POLICY

31 August 1944

FDR was proposing a toast to Dr. Ramon Grau San Martin, President-elect of Cuba, at a State Luncheon.[1]

THE PRESIDENT: . . . the President-elect is largely responsible for the good neighbor policy. I don't know that he is aware he is in large part responsible, because of the fact he was mixed up in the revolution in Cuba in 1933. And there was a real reason for dissatisfaction in Cuba with its own government; and firing started.

And there were a great many people in this country who said "Ah, now you must intervene under the Platt Amendment for the third time."[2] And I got letters and telegrams that we must do something about this problem in Cuba.

And thinking it over for a week or two, as the trouble was continuing, I asked the ambassadors and ministers of all the other American Republics to come to the White House. They came into my study and sat

[1] Toast to the President-elect of Cuba at a State Luncheon, 31 August 1944, *Public Papers and Addresses, 1944*, pp. 252–53.

[2] The Platt Amendment, named after Senator Orville Platt of Connecticut, required Cuba to permit the United States to intervene to protect Cuban independence and to maintain a government "adequate for the protection of life, property and individual liberty." Only after the Cubans agreed to incorporate the articles of the Platt Amendment (22 May 1903) did the United States agree to terminate its military occupation of the island. Apart from the two interventions referred to by FDR (1906–1909; 1917–1923), the Cubans frequently complained of meddling and interference by the United States. Roosevelt took the lead in promoting the concept of the "good neighbor" and the Platt Amendment was repealed on 29 May 1934.

down, and I said, "Gentlemen, I am going to make a very revolutionary announcement. I have decided not to send the armed forces of the United States into Cuba. I am going to send some Coast Guard cutters, and other gunboats and small craft to the ports of Cuba, and send word to every American in Cuba that if they are afraid for their lives, to go down to a port and they will find a Coast Guard revenue cutter they can get on, and we will take them home to the United States without any expense. And having done that, we will send word to all the people of Cuba to go right ahead and have the revolution. We think it's rather silly not to work it out some other way, but we are not going to interfere under the Platt Amendment.

Well, the result was there was a certain amount of trouble in a short time. We never fired a shot. The Congress of the United States repealed the Platt Amendment, and Cuba since that time has had no trouble at all.

THE BIG, BLANK SPACE ON THE MAP
21 October 1944

THE PRESIDENT: . . . I cite as an illustration in the field of foreign policy something that I am proud of. That was the recognition of Soviet Russia.

And may I add a personal word. In 1933, a certain lady—who sits at this table in front of me—came back from a trip on which she had attended the opening of a schoolhouse. And she had gone to the history and geography class with children eight, nine or ten, and she told me that she had seen there a map of the world with a great big white space upon it—no name—no information. And the teacher told her that it was blank, with no name, because the school board wouldn't let her say anything about that big blank space. Oh, there were only a hundred and eighty to two hundred million people in that space which was called Soviet Russia. And there were a lot of children, and they were told that the teacher was forbidden by the school board even to put the name of that blank space on the map.

For sixteen years before then, the American people and the Russian people had no practical means of communicating with each other. We reestablished those means. And today we are fighting with the Russians against common foes. . . .[1]

[1] Radio address at a dinner of the Foreign Policy Association 21 October 1944, *Public Papers and Addresses, 1944*, p. 344.

BRING THEM IN!

25 October 1944

Good news or bad news—FDR smiled through it all.

It was past 5 o'clock in the evening. Roosevelt asked Steve Early to round up any reporters who might still be found in the press room and bring them into his office. Seven reporters were ushered in a little later and they wondered what FDR was up to at that late hour.

STEVE EARLY: Here they are, sir.

THE PRESIDENT: Well, what are they doing around?

CORRESPONDENT: We were just asking that ourselves. . . . .

THE PRESIDENT: Well, this is good. I love to see them working. Just look! It always breaks my heart.

CORRESPONDENT: Like the old days at Hyde Park, in the study.

THE PRESIDENT: Yes. Some of you are putting on a little waistline.

CORRESPONDENT: We are all sober today.

THE PRESIDENT: . . . Chocolate soda?

CORRESPONDENT: At this time of day, Mr. President, please take it a little slow!

Roosevelt then thrilled the reporters by telling them that a flash message had been received from Admiral William Halsey to the effect that "the Japanese Navy in the Philippines area has been defeated, seriously damaged, and routed by the American Navy in that area." The great Battle of the Leyte Gulf had ended in a clear victory for American arms.

THE TALE OF THE MISSING DOCUMENT

19 December 1944

Roosevelt had answered some questions about the Atlantic Charter and he went on to recall an incident connected with the ceremony in Washington on 1 January 1942 when the Declaration of the United Nations was signed by representatives of the Allied nations.

THE PRESIDENT: Yes, that was done on the first of January 1942. . . . . There was one amusing thing that happened to it. The original was, I think, typewritten in the State Department. And, finally, on the first of January, 1942, came in—the Ambassadors came in a great part of that day. We had two or three sessions and we all signed up. And then a little later on Brazil and a couple of other countries signed, over in the Dining Room in the White House, which was all decorated with flags.

. . . That's where I got caught. Nobody caught on. The press was there, though.

And . . . the Brazilian Ambassador was sitting on my right, and the copy was not there! I delivered a speech and asked the signatory powers to sign. But there was nothing to sign. It was in the Department safe, and the keeper of the Department safe who knew the combination was in Bethesda—which didn't help at all.

And I said, all right, we haven't got the document for you to sign; and I wrote out [in] longhand very simple words: We hereby approve and join in the document of the United Nations set up on the first of January last.

But before writing it, I looked for a pen, and there wasn't any pen—because the pen wouldn't work—didn't have any ink in it! It finally ended by my borrowing the pen—I used really strong language—luckily I wasn't on the air—as to the lack of pens, and I borrowed the fountain pen of the Brazilian——

CORRESPONDENT: Mexican.

THE PRESIDENT: Mexican Ambassador—Najera, that's right. I think they have got that.

STEVE EARLY: That's it.

DEAR OLD WINSTON'S BLIND SPOT

23 February 1945

The Yalta Conference of the Big Three had ended and Roosevelt was returning from Algiers to Newport News, Virginia, on board the U.S.S. "Quincy." In a talk with reporters on board the ship he talked about his concept of international trusteeship for Indo-China to prepare the people of that country for self-government.

THE PRESIDENT: Stalin liked the idea. China liked the idea. The British don't like it. It might bust up their empire, because if the Indo-Chinese were to work together and eventually get their independence, the Burmese might do the same to the King of England. . . . It would only get the British mad. Chiang would go along. Stalin would go along. As for the British, it would only make the British mad. Better to keep quiet just now.

CORRESPONDENT: Is that Churchill's idea on all territory out there, he wants them all back just like they were?

THE PRESIDENT: Yes, he is mid-Victorian on all things like that.

CORRESPONDENT: You would think some of that would be knocked out of him by now. . . . This idea of Churchill's seems inconsistent with the policy of self-determination.

THE PRESIDENT: Yes, that is true.

CORRESPONDENT: He seems to undercut the Atlantic Charter. He made a statement the other day that it was not a rule, just a guide.

THE PRESIDENT: The Atlantic Charter is a beautiful idea. When it was drawn up, the situation was that England was about to lose the war. They needed hope, and it gave it to them.

CORRESPONDENT: ... Do you remember the speech the Prime Minister made about the fact that he was not the Prime Minister of Great Britain to see the empire fall apart?

THE PRESIDENT: Dear old Winston will never learn on that point. He has made his speciality on that point. This is, of course, off the record.

VI

FOURTH ESTATE FIESTA

PERFECT HAPPINESS

7 April 1933

THE PRESIDENT: If anybody wants to see something that is really a joy, here it is. This is just strictly in the family. The most correct paper in the United States is the *New York Times*. Here is the loveliest thing that ever happened. You see on the right-hand side a picture of a boat which is laying on its side in the mud and the story alongside it says "liner stabilizer found successful."

I got that this morning when I wasn't feeling at all well and I have been perfectly happy ever since.

THE PRESIDENT IS MISSING!

7 July 1933

The Hundred Days were over. The New Deal had been launched FDR was ready for a vacation and the sea called him. For nearly three weeks in June he sailed in the Atlantic Ocean in a small forty-five foot schooner, "Amberjack II." Eight correspondents— landlubbers all— lodged in two boats, watched Roosevelt's seamanship with admiration while nursing queasy stomachs with their favorite libations. Apparently during the vacation the President traded jokes with the reporters on spirituous matters.[1] He also played a prank on them and, on his return to Washington, he recounted the story to their colleagues duly embroidered to suit the occasion. It all began with a question on drinking!

CORRESPONDENT: Mr. President, what do you think of drinking out in the State Department Press Room? No kidding.

THE PRESIDENT: You know what we ought to do. We ought to take them on up to Roque Harbor, Maine. Did you people hear about it? It was the only time I got away with it on the cruise. The Press turned absolutely blue with fright.

In the fog there, in this little bit of a harbor that was just off the big harbor, there were the two Press boats, the regular Press and the prima donnas.[2] They were anchored just inshore from me, not more than two hundred or three hundred feet away. You could just barely see them. Outside of me there was the old "Cuyahoga," and outside of the "Cuyahoga" was the destroyer.

One morning we wanted some water on the "Amberjack"; so we took the little rowboat and tied the anchor light on the rowboat and then [the "Amberjack"] cast off and got away under the engine and went out past

---

[1] Charles Hurd who covered the cruise for the *New York Times* recalls the following conversation between FDR and reporters when the latter paid a visit to the "Amberjack." Reporters had described to the President the daily routine on their ship which included, of course, cocktails in the evenings. FDR immediately pricked his ears and the following discussion reportedly ensued:

THE PRESIDENT: Drinking? Have you got liquor on board?

REPORTER: We have a few medicinal supplies, Mr. President.

THE PRESIDENT: Well, that's all right—especially since you're not accustomed to the cold and wet. You have enough?

REPORTER: We are husbanding it carefully sir. You're very thoughtful. How about yourself?

THE PRESIDENT: (speaking firmly): Of course, we've no liquor. For the time being this boat is a commissioned Navy craft. The Navy is dry.

REPORTER: We had thought . . . it's too bad you can't join us, sir.

THE PRESIDENT: (impatiently): But we have ice and glasses and water, and if someone would occasionally bring along —

REPORTER (reaching for a bottle rolled in his rain coat): Mr. President, we'd be honored.

THE PRESIDENT (pointing): You'll find the ice chest in the galley forward. And the glasses are on a shelf just above it.

Charles Hurd, *When the New Deal was Young and Gay* (New York, 1965), p. 158.

[2] The prima donnas were the representatives of the wire services: Francis Stephenson of Associated Press; Frederick A. Storm of United Press; George A. Durno of International News Service; and Edward A. Roddan of Universal News Service.

the "Cuyahoga" to the destroyer and tied up alongside, and it took us about half an hour to get water.

Well, Steve [Correspondent Francis Stephenson] or somebody came on deck and looked over to where the "Amberjack" had been ten minutes before and she was gone! All that there was in place of the "Amberjack" was one rowboat. . . .

STEPHENSON: And did we jump out!

THE PRESIDENT: And I believe that the Press Association let out one wild yelp and sent over two boats.

CORRESPONDENT: You sure did scare us, Stevie.

THE PRESIDENT: That is the only time I got away!

TRAINED IN THE *NEW YORK TIMES*
9 August 1933

FDR was a past master in the art of getting a laugh by linking wholly unrelated and incongruous bits of information.

THE PRESIDENT: By the way, George McAneny is coming in this morning.

We will talk about sewers, I suppose.

CORRESPONDENT: Who is Mr. McAneny?

THE PRESIDENT: Late of the *New York Times*, now the Commissioner of Sewers in New York.

CORRESPONDENT: Well trained, wasn't he?

DUCKS
26 January 1934

THE PRESIDENT: I have a rather important piece of news: The ladies have been in to see me and they want a special stamp for Mother's Day. All the sportsmen of the country are united behind a duck stamp bill.[1]

[1] FDR took a keen interest in the quality and design of stamps issued by the US Post Office. Some months earlier Postmaster General James Farley had sent him a special National Recovery Administration stamp that depicted a farmer, a blacksmith, a businessman, and a woman. Wrote Roosevelt to Farley: "The honest farmer, who looks like me; the honest businessman, who looks like Grover T. Whalen; and the honest blacksmith who looks like Lionel Barrymore, are magnificent. But Oh Heavens what a girl! She is wearing a No. 11 shoe, also a bustle, and if recovery is dependent on women like that I am agin recovery." The President to Farley, 17 August 1933, FDRL.

CORRESPONDENT: What is this, stamp day?
THE PRESIDENT: No, you stamp the duck.
CORRESPONDENT: Try to do it!

YOU LITTLE KNOW WHAT YOU ESCAPED!

26 September 1934

Roosevelt and the correspondents had returned to Washington by special train from Poughkeepsie. He told them how he had planned to play a joke on them.

THE PRESIDENT: You little know what you escaped last night. We had it all planned on the train. I got Starling [Colonel Starling of the Secret Service] in and we had it all planned. We were going to let you fellows stay asleep and at one minute before midnight we were going to get off the train and go back home and all of you people would have waked up in Washington with no President.

CORRESPONDENT: And no job! . . . .

THE PRESIDENT: We came very near doing it. You little know what you escaped.

. . . I do not think there is any news except the sartorial announcement that I am still wearing a high hat. Otherwise, I do not know a thing!

A WHOLE LOT OF PURE BUNK

7 November 1934

The mid-term Congressional elections of 1934 resulted in a triumph for the President's party.

CORRESPONDENT: If you were in our position, called upon to write an interpretive piece, would you interpret the verdict as an approval of what had happened or as a mandate to proceed further?

THE PRESIDENT: You must have got to bed early to talk about interpreting stories today. He has a very strong mind!

CORRESPONDENT: I think it was a slug at [*sic*] gin this morning.

THE PRESIDENT: It must be hell to have to interpret. . . . It must be terrible. But you know, that is one reason why . . . the American public today are paying less and less attention to news stories because so many of them have become interpretive. That really is true. You pay your money and takes your choice.

. . . It is a very serious question for the American press. . . . In other words *reductio ad absurdum.* That is the substance, because if I take Henry Morgenthau from Washington back to Dutchess County, there isn't anything behind the fact. But the story says, "In all probability this means that foreign debt was discussed," or something like that. That is not news, that is just a wild stab in the dark, which is wrong, 99 per cent wrong at times. But, on the other hand, your own offices call for that sort of thing and what the hell are we going to do about it? . . . .

CORRESPONDENT: Do you think there is a public demand for that sort of thing? Is it because they have been educated up to it?

THE PRESIDENT: I think there is a big demand . . . and, of course, it has been aided and abetted by the popularity, quite frankly, of people like Mark Sullivan. . . . For instance, Mark Sullivan—a great friend of mine—if Mark wrote once a week he would be much more effective than if he wrote once a day. No human being can write a story once a day. He has to write a whole lot of pure bunk in order to fill his space.[1]

[1] Mark Sullivan was a columnist for the *New York Herald Tribune.* On many occasions FDR stated that it would be bad for the country and for the press if the phrase—"Oh, that is one of those newspaper stories" —gained currency. "People like to read the Walter Winchells and Paul Mallons and the other columns; they like to read the amusing stories, the Pearson and Allen stuff, and so forth and so on. But in the long run, they are getting to the point of saying, 'Oh, it is funny, it is grand; I love to read it every morning but what can I believe? I have read so much of this sort of stuff now for years and years.'" Special Press conference with members of the American Society of Newspaper Editors, 21 April 1938.

OUR GANG IS IN CONTROL
27 February 1935

Roosevelt learned that reporter Al Warner had been elected as president of the White House Correspondents' Association, succeeding Francis Stephenson of the AP.

THE PRESIDENT: Stevie, they threw you out.

STEPHENSON: Just the very minute I left town. . . .

THE PRESIDENT: Lovely. I think that is grand. "Truly" Warner will make a very, very dignified presiding officer. It will be all right.

STEPHENSON: He will have it all over me.

THE PRESIDENT: You will have to preside at this dinner.

STEPHENSON: I will start it off.

CORRESPONDENT: He has been rehearsing his speech during his visit up here.

THE PRESIDENT: Is that why he is late, or is there some other reason?

CORRESPONDENT: I have another reason.

STEPHENSON: You know too much.

THE PRESIDENT: That is all right; that is the first thing I got on the telephone. I keep in very close touch with the Poughkeepsie office. . . . [turning to Stephenson] Who was it ran against you last year in that hot contest? Was it "Truly" Warner?

CORRESPONDENT: Yes, sir.

THE PRESIDENT: Then it is a matter of justice. . . .

CORRESPONDENT: We are going to come out for Hoover, then, in 1936.

THE PRESIDENT: Succeeding Francis M. Stephenson, retired. Do you get a pension?

STEPHENSON: I am going to take that up. . . . .

THE PRESIDENT: This is perfectly grand. I did not know that Warner was an Amherst graduate. He belongs to that wicked crowd of brain-trusters.

Gosh, they put Fred [Storm of UP] and Charlie Hurd [of the *New York Times*] on the Executive Committee.

CORRESPONDENT: I am against the whole ticket.

THE PRESIDENT: [to Storm] How come you are on the Executive Committee?

STORM: I was out of town and could not do anything about it.

THE PRESIDENT: The Executive Committee really runs it, don't they?

CORRESPONDENT: I don't know. . . . .

CORRESPONDENT: . . . it has never met yet, Mr. President.

THE PRESIDENT: I don't know; I think our gang still controls. It is all right. We still have a majority vote in there.

LET US GET UP A POOL

27 February 1935

FDR was ready to incite the reporters to get up a betting pool whenever he was in a mood to do so—which was often!

THE PRESIDENT: Who has been doing the winning?

CORRESPONDENT: Well, it's about even, I think.

MARVIN McINTYRE: No, it is not. They got me way down low.

THE PRESIDENT: It is a bad month.

McINTYRE: I started a bad streak a few nights ago. . . . .

CORRESPONDENT: The bets are between mid-May and mid-June on adjournment [of Congress].

THE PRESIDENT: Let us get up a pool. There is something for you to do! Get up a dollar pool on the date of adjournment. I will put in a dollar too. Sealed bets.

CORRESPONDENT: Not to be opened until Christmas?

CORRESPONDENT: Unless Congress adjourns before then.

THE PRESIDENT: I think it is a good idea—let us get up a pool.

McINTYRE: We will work it up on the train.

CORRESPONDENT: You will have to do it now.

McINTYRE: That is what I mean—collect it now. I want everybody together.

CORRESPONDENT: Everybody still on the expense account?

CORRESPONDENT: Who is going to hold the money until the end of June?

CORRESPONDENT: I am treasurer of the Association!

"BUNKY"

4 September 1935

The President teased reporters for persisting in asking him what he had discussed or intended to discuss with visitors. A reporter had asked what he intended to discuss with Post Master General James Farley who had returned from a trip to Hawaii.

THE PRESIDENT: I am awfully sorry to have to tell you—some people are so far out on the limb I don't know how they are going to crawl back. . . . If I had been writing the story again, I would have said what would probably be true—which is a dirty dig, a damned dirty dig—I would say that probably Jim didn't go on a political trip. Of course he talked to a few people, but the primary object of this trip was to have a damned good time taking his Missus out to Hawaii. I do not think we will talk politics. I think he will tell me all about the trip. I do not anticipate for a minute that we will talk politics any more than the stories are true when I go out on the "Sequoia"[1] with the Comptroller, that we solemnly talk about the affairs of the Government and the Comptroller Generalship. This is a lot of bunk. So don't get bunky. It is not done.

[1] The "Sequoia" was the yacht which the President used on the Potomac River.

JOURNALISTS, CLERGYMEN, AND LAWYERS

27 December 1935

At an "off-the-record" press conference with members of the American Association of Schools and Departments of Journalism and the

American Association of Teachers of Journalism, Roosevelt explained his views on press conferences and spoke of the difficult art of financial journalism.

THE PRESIDENT: . . . occasionally we have special conferences, such as when we explain the textbook. The textbook every year is the Budget, and then I have in primarily the people who are going to write the Budget stories. . . . Of course, the Budget Message is a terribly difficult thing to write a good story about—an accurate story about. Of course, as you know, the average of the newspaper profession knows less about dollars and cents—c-e-n-t-s—than almost any other profession—except possibly the clergy. That is the reason for a great many of these perfectly crazy, wild stories that come out of Washington about Government finances, though I am trying all I can to keep the accuracy of these financial stories on a little higher level. . . . .

QUESTIONER: Do you have any trouble at all with intentional violations?

THE PRESIDENT: Only from a very small percentage of the Press. After all, the people in the newspaper profession, I suppose, have a little higher average of straight-shooting than the profession I belong to—lawyers!

DESSERT

10 March 1936

In the midst of his immense responsibilities, FDR managed to keep himself well posted on the goings-on in the world of the White House correspondents. He never missed an opportunity to tease them in good-natured fashion.

The White House correspondents had given a dinner in which apparently somebody "goofed" and no dessert had been served. At the next press conference:

CORRESPONDENT: Mr. President,—

THE PRESIDENT: (interposing) What is this, fudge?

CORRESPONDENT: Can you tell us anything—

THE PRESIDENT: (interposing) Yes, I like ice cream but—but it is bad for me.

CORRESPONDENT: We are going to have a dinner for the Vice President and we promise to serve ice cream at that one.

THE PRESIDENT: Beginning with ice cream!

A SAD PARTING
32 March 1936

The press conference took place on the wharf at Port Everglades, Florida, as Roosevelt stood at the foot of the gangplank prior to boarding the destroyer "Monaghan." He was feigning sadness over leaving the correspondents behind.

THE PRESIDENT: I am feeling awfully bad leaving you behind. I don't know what to do.

CORRESPONDENTS: You look it.

THE PRESIDENT: I am awfully sorry you are being left behind. . . . .

CORRESPONDENT: Is there anything you want to say before you go?

THE PRESIDENT: Only don't change the language on me. [He was referring to a previous trip on which his messages from the boat had allegedly been paraphrased by the Press] George,[1] don't change the language on me when you get it. Don't vary one word.

CORRESPONDENT: Well, Mr. President, happy trip.

THE PRESIDENT: I will send you the names of the fish in Latin.

CORRESPONDENT: We couldn't even spell MONAGHAN. . . .

THE PRESIDENT: We have one chief objective. Colonel Watson[2] has wanted to catch a rare fish. We hope so. He wants to catch one particular fish.

CORRESPONDENT: What is that?

THE PRESIDENT: He does not know the exact name but he thinks it is a "Denizen of the Deep." So, if we catch a denizen of the deep, I will send it by radio.

[1] George A. Durno of the International News Service.
[2] Colonel Edwin M. ("Pa") Watson, Army aide to the President.

GETTING AWAY FROM THE AMERICAN PRESS
12 November 1936

FDR was to make a visit to Argentina. Arthur Krock of the *New York Times* suggested to him that he should invite leading world statesmen to set out on naval vessels secretly and meet him in the Azores or some such haven to discuss problems of world peace. Roosevelt, in his reply, referred to the problem of throwing American reporters off the scent.[1]

THE PRESIDENT: The idea is perfectly pious but as to the execution,

[1] Arthur Krock to the President, 9 November 1936; the President to Arthur Krock, 12 November 1936, FDRL.

alas! when I dropped anchor in the harbor of X, I would find Bob Allen, Drew Pearson, Paul Mallon and Walter Winchell[2] appearing, pencil in hand, from the mouth of a sea-going whale!

As you know stockbrokers would say, "when, as and if" the foregathering should come to pass, it could obtain privacy only if the United States Marine Corps is put in charge. This is the only organization I would back against the American press. . . .

[2] Prominent commentators and broadcasters.

SEATING ARRANGEMENTS

12 February 1937

A large number of correspondents troooped in and FDR greeted them.

THE PRESIDENT: As they used to say when we had a joint session of the Legislature in Albany twenty-five years ago, the old Lieutenant Governor would be there on the rostrum and in would come the Senate— "The Senate will take their accustomed seats on the floor."

SAGE COUNSEL FROM THE FIRST ALUMNUS

10 June 1937

Walter Trohan of the *Chicago Tribune*, Chairman of the Board of Regents of the mythical J. Russell Young School of Expression, invited the President to attend the commencement exercises of the School to be held in the Italian Gardens of the Mayflower Hotel. He informed Roosevelt that three members of his official family were to be inducted into the faculty of the School on that occasion: "Mr. Stephen T. Early is to take the recently endowed chair of Golf Language, Mr. Marvin Hunter McIntyre will take that of Romance Languages and Col. Edwin M. Watson will hold down that of Fish Stories with a Southern Exposure." The exercises were to be preceded by a solemn march of the alumni in cap and gown led by the Honorable James A. Farley, Postmaster General.

THE PRESIDENT: . . . I should be delighted, in ordinary circumstances, to return to the campus for the annual commencement exercises of the J. Russell Young School of Expression but on June twenty-sixth I shall be in strict training for the famous international wedding four days later. I am, however, enclosing three dollars to help defray expenses because I recognize that some of the undergraduates are prone to break china.

As the oldest alumnus I feel that I should offer a constructive suggestion to the undergraduates. I make this suggestion in view of the fact that so many prominent newspaper publishers may, as a result of the forthcoming investigation into the technique of income tax evasion, matriculate at Alcatraz, or become expatriates. In either case the Washington representatives of these publishers no longer will be able to pay their tuition in the Young School of Expression.

There ought to be money in a College Daily and I suggest that the undergraduates establish one. As former Editor-in-Chief of the *Harvard Crimson* I shall be glad to conduct a course for you on how a newspaper should really be run. Although I have great faith in this proposal I am none too sanguine concerning its acceptance. In fact, I feel about as sceptical as a famous Speaker of the House did in the heat of a political campaign years ago. To a friend who inquired whether he expected his party to nominate him for high public office he replied: "They might go further and do worse and probably will."[1]

[1] Walter Trohan to the President, 4 June 1937; the President to Trohan, 10 June 1937, FDRL.

EMPTY

20 July 1937

The reporters clamored for some news. It had been a particularly lean day.

CORRESPONDENT: Is there anything we have not asked you that you could suggest?

CORRESPONDENT: We would like to get a little pay-dirt here today.

THE PRESIDENT: Let's see. I said to Steve at 3 o'clock, "Have we got anything on our chests?" And he said, "No."

CORRESPONDENT: He was kidding you.

THE PRESIDENT: I almost said, "Have we anything on our minds?" He might have said, "No," the same way.

PRESERVING THE TRADITIONS OF THE SCHOOL

28 January 1938

Roosevelt heard that Joseph Kennedy, Ambassador-designate to Britain, and Edward Moore, Adviser, Vocational Service for Juniors, were to receive the accolade of "The Silver Tongue" from that great center of higher learning, the J. Russell Young School of Expression. As the first graduate of the School he was concerned whether the highest traditions of the School were being maintained.

THE PRESIDENT: All the old grads are naturally elated to learn that Joe Kennedy and Eddie Moore are to receive due recognition as twentieth century upholders of the tradition of Demosthenes and Daniel Webster.

But I regret to say that my delight is conditioned by certain grave fears, nay, apprehensions—a veritable dread that our Joe's accent may suffer a change with the change of air just ahead of him. Not a few travelers to the bourne whither he is bound have returned with an intonation wholly unintelligible to American ears. As one who has at heart the preservation of the best traditions of the Young School of Expression I want to suggest that Joe Kennedy's diploma be awarded provisionally, the provisional award to receive formal ratification if, as and when Joe, at some future time, shall demonstrate that he still speaks our mother tongue in its full American purity, free from all foreign entanglements. One more admonition: impress upon Eddie Moore that when Carlyle said silence is golden he meant it was the best form of expression. I hope Eddie will grasp the wisdom of that hard saying.[1]

[1] The President to J. Russell Young, 28 January 1938, FDRL.

HOW TO HANDLE NEWSMEN

15 March 1938

THE PRESIDENT: . . . for the benefit of that very small but persistent minority who think that they are living under a dictator in the United States, I call the attention of that little minority to the *Washington Times* front page: "Newsmen held under Guns as Hitler talks to Austria"!

CORRESPONDENT: That is the way to do it!

THE PRESIDENT: I am afraid my technique has not improved very much!

IF LINCOLN. . . .

18 March 1938

CORRESPONDENT: Mr. President, on the subject of national defense, may I ask your judgment as to whether we would have had attacks upon our ship, after other aggressions that led us into the World War, had we then had a Navy and other national defense adequate enough to deter attacks?

THE PRESIDENT: I am afraid it is too hypothetical.

CORRESPONDENT: I avoided the word "if."

THE PRESIDENT: It is a little bit too much like saying, "If Abraham Lincoln were alive in this particular Bituminous Coal Commission problem, what would he have done?"

FDR ON HOW TO RUN A NEWSPAPER

21 April 1938

THE PRESIDENT: I am thinking about the American public and I am thinking about the newspapers of this country. I do not want them to lose their influence as newspapers giving all the news. I feel very, very strongly about it for the sake of the public and even for the sake of the Press and if, from now on, we can have a presentation from the Press of both sides of the news, it will be a perfectly magnificent thing.

I will tell you a story: A year and a half ago, when John Boettiger[1] went out to take charge of the *Seattle Post-Intelligencer*, we all know he had a hot potato. In the first place, he had a paper that ran between three and four hundred thousand dollars a year in the red. That is no joke. In the second place, he had old man Hearst as a boss, which is no joke either!

However, he had got a pretty good understanding out of the old man, Hearst, that he would not have to run those box editorials that Hearst wrote. Well, that was something! That was a gain. Then, in addition to that, he was going to a city that has had more violent labor troubles than almost any other city in this country.

He said, "What would you do?"

I said, "Two pieces of advice from a student of publicity. Eliminate your editorial page altogether. Nobody reads it!"

Now, that is horrible for me to say that to you. Old man Ochs[2] told me a great many years ago—not so many, about four or five years ago—that in his judgment only eight per cent of the readers of the *New York Times* read any of the editorials, and less than half of one percent read one editorial all the way through. Now that is Mr. Ochs.

So, I said, "John, cut out your editorial page entirely. Run some features on it, run some cartoons on it, run letters to the editor on it and clip editorials that appeal to you from other papers or weeklies or monthly magazines!"

I said, "Number 2: On your news stories, you are a newspaper. You are in a labor dispute town. The next time you have a strike down on

---

[1] FDR's son-in-law; husband of Anna Roosevelt.

[2] Adolph S. Ochs, publisher of the *New York Times*.

the water-front, take two of your best men and say to Mr. A, 'You go down and you cover the water-front story for tomorrow's papers and you get in your story, the story of the strikers from their point of view, and write your lead that the strikers claimed yesterday that so and so and so and so and so and so, and that the leader of the strikers, Bridges'[3] man, said so and so and so and so.' And then say to Mr. B, 'You go down there and you write your story from the point of view of the shippers, the owners of the freight that is tied up, the point of the view of the steamship owners whose ships are tied up, and you write your lead that yesterday on the water-front the shippers and ship owners claimed the following.' You run those two stories in parallel columns on the front page and do not make them too long so that the reading public would get both sides at the same time."

CORRESPONDENT: Did he follow your suggestion, sir?

THE PRESIDENT: He did not!

He is in the black probably because he did not take my advice! But I will say this, he did honest reporting.

[3] Harry Bridges, head of the longshoremen's union on the West Coast.

WAVING THE FLAG

9 September 1938

The President was on a visit to Hyde Park. Reporters went out for a game of golf; and with Marvin McIntyre around money inevitably changed hands. At the golf course itself a strange-looking flag had been delivered to the players with compliments of FDR.

THE PRESIDENT: Well, how is everybody? How is your golf?

CORRESPONDENT FRED STORM: I took eight bucks from Mac yesterday.

THE PRESIDENT: Were you his partner?

CORRESPONDENT FELIX BELAIR: I was, Mr. President.

CORRESPONDENT: That was the grandest flag of all; grand design; pony express flag.

THE PRESIDENT: Yes, I thought you would like to have that. George needed something to wave.

CORRESPONDENT GEORGE DURNO: Absolutely.

THE PRESIDENT: . . . You really have something to wave.

DURNO: I have been waving.

THE PRESIDENT: You cannot just go around through life, just waving your arm. You get tired. You have to have something in your hand!

THE WAYWARD PRESS

18 October 1938

Colonel Arthur Murray, an old British friend of the President, and Mrs. Murray were guests at Hyde Park. FDR noted with amusement that newspapers were giving varying descriptions of his visitor.

THE PRESIDENT: Colonel and Mrs. Murray over here in the corner. We have all had the best time yesterday that ever happened because when the good people landed on the "Cameronia" and joined us on the train, the first stories that went out were that Mr. Arthur Murray, famous dancing teacher, and his third wife were coming up to spend the day at Hyde Park. That was good. And the next morning Colonel Murray and Lady Murray were staying here—that was yesterday morning's papers. And yesterday afternoon's papers said that "Sir Arthur Murray, railway magnate, and Lady Murray." So they have come to the conclusion that if they are not made Marquis and Marchioness before they leave, they will be quite hurt!

I SEE BY THE PAPERS

6 January 1939

THE PRESIDENT: The only news is that I have not yet—a most curious thing happened. Last night I read the papers and I found that I had read the Defense Message to . . . four gentlemen yesterday morning. Actually I have not begun to write it yet, twenty-four hours later. However, of course the papers cannot be wrong so I think I must have a dual personality.

PRAISE FROM THE *HERALD TRIBUNE*

10 February 1939

Postmaster General James Farley informed the President that the *New York Herald Tribune* had written a favorable editorial on a baseball postage stamp that he had issued. "It is very seldom that I even get a tumble on the editorial page of the *New York Tribune* and when I do I am generally knocked all over the lot," he stated.

THE PRESIDENT: Good for you! To draw a word of commendation from the *Herald Tribune* is like being allowed to sit on an iceberg for a whole day when you are in hell.

It is worth remembering that knocks by the *Herald Tribune* in 1939 are nothing new. Turn back to their files in 1933 and 1934 and you will find that they were the opposite of generous, even when we were saving their bank accounts.[1]

[1] James A. Farley to the President, 9 February 1939; the President to Farley, 10 February 1939, FDRL.

HAVING A BABY

7 March 1939

Opening the press conference, FDR greeted a woman correspondent who had reported for work after a spell of absence to have a baby.

THE PRESIDENT: Evie, how are you? Congratulations; glad to see you back.

EVIE: Thank you, Mr. President; glad to be back. . . . .

THE PRESIDENT: It is all right. How is the flu in town, by the way?

CORRESPONDENT: Breaking up; we had an awful lot.

THE PRESIDENT: It certainly does pull you down.

CORRESPONDENT: Get over yours all right, did you?

THE PRESIDENT: I'd almost rather have a baby than have the flu.

EVIE: Oh, you don't know.

THE PRESIDENT: I thought I'd get a rise.

HOPE

20 April 1939

Even hardened critics could find it no easy task to resist FDR's charm in a face-to-face meeting.

William Allen White, editor of the *Emporia* (Kansas) *Gazette*, had brought in about two hundred members of the American Society of Newspaper Editors for a press conference.

WHITE: Mr. President, on behalf of the Society I want to thank you for your invitation. I want you to know that this is the largest assemblage of our Society that has ever gathered in the White House. You are still the most interesting person. For box office attraction you have Clark Gable gasping for breath.

We wish to say this: Most of us have agreed with most of the things that you have tried to do. If some of us have disagreed with a few of the things, it was in sorrow, not in anger, and it hurt us much more than it did you!

THE PRESIDENT: I am very glad that Bill put it that way. Of course I have got to admit that those things in which you have not agreed with me, I have not even felt sorrow, let alone anger.

WHITE: Withering indifference?

THE PRESIDENT: No, merely a hope deferred, a hope deferred.

MEDICINE FOR NEWSMEN

25 April 1939

A medicine cabinet that had reportedly been stolen from the White House in 1814 had been returned by a Canadian.

CORRESPONDENT: What is the scarlet ribbon for?

THE PRESIDENT: This, it came around a thing that was taken out of the White House—a medicine chest.

CORRESPONDENT: . . . That medicine chest is the one that the Canadian's grandfather stole out of the White House?

THE PRESIDENT: Yes.

CORRESPONDENT: I asked Colonel Watson what it was this morning and he said it looks like something you might be able to carry two quarts of liquor in.

THE PRESIDENT: Well, that's not my crack.

. . . In this medicine cabinet that was stolen from the White House in 1814 and has just been returned, there is one drawer that still has some medicine in it. It is hemlock bark and that is a specific against scurvy. Steve [Early] suggested that I hand it over for distribution to the Press. Now, I do not think that is nice.

CORRESPONDENT: Let Steve try it.

CORRESPONDENT: Hemlock bark is worse than the bite!

CORRESPONDENT: I thought that hemlock was a poison.

THE PRESIDENT: Well, perhaps Steve had that in mind; I do not know.

PRETTY NEWSMEN

23 September 1939

THE PRESIDENT: All you people look very well. The French call it *soignée*.[1] You are looking in the pink of condition. You probably went to a beauty parlor. I think it is so nice to see people who have been to a beauty parlor!

[1] Adjective, feminine, meaning "wellgroomed" or "carefully done."

A SENATOR'S PLEA TO REPORTERS

22 September 1939

THE PRESIDENT: [addressing correspondent Earl Godwin] Did you have a good holiday? . . . When you were away last week there were all kinds of ribald remarks made about your absence. It was all right.

GODWIN: I know it; I got a report on it.

CORRESPONDENT: The Boss made a couple himself, too, Earl.

THE PRESIDENT: No quarter, isn't that right?

GODWIN: Do you remember [Senator] Ham Lewis[1] said, "Mention me, kindly if you will, but mention me."

[1] Senator James Hamilton Lewis of Illinois.

A FARMER'S TALE

10 October 1939

Some reports had appeared in the press concerning peace feelers. Newspapers also noted the arrival in Washington of Lord Beaverbrook, the powerful British publisher.

CORRESPONDENT: Can you tell us about your conversations with Lord Beaverbrook?

THE PRESIDENT: No, I do not think so. He is an old friend of mine. . . . I told him a newspaper story—and some other things.

We got reminiscing about a phrase that is used over here a good deal by certain people, a phrase beginning, "It is learned on the highest authority," or, "Sources close to the President allege," and so forth.

So I—we got to talking about this Berlin story and I told him a story, which I think he liked, about an old farmer who lived near me in the country—

CORRESPONDENT: Talk a little louder.

THE PRESIDENT: Well, the old farmer didn't talk loud, he just talked this way!

I saw him one morning and I wanted to call his attention and get his opinion on something.

I said, "Pete, did you see by the paper—"

He said, "Wait a minute, son. Did I see by the papers? Did you know an old friend of mine named Adam? Well, Adam got into trouble one afternoon and his wife told him that if he would eat one of those nice McIntosh apples he would get wise. Adam ate the apple and he and his wife both got thrown out of the Garden of Eden that same evening and they spent an exceedingly unprofitable night in the fog, without a blanket, and the next morning Eve was sort of trying to make up to Adam for this thing she had brought on to them both, and she sort of snuggled up to him and said, 'Adam, I see by the paper—' He said, 'Wait a minute, honey, wait a minute. Do I see by the paper? Oh, yes, don't forget, since yesterday afternoon I am wise.' "

I think it was a rather nice parable in regard to a good deal of this peace talk we have been seeing lately.

WHY FDR ADVANCED THANKSGIVING DAY

25 October 1939

Opening the press conference Roosevelt picked on correspondent Russ Young who had recovered from a bout of illness.

THE PRESIDENT: How is he behaving?

CORRESPONDENT: Well, we were talking about drinking out there.

THE PRESIDENT: He ought to know he cannot do that. [Turning to Young] You can't do it yet; not yet. You have got to stay on the wagon for quite a while.

CORRESPONDENT EARL GODWIN: I was on the right side.

THE PRESIDENT: You represented the W.C.T.U.[1] and he represented Hennessy 5-Star? Right?

No, you have got to stay on the wagon until Thanksgiving. I put it a week early for that reason. I put it a week early on account of Russ! ....

RUSS YOUNG: That is fair; that is all right.

[1] Women's Christian Temperance Union.

A RED NOSE

7 November 1939

THE PRESIDENT: Good people, how are you?

VOICES: Good morning.

THE PRESIDENT: George, you have a red nose, old top. Where does that come from?

CORRESPONDENT GEORGE DURNO: This cold air.

THE PRESIDENT: Snappy air. It is all right. Do you people all agree with the diagnosis I have just heard from the patient? ... George swears that his red nose comes from the cool air. Is that all right?

DURNO: I would say they all had better!

FIRESIDE CHAT

14 March 1941

THE PRESIDENT: The White House Correspondents' Association is having a dinner tomorrow night, and I would very much like to make a speech.

THOMAS F. REYNOLDS, PRESIDENT OF THE ASSOCIATION: I think, sir, that could be arranged!

THE PRESIDENT: It is, what?—this topsy-turvy world, the President pleading with the press association to be allowed to address them! If that's all right, Tom, I'll go on the air at the same time.

CORRESPONDENT: Will that be the fireside chat you have been planning?

THE PRESIDENT: It may be what could be called fire*works*!

CORRESPONDENT: Firewater!

CORRESPONDENT: . . . Can you tell us what the general topic of this speech will be, sir?

THE PRESIDENT: I don't know; I think it will cover a multitude of sins!

SOMETHING FOR THE "DEAN"

29 March 1940

FDR had something in store for one of the correspondents for whom he had special affection, Russ Young—"Dean" of the J. Russell Young School of Expression.

CORRESPONDENT: Mr. President, "Boss" Young has asked me to take this seat, with your approval.

THE PRESIDENT: All right. . . . I have got a lot for you. Loaded for bear.

In about three minutes there will be presented to the Senate . . . the name of a new Commissioner of the District of Columbia.

I have had a good deal of difficulty in finding somebody to take George Allen's place because I had set my heart on finding somebody in the District who had certain qualifications: first, preferably somebody who had been born in the District; secondly, somebody that had very distinctly the atmosphere of scholarship, and secondly [thirdly], somebody who was somewhat skilled in politics. After a good deal of search I found just the man for the place, a man who was the first white child born in the District; secondly a man who was the president of a great college, a great institution of learning; and thirdly, a skilled politician—

Mr. John Russell Young. (Prolonged applause)

So that makes it unanimous. Now you have all got a job. We all know it is going to be terribly difficult in the Senate to get him confirmed, so every one of you is appointed a committee of one to see that we get him past the Senate of the United States!

CORRESPONDENT: That is lobbying.

CORRESPONDENT: Mr. President, we are all volunteers.

THE PRESIDENT: Well, I am very, very happy. It is richly deserved, Russ, and some day you have got to make a speech in reply—you can do it now!

RUSS YOUNG: Mr. President, I wish you had given me a little time. A lot of my scholars are here and I am afraid I won't show up to good advantage.

It came a little sudden but I will say, sir, that I hope this has no political significance to it and I hope I am not held down to any particular terms! Anyhow, I will do the best I can, sir.

THE PRESIDENT: You know, I told him, I told Russ this morning that he was just my age and I thought he ought to begin public life before it is too late, because, of course, he will be fairly old when the question of a third term comes up!

THE ORACLE

18 April 1941

CORRESPONDENT: Mr. President, have you any general thought on the progress of the war in Europe?

THE PRESIDENT: No! ... Well, you see, you haven't greased the palm of the Delphic oracle sufficiently for me to answer that question. ...

CORRESPONDENT: Mr. President, the motor car manufacturers have agreed to decrease production by 20 per cent into next year. Is that the forerunner of other curtailments in consumer goods?

THE PRESIDENT: I ain't no seer!

THE DROUGHT

3 June 1941

From time to time reporters would seek to find comic relief by asking the President to give his views on the problems of some obscure hamlet—Passamaquoddy, Maine, for instance! FDR could be depended upon to come up with an appropriate response.

CORRESPONDENT: Mr. President, I would like to ask a local question. It has been a long time since I said anything about Passamaquoddy. Now that the drought has caused a dearth of power from rivers, are you considering the revival of the tidal project?

THE PRESIDENT: Well, you are too young to remember, but even in prohibition days in Maine we never had a drought up there!

A GUARANTEED RECIPE FOR WEIGHT REDUCTION

28 October 1941

FDR often traded jokes with Earl Godwin, a corpulent newsman who tipped the scales at 235 pounds.

THE PRESIDENT: I'd get a better chair, Earl! . . . You have been putting on weight, you know that?

GODWIN: The more I exercise the more appetite I get. You know how it is.

THE PRESIDENT: Let me ask you if you knew Doc O'Connor.[1] Ten years ago he used to be terribly fat. He's as thin as a rail now. I asked him how did he do it. He said, "Perfectly simple. I keep my mouth shut at the table!"

A lot in that.

[1] D. Basil O'Connor was a law partner and a close business and political associate of FDR.

"DISCOMBOBOLATION"

24 February 1942

The great British naval bastion of Singapore had fallen on 15 February 1942, and news from other fronts was equally grim. But FDR's indomitable playfulness remained unaffected. Nothing could deter him from "discombobolating"—whatever that meant!

CORRESPONDENT MAY CRAIG: Mr. President, I have a very small question. Every spring a great many high school seniors come here for a spring trip. They are writing in now to us asking whether they should or should not come to the crowded city here. Do you have any thoughts on that? . . . .

THE PRESIDENT: I would say if they can come here and have a good time, and go away without "discombobolating" Washington, it would be all right!

MAY CRAIG: Most of them make their reservations the year before, but the hotels now would like them to give them up because they are crowded.

THE PRESIDENT: Well, I don't know whether they discombobolate[1] or not. It is a thing for them and the hotels to work out!

[1] FDR told reporters on 15 December 1942 that it was asserted in certain quarters that "if we did attempt to raise, train a large enough Army from the military point of view, that it might discombobolate our domestic economy!" The dictionary reveals the existence of a word, "discombobulate," which means "to upset, confuse, disconcert."

FDR SPEAKS OUT!

27 January 1942

CORRESPONDENT: Have you any views? Maybe we could have some views, if you haven't any news. . . .

THE PRESIDENT: I have got an awful lot of views, and I am not allowed to express them except to myself, in my sleep!

FDR GIVES A GAVEL TO "THE PRESIDENT"

27 February 1942

The White House Correspondents' Association had elected a new President, John Henry.

THE PRESIDENT: [To Henry] How is it weighing on your shoulders?

HENRY: Taking it all very lightly.

THE PRESIDENT: Don't you think he looks older? . . . .

HENRY: I certainly look much balder!

CORRESPONDENT: That is because of his "coronation." . . . .

THE PRESIDENT: Yes, yes, yes, yes. When are we going to have the induction? . . . We ought to have one.

HENRY: We will have to wait until Steve gets back.

THE PRESIDENT: Has your Association got a gavel of its own? It has, hasn't it? . . . I have got about 20 or 30 gavels at Hyde Park. I think I will have to give you a gavel—with an inscription.

31 March 1942

THE PRESIDENT: Come in, Pa. I am going to talk about you. What do you want to say?

EDWIN M. ("PA") WATSON: I haven't been to one for such a long time, I thought I would come in.

THE PRESIDENT: It's your turn to get talked about.

WATSON: I don't know anything good that you can say about me.

THE PRESIDENT: That's the trouble. . . . Where is Henry? . . . Bringing up the rear? Tell him I want to see him.

CORRESPONDENT: Got the gavel for him?

THE PRESIDENT: I have got the gavel for him. A very nice one. . . . I am going to have it inscribed. It came out of George Washington's cherry tree.

HENRY: It's a bigger tree than we thought.

CORRESPONDENT: Not out of the Mayflower, Mr. President?

THE PRESIDENT: Stay afterwards, John. We will decide on the inscription, whether it is to be ribald or not!

HENRY: In keeping with our dignity!

10 April 1942

THE PRESIDENT: Where's the hammer? Where's the hammer?

STEVE EARLY: Sir?

THE PRESIDENT: Oh, here it is. [He displayed a gavel]

CORRESPONDENT: Might keep us in order?

THE PRESIDENT: Yes. [To John Henry] All ready to make your speech?

HENRY: Well, not a very good one, Mr. President.

CORRESPONDENT: We'll cheer anyway, John. . . .

THE PRESIDENT: I have a little—carrying out a promise—a little present to give to the President of the White House Correspondents' Association. I found it at Hyde Park. It is one of the gavels that was used in the 1936 Democratic National Convention. And it is very simple. It says, "White House Correspondents' Association, from F.D.R., 1942." And you will note that I am handing it handle first to John Henry!

HENRY: Thank you, sir. I hope I will be able to preserve the old order and not the new order!

ON HENS AND EGGS

13 November 1942

THE PRESIDENT: I am afraid I have nothing. I have got a number of hens that are "setting," but they haven't laid any eggs yet.

CORRESPONDENT: Do "setting" hens lay eggs?

THE PRESIDENT: . . . I am not going to tell you too much about hens.

May Craig: Mr. President, is the Hatch Act[1] stopping you? . . . .
The President: Oh, May, May, really!

[1] The Hatch Act (1939) prohibited Federal office-holders from active
participation in political activity.

A POLITE TERM

6 November 1942

The President: Now I went to a camp where they had a special little
group of 800 men. Well, I took a look at them—they were all lined up—
and I was just looking at [their] figures.

Suppose they lined you people up, or me!—we would look like Hell!
All right. Now, it's a type called a "postural defect"—which is a polite
term for a big belly!

FREEDOM OF THE PRESS

18 May 1943

An international conference on food was scheduled to begin at Hot
Springs, Virginia.

Correspondent: Mr. President, do you have any comment at all on
some of the reports that the restrictions on the press coverage at Hot
Springs constitute restrictions on freedom of the press?

The President: I haven't had anything, except the suggestion from—
he is not a member of the White House Correspondents' Association, but
he is a very reputable and experienced newspaperman. He intimated to
me that he thought it would be awfully nice if we could have in the
Cabinet Room there a nice little tier of benches put up so that there will
always be twenty or thirty of the press in attendance at Cabinet meetings!

And I—going him one better—I suggested, as I see—Oh, ten or fifteen
people in here every day—all kinds—Government, civilian, and otherwise
—Army and Navy—and we would, right in the back of the room, have
another little tier of benches put up, so that they would all be present,
you see, when——

Correspondent: What's wrong with that?

The President: A good idea. I'm all for it.

Correspondent: When may we expect that, sir?

The President: You will be asking to come in next to watch me take
my bath! After all, there are certain limits!

HOW TO WIN AN ELECTION

3 March 1944

THE PRESIDENT: What's this I hear about an election? Is that true?

CORRESPONDENT: Meet the President, Mr. President! [Introducing Merriman Smith of the United Press, newly-elected President of the White House Correspondents' Association]

THE PRESIDENT: I hear that they haven't counted the ballots!

SMITH: They most certainly have.

STEVE EARLY: How many?

SMITH: One.

THE PRESIDENT: Grand. . . . I was made very happy a few minutes ago to learn that Merriman Smith has been made the—I said made—the President . . . of the White House Correspondents' Association with Mr. Fox as Vice-President. Steve told me that the votes haven't been counted yet, but they are both elected! Congratulations. It's all right.

VII

SPORT AND PASTIME

THE OLD QUAIL WAR

4 March 1935

Colonel Edwin Watson, Army Aide to the President, and Admiral Cary Grayson, head of the American Red Cross, were vacationing at "Hobcaw Barony," the estate of Bernard Baruch in South Carolina. Aware of the President's keen interest in the achievements of his comrades, Baruch filed a telegraphic "daily report" on the "Hobcaw Quail Front." He informed the President that the Army score was perfect, if one were to count feathers and heads as dead birds. The Navy, however, was lagging behind because it was "too busy feeling pulses and prescribing." The Commander in Chief immediately swung into action.

From: Commander in Chief, U.S. Forces

To: Hospital Apprentice Third Class Cary T. Grayson and Gunner Third Class E. M. Watson

Subject: The efficiency record in artillery defense in severe engagement in old quail war.

1. Field Marshal Baruch reports that in repelling the enemy's landing party on the coast of South Carolina more corpses were found in front of your gun than in any other sector.

2. The C. in C. has in person dissected sufficient samples of said corpses to certify that many of them perished from shell

fire—only a minority showing the effects of death from sheer fright.

3. You are, therefore, presented with the Order of the Red Cross, First Class, with sago palms.

4. You are from this date detailed to serve in the Tear Gas Squad of the President's personal bodyguard.[1]

[1] The President to Cary T. Grayson and E. M. Watson, 4 March 1935, FDRL.

THE WATSON-GRAYSON AFFAIR

November-December 1935

We give below the basic documents relating to what will be described by historians of the future as the notorious Watson-Grayson Affair that rocked Washington in the weeks before Christmas, 1937. The documents still leave us in some doubt as to whether the affair actually culminated in a Court Martial at the White House presided over by the Commander in Chief. According to one printed document in the Presidential files, of doubtful authenticity if not of parentage, the Court Martial was actually held and the verdict, delivered "dryly" by the Commander in Chief, strongly hinted at the possibility that it might have been a "wet day" for all parties concerned when the events relating to the Affair actually took place.[1]

COLONEL EDWARD M. WATSON TO THE PRESIDENT:
I trust that I am not unduly bold or boastful, in reporting an incident, almost unheard of in shooting circles. This morning . . . I shot and killed two wild turkeys (a fine large gobbler and a magnificent hen) with *one shot*. I have taken the precaution of having the secretary of the Woodmont Rod and Gun Club certify to this feat of precision and skill.

THE PRESIDENT TO COLONEL WATSON:
My congratulations to you all along the line!
WHAT A MAN?
(a) You got a bigger fish than the Navy.
(b) You beat the score of Rear Admiral Grayson with the Wild Tur-

[1] Colonel E. M. Watson to the President, 21 November 1935; the President to Watson, 3 December 1935; Bernard Baruch to the President, n.d., December 1935?; Watson to the President, 19 December 1935; the Commander in Chief to Baruch, 20 December 1935; printed galleys of proceedings of the Court Martial in the executive office at the White House on 23–24 December 1935; FDRL.

keys by killing two birds with one shot instead of one bird with ten shots! . . . .

AGAIN I SAY—WHAT A MAN?

BERNARD BARUCH TO THE PRESIDENT:

There is a rumor, very persistent, that your military aide known as "Pa" Watson shot two blind turkeys. Also that he is endeavoring to get publicity to overcome the prowess of that well-known hunter and horse trader, Cary T. Grayson. The latter has them tied to a tree before he shoots them.

COLONEL WATSON TO THE PRESIDENT:

In reference to the report of General Baruch, I beg leave to present a small word picture of what is now alluded to around Woodmont way as the "two-in-one shot by Watson."

My companion was in a prone position behind a thick bush, calling to the wild ones—I, in a more alert posture, was behind an equally thick bush, gun in hand—suddenly two fine turkeys sprang into view. So keen were their senses and so swift their reactions that they were practically in full flight before I could get in a shot "from the hip." The results of this shot are now matters of local pride and history.

As to the "Grayson Affair," I ask in a Yuletide spirit that we draw over it the veil of charity.

THE COMMANDER IN CHIEF TO GENERAL BARUCH:

Subject: Charges filed against Colonel E. M. Watson

1. Copy of Colonel Watson's reply is forwarded herewith.

2. Rather than incur the expenses of a Court Martial it is suggested that General Baruch tie Colonel Watson and Admiral Grayson to convenient trees, distant one hundred paces, that each be armed with a bow and arrow, that each be blindfolded, that each be required to emit turkey calls and that thereafter firing shall begin.

It is believed that this will prove:

(a) That neither of them ever shot a turkey.

(b) That they would not recognize a turkey at ten feet.

(c) That both of them should be released on good behavior in your custody.

ADMIRAL CARY GRAYSON TO THE COMMANDER IN CHIEF:

I respectfully acknowledge receipt of your memoranda to General Baruch preferring certain charges against Colonel Watson in which by some unexplainable reason he chose to involve me. I beg to state—

a. That in view of my personal observation of Colonel Watson's marksmanship in the past, it would give me no cause for concern to be a target for him whether tied to a tree or not; regardless of whether he be blindfolded or not; whether he uses a bow and arrow or a gun.

b. That Colonel Watson's explanation of his "two-in-one shot" failed to reveal that the turkeys in question were not only blind but also bore white tail feathers, evidence of being tame and not wild and I, better than anyone, know from experience what a tame turkey looks like.

c. That, however heinous may be Colonel Watson's offense or my offense, I implore you to consider that the crimes charged against us, even if sustained, though perhaps warranting death by bow and arrow, can hardly justify the extreme penalty of being consigned to the custody of General Baruch.

* * * *

Was that really the way the Watson affair ended? Our mischief-loving friend, President Franklin Delano Roosevelt, has sought to confuse us by leaving in his files galley proofs purporting to be a record of the proceedings of a Court Martial held in the executive office at the White House on 23-24 December. According to this important document the Court Martial was presided over by the Commander in Chief himself and was composed of a galaxy of generals and admirals. Major General Douglas MacArthur was described as counsel for the accused, Colonel Edwin M. Watson. The charge against him was: "Violation of the 25th Article of War—'No officer or soldier shall use any reproachful or provoking speeches or gestures to another.' "

According to this historic document, two specific charges were levelled against the hapless colonel:

Specification 1—In that Col. E. M. Watson, FA, Military Aide to the President of the United States, did at Washington, D.C., during period Dec. 18 to Dec. 22, both days inclusive, deliberately and maliciously allege that Rear Admiral Cary M. Grayson, USN-Retd., had shot a turkey when tied on the estate of one Bernard M. Baruch in the State of South Carolina, and that the said Grayson could not have hit the said turkey otherwise, and that in so doing the said Watson brought contumely and shame upon the said Grayson and thereby was guilty of making a provoking speech within the prohibition of the 25th Article of War.

Specification 2—That the said Watson, as aforesaid, well knowing at the time the provocation of his language, did boast and declaim that he killed two turkeys with one shot at the Woodmont Gun Club on or about Dec. 16, which boast and claim could not be based upon fact since two turkeys cannot be in the same place at the same time, and that even assuming the impossible he must have fired a burst of shot and not one shot; and, further, this boast and claim was uttered for the deliberate and malicious purpose of humiliating the said Grayson, as aforesaid, and the said Watson as aforesaid was thereby guilty of making a provoking speech within the prohibition of the 25th Article of War.

The record further shows that witness Baruch testified to the correctness of the charges against Watson. However, he fell into considerable confusion as the defense counsel, General MacArthur, questioned him vigorously. At one point Baruch protested when MacArthur asked him whether others besides the turkeys were blind. Baruch raised a strong objection when the General insisted on questioning him about the "shot." At that point, according to the record, the Commander in Chief intervened and said: "Objection sustained. Counsel for the accused will refrain from asking about shots or the number of shots or whether it was wet or dry, or anything of a similar character."

As MacArthur continued his cross-examination, says the record, Baruch described as a "fowl slander" Watson's claim that Grayson could only hit a turkey when it was tied. He was, however, quite vague on whether the birds had actually been tied to the trees and whether indeed it had been Admiral Grayson himself who had tied them.

In his concluding arguments before the Court, according to the record, MacArthur argued that it was Baruch and his associates who had in reality caused humiliation to Admiral Grayson. As far as his client was concerned, he had merely spoken the exact truth. As there could be no libel in truth, the case against him should be dismissed. The record describes what transpired subsequently in these terms:

> THE COMMANDER IN CHIEF: (dryly)—The Court has decided to treat—to treat both specifications at the same time. It is our judgment that it was a wet day on both occasions, and that no one can tell how many shots or rounds were employed in the despatch of the flying turkeys or the turkey that was tied.
>
> Sentence: That Colonel Watson and Admiral Grayson be admonished by the President of the United States, the said Colonel Watson for taking only one shot to kill two blind birds, and the said Rear Admiral Grayson for his failure—in this case we give the Admiral the benefit of the doubt—his inability to note the fact that the bird at which he aimed was tied.

WAS FDR HIT BY A DUCK OR BY A GOOSE?

5 December 1939

It was duck season and a Washington lawyer, Harry B. Hawes, remembered a story that FDR had told him shortly after he entered the White House in 1933. He recalled Roosevelt as telling him: "I was sitting in a duck blind, a duck was flying high overhead. I shot at it and wheeled to shoot one coming in and the overhead bird hit me on the head and nearly killed me." Hawes wrote to the President that he had recounted the story recently to a bishop who had responded, "Hell, . . . if that duck had been a goose the history of the world would have been changed."

THE PRESIDENT: Tell your friend that that duck was a goose and whether he likes it or not the history of the world was not changed. Actually five geese were coming into the blind. I hit the leading goose, swung left to try to get another with my left barrel and at that moment the first goose hit me a glancing blow on my right shoulder. I understand there are a number of people in Russia, Germany (and the United States) who regret the poor aim of that goose.[1]

[1] Harry B. Hawes to the President, 4 December 1939; the President to Hawes, 5 December 1939, FDRL. Hawes responded: "The 'Goose' did not get you but you will have to stay in the 'Duck Blind' another four years despite your objections and without consideration of the matter of continued bad weather." Hawes to the President, 6 December 1939, *ibid*.

THE GREAT CATCH
8 April 1935

In spinning yarns about fishing exploits, FDR was a past master. His stories were very elaborate. In minute detail he described the preliminaries and built up the tempo step by step for the big climax—or anticlimax.

The setting for this story is the President's special train. Roosevelt was returning home after a vacation cruise near the Bahamas.

THE PRESIDENT: It looks like an outdoor tan, doesn't it?

CORRESPONDENT: Mr. President, I got an indoor one too.

THE PRESIDENT: Was your behavior good . . . ?

CORRESPONDENT: I slipped a couple of times, Mr. President.

THE PRESIDENT: We had a grand time. We did not have a single bad day. . . .

CORRESPONDENT: I wish you had caught a real one like we did on the destroyer coming down here last summer. . . .

THE PRESIDENT: Didn't you get the message about adjectives? [Apparently FDR had tried to send a jocular telegram to the correspondents on their use of adjectives.]

CORRESPONDENT: No, we did not get that. . . .

THE PRESIDENT: There was no color in your stories; I read them. . . . there was no color so I supplied color and Mac [Marvin McIntyre] held it out on you.

McINTYRE: I did not really hold it out—I just could not get it mimeographed in time.

CORRESPONDENT: Mr. President, off the record, let us have it. What was it? Just for our information. . . . .

THE PRESIDENT: Somebody wrote a lovely story about my sitting on a swivel chair on the afterdeck of the "Nourmahal."[1] That did tickle my fancy.

WALTER TROHAN OF THE CHICAGO TRIBUNE: It looks like me.

CORRESPONDENT: I wrote a nastier one than that but I did not write that one.

CORRESPONDENT: I said you had trolled hundreds of thousands of miles and did not get a bite.

THE PRESIDENT: I think they all carried the story that we had been catching fish for the aquarium and they also said that we had been netting fish for the aquarium.

CORRESPONDENT: I wrote that.

THE PRESIDENT: We hauled the seine one day, with the aid of the destroyer's crew and everybody on board. You pick a sandy beach—you have to find a place where it is more or less rocky bottom off shore, and then you take one end of this net, which is about eight or nine feet deep and about 400 feet long. It is weighted on the bottom and there are floats on the top. You take one end and anchor it on the beach and then gradually work it out, with people in the water wading, and the rest in a boat, and you work it out like that and around in a great big circle, and back to the beach, and, having made a complete circle, outside the circle they all splash. They make a great deal of noise and gradually you work it in and work it in until it gets down to bottom and then you work it in from there to the shore. It is a tremendous performance and a tremendous net and finally it got narrower and narrower circle and then it got down to 30 feet across and then 20 and finally they hauled it on to the beach, expecting a large catch. In it were two fish that long [indicating with his hands]—two fish that long, and one fish that long [indicating].

CORRESPONDENT: Who watched out for the barracuda while all this was going on?

THE PRESIDENT: I sat on the shore and right outside was a big shark. It would not come in with a crowd like that.

. . . Every morning at breakfast we would get the U.P. news coming out over the radio marine and Vincent[2]—this is off the record— and Vincent had a perfectly swell game. About every second or third night he would send up to the radio operator some crack on somebody on board. . . . The night before last an item appeared in the ship news which read as follows:

> The secretarial office in Miami is being closed and Mr. Mc-
> Intyre and staff will join the President sometime tomorrow. . . .
> In a final statement Mr. McIntyre intimated that the President

[1] "Nourmahal" was a luxurious yacht belonging to FDR's friend and neighbor, Vincent Astor.
[2] Vincent Astor.

had enjoyed great relaxation on this trip, especially in view of the fact that the mental calibre of his associates scarcely required effort on his part.

Well, Freddie Kernochan caught on; Kermit swears he did but I know damned well he did not. . . . George St. George was pretty sore and Will Stewart was really awfully angry all the way through and Russell Heiter also thought that Mac was drunk again.[3] He [Astor] did have them fooled completely.

[3] Frederic Kernochan, a judge in the Court of Special Session in New York City; Kermit Roosevelt, son of former President Theodore Roosevelt; George St. George, A Tuxedo Park dignitary; Leslie Heiter and Will Stewart were friends of Vincent Astor.

EDITORIAL COURTESY

7 May 1937

Roosevelt talked with reporters on board the "Potomac." He had been fishing off Galveston, Texas. Among those who had called on him was Jesse Jones, Chairman of the Reconstruction Finance Corporation. Jones, a Texan, had a financial interest in the newspaper *Houston Chronicle*.

THE PRESIDENT: It is a good place in here. There is fine fishing. I think I have taken off two inches. It is all right.

CORRESPONDENT: Did you see Mr. Jones while he was here?

THE PRESIDENT: Yes, he came on board. He went out fishing but did not get anything. The *Houston Post*, however, credited him with four fish. That is what they call editorial courtesy.

STEVE'S TROUT

27 September 1937

Press Secretary Steve Early, vacationing in Ohio, sent some trout to the President who was then travelling West by train. He said in his letter: "I solemnly swear that each and every one was caught with fly and rod. They come from Cold Creek which flows at the rate of 50 million gallons a day, winter and summer, and always is at 48°. The creek flows underground from somewhere in Kentucky and reappears on this Ohio farm. It is literally filled with trout, rainbows, browns and speckled." Steve voiced the hope that even from the rear-end of a railroad train,

FDR "will catch more 'fish' than we who ply the rod and reel. Of course, 'Pa.' will be a big help," he added. Roosevelt rose to the bait.[1]

THE PRESIDENT: In spite of the general cynicism of the members of your profession on our train, I personally do not believe that those magnificent trout were netted. It is true that a careful examination of their mouths show no hook marks. I attribute this to the dexterity of your wrist in casting the nimble fly, and any time you want I will testify in your behalf if you bring a slander suit. The only individual on the train who did not praise their flavour was your sadist friend, Franklyn Waltman, and he was heard to express the wish that you had fallen into that underground river and never come to the surface again.

Apparently a few members of the reportorial staff are sending news—crowds, speeches, etc., while the majority are writing columns on whether I shake hands with Mr. X with my left hand, or looked away when Mr. Y greeted me, or spent forty seconds longer talking with Mr. Z than with his colleague. It would be a lot cheaper if all your newspapers would hire Walter Winchell[2] and save railroad fares.

[1] Steve Early to the President, 22 September 1937; the President to Early, 27 September 1937, FDRL.

[2] Well-known "gossip columnist" and radio commentator.

"PA" AND THE SHARK

17 August 1938

FDR reported to Harold Ickes about the latest feats of "Pa" Watson.

THE PRESIDENT: You should know the following: Pa hooked a fish—brought it to within ten feet of the boat, looked at it and screamed, "A huge shark! Sergeant, Sergeant, shoot the blank of a blank." The Marine shot said fish through the head, whereupon Pa brought him in and he turned out to be an innocent little two-foot mackerel. When you get back, I will tell you how Pa lost $30 and I won—another shark episode.[1]

[1] The President to Harold L. Ickes, 17 August 1938, FDRL.

THE MOST DELICIOUS FISH THAT FDR EVER ATE

1 August 1939

CORRESPONDENT: What about the big seventy-pound fish you did not catch?

THE PRESIDENT: Yes. Did you notice the newspaper accuracy on that?

CORRESPONDENT: There has been a good deal of faking on that since Jonah's whale.

CORRESPONDENT: Pa [Watson] says that he has $50 that says he caught the biggest fish.

THE PRESIDENT: Pa always catches the biggest fish![1] No. As a matter of fact, I caught far and away the best fish on the trip. I never saw one before. It was a ten-inch mackerel! I had him for breakfast and it was the most delicious fish I ever ate.

CORRESPONDENT: How did you know it was a mackerel?

THE PRESIDENT: It had all the fins.

CORRESPONDENT: How big are they ordinarily?

THE PRESIDENT: Three feet; two or three feet.

CORRESPONDENT: Hadn't you ought to have thrown him back?

THE PRESIDENT: I don't know if there is any law on that; but anyway it is inside of me now, so it is safe! Gosh it was good. It was the most delicious I ever tasted.

[1] FDR used to warn reporters jocularly about "Pa" Watson's claims of having landed the biggest fish or made the biggest betting gains among members of the President's party. At a press conference on 3 March 1939 on board the cruiser "Houston," for instance, a reporter told Roosevelt that "Pa" claimed to have won 75 per cent of the betting pool on fishing. Retorted FDR: "Well, I suppose, strictly speaking, that that statement was true but it should be coupled with a very careful investigation by a grand jury, as to how he won it."

HOW TO FEEL BETTER IF YOU
ARE INVOLVED IN A CONTROVERSY

16 January 1940

CORRESPONDENT: Have you heard of any differences between the Governor of Alaska and the Navy Department concerning labor on Kodiak Bay?

THE PRESIDENT: I never heard of it. All I know is Kodiak bears.

CORRESPONDENT: Aside from the bears, there is supposed to be quite a discussion up there about Governor [Ernest] Gruening's ruling that one hundred per cent of all the labor employed at the base be drawn from the Territory.

THE PRESIDENT: The Aleutian Indians, is that it?

CORRESPONDENT: I understand that is it and the Navy Department does not want it.

THE PRESIDENT: Well, the answer is, "Go and catch a salmon. You will feel better!"

GUARDIAN OF THE POSSUMS

8 December 1938

FDR had "appointed" Marvin McIntyre as Superintendent of the mythical Marvin McIntyre Memorial Possum Reserve in Georgia.[1]

THE PRESIDENT: As an American citizen who wants to see the New Deal succeed, I am hopeful that you will adopt a "pay-as-you-go" policy in running this magnificent Reserve, which will do so much to prevent the extinction of that glorious symbol of our freedom—the American Possum.

I am glad to hear from friends that you will start next Spring to charge admission to the public when they visit the Reserve.

I realize that the admission fee is not yet in effect, but the other day I visited the Reserve with nine friends. It was a cold day. We found it necessary to avail ourselves of the excellent facilities which you have established. The normal fee for the use of such privileges is five cents per capita, and I am, therefore sending you fifty cents, with the happy thought on the part of all of us that the splendid improvements built under the direction of Mr. Hopkins and the WPA will remain as a Memorial to you for all time.

[1] The President to Marvin H. McIntyre, 8 December 1938, FDRL.

THE COWS OF HYDE PARK

22 March 1935. Press conference for editors of farm journals.

THE PRESIDENT: I believe that I have the most extraordinary herd of cows in the world up at Hyde Park. In 1848 my father, running a farm, got it into his head that he wanted to bring over some Alderney pure-blooded stock; so he got two or three bulls and about twenty or thirty Alderney cows and kept them for about twenty years—all registered—and at the end of twenty years he decided that they were too delicate for our Hudson River climate. So he began buying Jersey bulls and he crossed the original Alderney cows with nothing but registered Jersey bulls from about 1870 to about 1895. Then he decided that he didn't like the Jerseys quite so much—I do not know what the herd was by that time; you can figure it out for yourself. But, mind you, nothing but registered stock; and about 1895, when I was a small boy, he was going to change that herd into Guernseys. So, from 1895 on, we had nothing

but registered Guernsey bulls. So you had better get a paper and pencil
and figure out what kind of a herd I have got! [1]

> [1] At a press conference on 6 April 1938 Roosevelt spoke proudly of
> "my famous herd, 98 per cent registered Guernsey, 1½ per cent registered
> Jersey, and one half of one per cent China. . . ."Asserting that "they are
> the best cows that are anywhere around," he announced his intention "to
> start a new breed."

A VOYAGE IN SEARCH OF THE CHERABLE ISLES
22 November 1940

FDR was an ardent admirer of Thomas Jefferson—the President who
had sponsored the expedition of Meriwether Lewis and William Clark to
explore the West. He was also keenly, if on occasion whimsically, interested in geography. Here we offer in their entirety, documents relating to
a geographical expedition that Roosevelt initiated, with Archibald Mac-
Leish, Librarian of Congress, and David C. Mearns, Superintendent of
the Library's Reading Rooms, as the New Deal's counterparts of Lewis
and Clark.[1]

THE PRESIDENT TO ARCHIBALD MACLEISH, LIBRARIAN OF CONGRESS:
Last Spring on leaving for a short cruise, I told the newspapermen a
cock and bull story about visiting the Andaman Islands, the Celebes
Islands and the South Shetland Islands. To this I added the possibility of
visiting the "Cherable Isles." One or two of the newspapermen sent the
story in just as I had given it to them and it was printed in a number of
papers by desk editors who had never learned geography.

Now I am in a bit of a quandary—for my dim recollection was that
the name "Cherable Isles" came from one of Edward Lear's Nonsense
poems. I can't find it in Lear! I am sure it is in a Nonsense poem but
where?

DAVID C. MEARNS, SUPERINTENDENT OF READING ROOMS, LIBRARY OF
CONGRESS, TO THE LIBRARIAN OF CONGRESS:

> To hunt for an island named Cherable
> Is a job that is almost unbearable
> Pray, accept our apologies,
> But nonsense anthologies
> Are giving us hemorrhages cerebral

> [1] The President to Archibald MacLeish, 22 November 1940; David C.
> Mearns to MacLeish, 26 November 1940; MacLeish to the President, 27
> November 1940; Mearns to MacLeish, 2 December 1940; MacLeish to
> the President, 3 December 1940, FDRL.

THE LIBRARIAN OF CONGRESS TO THE PRESIDENT; ENCLOSING THE POEM FROM THE SUPERINTENDENT OF READING ROOMS:

May I respectfully submit an interim report upon your inquiry of the other day having to do with the Cherable Isles. My last information is that cerebral hemorrhages are doing nicely.

THE SUPERINTENDENT OF READING ROOMS TO THE LIBRARIAN OF CONGRESS:

Our first ill-fated expedition in search of the Cherable Isles set out in the late afternoon of February 15th, 1940.

The President was on board the U.S.S. "Tuscaloosa," in the Gulf of Mexico and the newsmen, who were quartered on the escort ship "Lang," were anxious to know where he was going. But the itinerary was not disclosed and in response to repeated questions he "turned to whimsy."

. . . He asserted some one had it all figured out—he thought it was Tommy Qualters, his personal bodyguard—that he was going to the Andaman Island (in the Bay of Bengal near India) the Celebes (East Indies) and stop on the way home at the Shetland Islands (in the North Sea and the war zone). Such a course would take him a very long way around the world. [The *Washington Post*, Friday, February 16, 1940, p. 2, col. (2).]

The *Post* in its report made no reference to the Cherable Isles but the rather long telegram to the Washington office of the Associated Press did and a representative was sent to the Library post-haste to track it down. He had been informed that it was probably to be found in one of the nonsense rhymes of Edward Lear, and we began a systematic survey of the published works of that distinguished landscape painter. It soon became apparent, however, that the Cherables had disappeared as completely as Atlantis.

It will be recalled that when Lady Jingly Jones (Mrs. Handel Jones) rejected, for excellent reasons, the proposal of Mr. Yonghy-Bonghy-Bo, that love-lorn gentleman fled from the coast of Coramandel and the Bay of Gurtle on the back of a Chelonian reptile.

> Rode the Yonghy-Bonghy-Bo
> With a sad primaeval motion
> Toward the sunset isles of Boshen
> Still the Turtle bore him well . . .

[Edward Lear's NONSENSE SONGS AND LAUGHABLE LYRICS; Mount Vernon, N.Y., The Peter Pauper Press, 1935, p. 57.]

Despite our best efforts we were unable to identify Boshen with the Cherable group, and the saddened reporter departed.

Several days later Mr. Hassett [Assistant Press Secretary to the President] re-opened the question and we tried and tried again, but again without result.

Since receiving the [Presidential] request of November 22nd, we
have extended the field and have literally ransacked the literature of
nonsense. We have even landed on an island or two:

> From east and south the holy clan
> Of Bishops gathered, to a man
> To Synod, called Pan-Anglican
> In flocking crowds they came.
> Among them was a Bishop, who
> Had lately been appointed to
> The balmy isle of RUM-TI-FOO,
> And Peter was his name.

[The Bishop of Rum-ti-Foo. THE BEST KNOWN WORKS of W. S.
Gilbert; New York, Illustrated Editions Company (c. 1932), p. 195.]

> And we all felt ill as mariners will,
> On a diet that's cheap and rude;
> And we shivered and shook as we dipped the cook
> In a tub of his gluesome food.
> Then nautical pride we laid aside,
> And we cast the vessel ashore
> On the Gulliby Isles, where the Poohpooh smiles,
> And the Anagazanders roar.

[The Walloping Window-blind. Charles Edward Carryl's DAVY
AND THE GOBLIN; Boston and New York, Houghton Mifflin Company,
1928, p. 108.]

> There were two little skeezucks
> Who lived in the isle of Boo in a southern sea;
> They clambered and rollicked in heathenish style
> In the boughs of their cocoanut tree.
> They didn't fret much about clothing and such
> And they recked not a whit of the ills
> That sometimes accrue
> From having to do
> With tailor and laundry bills.

[Eugene Field: POEMS; COMPLETE EDITION; New York,
Charles Scribner Sons, 1910, p. 345.]

> The Mouse and the Elephant lived at ease
> On the island of WHERE-AND-WHY
> But the Elephant mourned,
> In his ponderous way,
> That he was so wide and high.

[Abured Beyard: AN ISLAND FABLE. In ST. NICHOLAS, vol. 26, no. 2, December, 1898, p. 107.]

> Far out from the shore on the river wide
> Lies the wonderful isle "Just Right."
> Here are bands that play all the livelong day,
> And rockets to light at night.

[Emma L. Stevens: A VOYAGE WITH THE OLD DREAM-KING. In ST. NICHOLAS, vol. 30, no. 4, February, 1903, p. 313.]

The anthological waters are, of course, dotted with conventional "silver-coasted" isles, "blessed" isles, "happy" isles and "golden" isles, and Alexander Woollcott has written of ENCHANTED AISLES but the Cherable Isles elude us. I am sorry, humble, and reluctant to have to admit defeat. I feel as though somehow we must have been thumbing through the Hole-Keeper's book which is mentioned in DAVY AND THE GOBLIN:

> . . . Davy saw, to his astonishment that there was nothing whatever in the book, all the leaves being perfectly blank, and he couldn't help saying, rather contemptuously:
> "How do you expect to find my name in *that* book?
> "Ah! That's just it, you see," said the Hole-keeper, exultingly; "I look in it for the names that ought to be out of it. It's the completest system that ever was invented. Oh! here you aren't!" he added, starting with great satisfaction at one of the blank pages. "Your name is Rupsy Frimbles."

The closest we have come to a word like Cherable has been found in the thirty-fifth chapter of NICHOLAS NICKLEBY. When Nicholas was recalled to London by a letter from Newsman Noggs he was fortunate enough to fall in with the beneficent Cheeryble brothers, prosperous merchants, who gave him a job in their office. When they retired their nephew Frank, and Nicholas carried on the business.

THE LIBRARIAN OF CONGRESS TO THE PRESIDENT, ENCLOSING A REPORT FROM THE SUPERINTENDENT OF READING ROOMS:

I attach an account of the voyage of Mr. David C. Mearns, Superintendent of the Reading Rooms in the Library of Congress, in search of the Cherable Isles. The narrative of this unhappy ship-wrecked mariner will, I think, enchant you as it has me. I shouldn't be at all surprised if Mr. Mearns came in time to resemble the bearded gentleman with the frenzied eye at the beginning of a certain poem of Mr. Coleridge's.

To this narrative I can add one bit of geographic lore supplied by our Geographer. This learned gentleman informs me that there are two reefs in the Laccadive Islands, west of India, named Chereapani Reef and

Cherlianiani Reef. Science, therefore, implies, but does not specifically state, that the Cherable Isle may be nothing more than a mispronunciation of a couple of East Indian reefs to which no President of the United States would ever think of voyaging. This conclusion I must indiscriminately reject.

I am sorry that we can't send you precise latitude and longitude for this—and for all your desires. What we do send you, however, in clear and precise and geographical form is the warm and affectionate hope of the Librarian of Congress that you will fish fortunately, sleep soundly, and come back rested and well.

WEIGHT CONTROL

5 July 1933

THE PRESIDENT: There is only one bad piece of news today. It will have to be corrected and I am taking immediate steps.

I found this morning that I had put on seven pounds and have to take drastic measures to get it off.

However, that will not be referred to London![1]

CORRESPONDENT: What is the total weight?

THE PRESIDENT: About 181 pounds, I am sorry to say. That is bad; I have to get it down to 174 pounds.

CORRESPONDENT: How are you going to get it down?

THE PRESIDENT: Eat less!

12 July 1933

CORRESPONDENT: Mr. President, how are the seven pounds?

THE PRESIDENT: I lost two. I just took the belt in a hole, that is all. I have not weighed yet—or may be the belt stretched, I don't know.

I hope you are all having a good time; I can stand it, and if you can stand it and the American people can stand it, we are all right!

[1] Apparently a reference to the World Economic Conference in London which at that very time was breaking up as a failure.

MUSICALE

17 January 1934

THE PRESIDENT: Too much musicale last night.

CORRESPONDENT: Have a crowd?

THE PRESIDENT: No, had a boy violinist and a lady who recited. Acute indigestion most of the night. I don't know whether it was cause and effect or not.[1]

[1] The performers at the musicale were Ruggiero Ricci, violinist, and Jessica Lee, diseuse.

THE MAGICIAN
21 October 1934

THE PRESIDENT: [Showing a pad with a cellophane top] This is the most fascinating thing anybody has ever seen. I take this pad and I write, "I owe you—let us suppose it is Fred Storm[1]—$1,000," and I sign it "F.D.R." Now Fred thinks that is perfectly grand and all I do is say, "You want it?" [Roosevelt was writing as he spoke and while handing over the pad to Fred Storm he lifted the leaf which erased the writing]. ... Isn't it perfectly amazing? [Turning to reporters who were crowding around] I am showing the crowd a little gadget by which you can write something that you do not want anybody to see and then you lift up the leaf and the writing is gone. It is very useful for politicians.

CORRESPONDENT: For politicians and poker players.

[1] Correspondent Frederick A. Storm of the United Press.

NEXT TO GODLINESS
8 November 1934; 13 November 1934

The chairman of the Saratoga Spring Commission requested the President's permission to name a new complex of bath houses after him.

THE PRESIDENT: That is a very complimentary suggestion that the new baths be named after me. I am entirely willing but think you had better reconsider because it is wholly possible that next year or the year after a lot of people would decline to take a bath in the house so named![1]

Immediately after the mid-term elections in which the President's party scored a tremendous victory, the Chairman of the Commission wrote to Roosevelt that he could not accept the latter's suggestion that there should be reconsideration of the suggestion for the naming of the bath houses. "That which happened on the 6th," he wrote, "suggests that there are at least seventy-five million people in the United States who would be glad to take a bath in a bath house named Roosevelt. As our

[1] Pierrepont B. Noyes to the President, 15 August 1934; the President to Noyes, 24 August 1934, FDRL.

equipment will not accommodate any larger number, we ought to be satisfied."

THE PRESIDENT: If you must you must! At least the Roosevelt bath house suggests the thought of cleanliness which they used to say is next to Godliness![2]

[2] Noyes to the President, 8 November 1934; the President to Noyes, 13 November 1934, *ibid.*

CHANGING THANKSGIVING DAY
25 October 1935

Reporters did not hesitate to pose whimsical questions and FDR responded in kind.

CORRESPONDENT: Mr. President, sometime ago your Fish Advisory Committee recommended that you make the last Tuesday in November Thanksgiving Day instead of Thursday because it found people had so much turkey on Thursday that they had no appetite for fish on Friday. Your proclamation is about due now and I wondered if we might have an answer to it.

THE PRESIDENT: I think the answer on that is that I will take the people who featured that on the next cruise and they will catch so darned much fish that it will be all right.

A FAT CAT IN A FIT
8 January 1936

THE PRESIDENT: I wish you could read some of the comments from my friends in New York City whom I call "fat cats." Did you ever see a "fat cat" having a fit? Not even a good veterinarian like you could cure one. The highest type of brain surgery has been tried on "fat cats" but it only makes them "fittier."

Nevertheless, I think the country will survive.[1]

[1] The President to Dr. Harvey Cushing, 8 January 1936, FDRL.

McINTYRE'S ROLL
8 September 1936

FDR was discussing some forthcoming appointments and he and the correspondents had some fun at the expense of his secretary, Marvin McIntyre.

THE PRESIDENT: I hope I shall have that Shipping Board [Maritime Commission] going inside of a week. . . .

CORRESPONDENT: There was a report that Secretary Marvin Hunter McIntyre was going to be named to that Commission. Can you clear that up for us today?

THE PRESIDENT: Well, I could say this: that he has proved to me many times that he does not know the bow from the stern of a ship and therefore he might be thoroughly valuable. However, he does know where the roll is.

THE DIFFERENCE BETWEEN AMERICA AND EUROPE

5 July 1937

Roosevelt spoke informally to a group at Mt. Marion, New York.

THE PRESIDENT: Yesterday, at Hyde Park, a very distinguished European writer, a great biographer, was visiting me; and yesterday afternoon, over back of our place, at what we call the cottage, we had a little picnic. We had some neighbors there, and we had some members of the Press there. And this great biographer was perfectly amazed because there we were, sitting around in our shirt sleeves, some going in swimming in the pool, and everybody having a good time with complete informality. He said, "You know, if this happened anywhere in Europe, whether it was a dictatorship or a monarchy or a republic, the head of the nation would have been surrounded by men in uniform, soldiers with bayonets, and the members of the Press would have appeared in frock coats and silk hats instead of shirt sleeves and bathing suits."

You can multiply a thousand times that example of the difference between our American form of living and the European. I am very confident of the future of this country as long as we maintain the democracy of our manners and the democracy of our hearts.[1]

[1] *Public Papers and Addresses, 1937,* p. 292.

A NICE STORY OF GOLF

29 November 1938

The President talked with reporters in front of the Press Cottage in Warm Springs, Georgia.

THE PRESIDENT: Have you played our golf course, Brother Whigham?

CORRESPONDENT WHIGHAM: Yes, I have.

THE PRESIDENT: How do you like it?

WHIGHAM: Very well laid out.

THE PRESIDENT: This is rather a nice story of golf which you will appreciate. I was driving over the course when it was under construction. We got to the eighth hole, and Donald Ross who laid out the course said to me, "This is a trick hole. It is a good deal further than it looks. It is pretty nearly a full midiron."[1]

Then we went up to it and it was trapped on both sides, with a precipice on one side and woods on the other end. If you did not land on the green, you were gone.

I said to Mr. Ross, "That is a terribly discouraging hill. A good player can take eight or nine on this hole and he is going to give up golf!"

"Oh," he said, "no. You know, it is a game of psychology." He said, "He will feel that way until the end of the eighth and then he will step over to the ninth tee and see all the kingdoms of the earth, and he can chop or slice or pull and he has no trouble. He will get to the bottom of the hill."

[1] A golf club used for fairway shots of medium distance.

THE ROOSEVELT DIARIES

10 December 1938

The President described to reporters his plans for the establishment of a Franklin D. Roosevelt Library at Hyde Park. He stated that his personal and Presidential papers would be deposited with the Library. The question was raised whether there would be any diaries among the items that would be deposited.

THE PRESIDENT: I think you will find among the papers three diaries that started on the first of January in three different years, far apart. I think the most voluminous one ran to the fourth of January!

CORRESPONDENT: That is like Mark Twain. He kept it up for a week, got up, washed and went to bed!

THE PRESIDENT: Yes. I tried it once and it went on for four days, I believe.[1]

[1] On entering the White House in 1933 FDR started a diary and kept it up for two days! For the diary entry for 5 March 1933 see Elliott Roosevelt, ed., *F.D.R. His Personal Letters* (New York, 1950), I, pp. 333–34.

PROPHECIES OF THE
GRANDSON OF AN OLD BACHELOR

31 January 1939

It was a day after FDR's birthday. He solemnly read to reporters certain prophecies that had supposedly been made by Steve Early at the birthday party a year earlier.

THE PRESIDENT: Hello, hello, how is everybody?

CORRESPONDENT: How are you?

THE PRESIDENT: I survived—I do not know why, but I did.

CORRESPONDENT: Steve did not look so good. . . .

THE PRESIDENT: . . . I was going to read to you, off the record, one of the several prophecies that were made at the Birthday Party last year. And really, this is off the record, just between us girls!

[He reads]

I suspect I am nearer to being the Son of a Prophet than—as I have often been accused of being—the grandson of that old bachelor misogynist, Jubal Early.

It matters not what I am—I must be bold—because I prophesy:

That McIntyre need never worry about employment . . . , he and Senator Capper have just found out that girls are willing to pay for the messages both of them now give away free.[1]

That the President, in the near future, will issue an Executive Order prohibiting accordion playing in and about the White House.[2]

That some friend is going to tell me before very long that the girls in my outside room are entirely too pretty for office work.

As for a third term—the boys in the Press Room say—FDR can have [it] for all they care if he will only start his Press Conferences on time; stop advertising Mark Sullivan; quit smoking Camels; buy Sister Perkins a new bonnet; cork up Harold Ickes and put a Mickey Finn in Henry Morgenthau's coffee at lunch some Monday; also quit talking about the Herald Tribune.[3]

[1] The import of this statement is not clear to the present writer. It is also not clear why the name of Republican Senator Arthur Capper of Kansas is linked up with that of Appointments Secretary Marvin McIntyre.

[2] This refers to Tom Corcoran who stood high in Roosevelt's favor at this time. FDR enjoyed listening to Corcoran playing the accordion.

[3] Mark Sullivan was a columnist of the *New York Herald Tribune*. Sister Perkins refers to Secretary of Labor Frances Perkins. Harold L. Ickes was the voluble Secretary of the Interior. Henry Morgenthau Jr., was Secretary of the Treasury. To "put a Mickey Finn" is to slip a potent narcotic or purgative in a drink offered to an unsuspecting person.

They say they are all for a third term if the President will promise to keep on riding to Hyde Park in the daytime instead of night; if he will take the B. & O. for a change to give them relief from those flat wheels of the Pennsy; if he will desist from picking out those farm-to-market roads when he goes automobiling; and if, for Pete's sake, he will tell the Pine Valley Mountain promoters to "go to hell" when they invite him to visit their settlement on the coldest day of the year.

THE PAPACY

3 March 1939. Aboard the cruiser "Houston," off Charleston, South Carolina.

THE PRESIDENT: I sent a telegram to the new Pope Pius the Twelfth. . . .

CORRESPONDENT: I just want to thank you for not appointing a Protestant!

THE PRESIDENT: You know they can, under the law, and it does not have to be a priest. Did you know that?

CORRESPONDENT: That is true. All he has to be is of sound mind and body.

THE PRESIDENT: I suppose he ought to be a Christian!

CORRESPONDENT: I do not think they require that. . . .

PRESIDENTIAL AIDE WILLIAM HASSETT: At least the first Pope was not always a Christian.

THE PRESIDENT: Yes, there were quite a lot of pagans they had there. I suppose, . . . although my good Catholic friends do not like to talk about it, there was once a woman Pope.

CORRESPONDENT: Pope Joan.

THE PRESIDENT: Pope Joan, sure.[1]

---

[1] According to the *New Catholic Encyclopedia* there is no historical basis for the story of a woman pope named Joan. The "fable" was based on the writings of certain 13th century chroniclers. The most "widely circulated and accepted story" was to the effect that "Leo IV (d. 855) was succeeded by a John Angelicus, Pope for 2½ years, who was in fact a woman. Joan, educated in Athens, was returning to Mainz dressed as a man when she stopped off at Rome and so impressed all by her learning that she became a curial notary, a cardinal, and finally pope. Her sex was discovered when, during a procession, she gave birth to a child in the road between the Colosseum and St. Clement's, or in the church itself." Evidently the story was accepted and the statue of "Pope" Joan was included among the popes in the cathedral of Siena (circa 1400 A.D.). *New Catholic Encyclopedia* (New York, 1967), VII, pp. 991–92.

A REMEDY FOR COLDS

24 March 1939

THE PRESIDENT: Good morning. I do not know whose cold I have caught.

CORRESPONDENT: How are you coming along sir?

THE PRESIDENT: Oh, just my whole nose is clogged up.

You know the Irish remedy for a cold is to sit with your nose over a peat fire. It is the greatest thing in the world. . . . I never tried it!

PURE, CLEAN PATRIOTISM

17 May 1939

Rear Admiral Wilson Brown, Superintendent of the US Naval Academy, received a gift from the White House. The items inside the box were found to be carefully wrapped and tied with a charming blue ribbon. We are not in a position to determine what exactly was the gift that Roosevelt had so lovingly sent. The letters exchanged between the President and the Superintendent leads us to believe that the gift probably consisted of a few cakes of washing soap.

THE PRESIDENT TO THE SUPERINTENDENT OF THE US NAVAL ACADEMY:

The White House staff, including my Naval and Military Aides, Secretaries McIntyre and Early, have been deeply disturbed by the unwashed condition of the young men under your command, a similar condition apparently in regard to the officers and professors of the Naval Academy. This matter has also been pressed by Miss Le Hand, Miss Tully and other young ladies to such an extent that I was compelled to take it up at Cabinet meeting last Friday.

Apparently no constructive action is intended to be taken by the Congress at this session and, as the President of 1940 will probably prevent action also next year, we realize the seriousness of the Naval Academy problem.

Therefore, the Executive Branch of the Government of which I have the honor to be the chief has felt as a matter of pure, clean patriotism that they should dig down into their pockets and in their behalf I am handing you herewith the necessary equipment for restoring proper hygiene at Annapolis.

We all wish you well.

THE SUPERINTENDENT TO THE PRESIDENT:

After fully unpacking the box containing your generous gift to the Naval Academy and upon realizing the completeness of the modern equipment provided by the Executive Branch of the Government—to say nothing of the careful wrapping of each article with the touching addition of blue ribbon, I beg leave once again to tender the heartfelt thanks of the Academy realizing as I do the inadequacy of my thanks at the moment of presentation owing to the surprise of the occasion.

I gather from your letter of transmittal that I have failed adequately to present all phases of our problem and that thereby I have unwittingly done an injustice to that distinguished Corps of Medicine that has as its main mission the health, comfort and sanitation of all naval personnel. I therefore hasten to explain that it is not the unwashed condition of the young men, officers and professors that gives us concern, as that is beyond reproach but that our concern is merely the desire to maintain that immaculate appearance of the inner and outer garments for which the Navy is so justly famous and in which it yields to no group except possibly the Army under certain conditions when not in bivouac or traveling on Presidential trains.

Owing therefore to the pending threat to our clothes washing supremacy, your timely gift will become one of our important inspirational exhibits supplementing the godliness of the chapel with the cleanliness of the laundry. We plan to blazon it forth with the stirring motto, "The Laundry! Long may she wash!" . . .

Assuring you, Mr. President, that we are all washing well, I beg to remain with great respect and affection.[1]

[1] The President to Wilson Brown, 17 May 1939; Brown to the President, 22 May 1939, FDRL.

THE LITTLE BOY WHO TELEPHONED THE PRESIDENT

30 May 1939

CORRESPONDENT: Did you have a five-minute talk yesterday on the telephone with a boy from a little town outside of New Orleans? . . .

THE PRESIDENT: No. . . . It may have been like that old Negro down in Mississippi that talked to me by telephone. Of course, I never heard of it. He told everybody he talked to me and I saved his home for him. It was all right. I was a popular hero!

AN UNOBLIGING GENTLEMAN
25 July 1939

THE PRESIDENT: This is off the record. I found this morning on the
table, beside my bed, a memorandum from Steve [Early] dated about a
month or six weeks ago, with respect to sending flowers to a certain
gentleman who was in hospital and was not expected to live. The gentleman in question is out playing golf now.

EARLY: You should tell him that the memorandum has been here a
month.

THE SAD TALE OF PA'S PLASTERS
8 August 1939

Roosevelt made it known that he planned a cruise to Campobello,
New Brunswick.

CORRESPONDENT: Have you any seasick remedies you might recommend?

THE PRESIDENT: Get one of Pa's[1] plasters. You know that? . . . it
saved their lives. You know that story?

We took the first cruise from San Francisco back through the Canal—
this is all off the record—with Secretary Ickes and Pa and Harry Hopkins.[2] It was their first cruise. Pa had gone to Abercrombie and Fitch and
he had spent thousands of dollars in buying the latest fishing outfits recommended by Abercrombie and Fitch. They had cost four times the
prices you can buy them at any other store.

He had the darnedest things. He had a fishing cap that had a darky's
visor which was eight inches long.

He had said to the clerk, "Do you know of any remedies for seasick-
ness?"

The clerk said, with an English accent, "Oh, yes, sir. The very best
thing we had is a plaster from London."

And Pa bought the plaster and read the directions and, about the
third day out, we were off the southern end of lower California and we
struck the tail end of what they call a Tampico twister.

It was a bit rough and Pa gave those [plasters] to Ickes and Hopkins
and they put it, each of them, one of those plasters squarely on their
abdomens and went to bed. Whether it was the bed or the plaster, they
were not seasick. They remained safely in bed.

[1] Edwin M. ("Pa") Watson, Army aide to the President.
[2] Secretary of Commerce and a trusted confidant of Roosevelt.

Then we got down to the Cocos Islands where it was wonderfully smooth and warm and we went into shore to swim—and they had these plasters on.

It took them about six weeks to get them off. We used hoses and gasoline and kerosene and could not get them off.

The last remains were off in about six weeks![3]

[3] Hopkins, Ickes, and "Pa" showed themselves to be poor sailors in a cruise on the "Potomac" in the spring of 1941. The weather was rough, the boat was being tossed about, and the three worthies lay in bed glancing anxiously at the wild waves crashing against the tightly closed portholes. Roosevelt chose such a time to communicate to them his conviction that if the "Potomac" were to capsize, "there wasn't a chance for a single one of us." Diary entry, 12 April 1941, in Harold L. Ickes, *The Secret Diary of Harold L. Ickes* (New York, 1954), III, p. 467.

GOBBLEDYGOOK

17 November 1939

CORRESPONDENT: Mr. President, Senator Wheeler[1] suggested a Congressional investigation of this faulty ship design. What is your information on that subject?

THE PRESIDENT: . . . when the ships were designed, when the plans were first drawn, there was a difference of opinion between naval architects—some of the naval architects and engineers in both Government and private plants felt that the metacentric height, which is not the same thing as the center of gravity—

CORRESPONDENT: What was the phrase you used?

THE PRESIDENT: Metacentric height, which is not the same thing as the center of gravity . . . was too high. . . . When the ships were tried out, the earlier ones, they found that the school of thought which had said in this highly scientific computation that the metacentric height was too high were correct. Since then they have made certain changes; they have lowered the metacentric height and it is all over.

That is all there is to it, this thing that calls for a Congressional investigation.

. . . Don't say I am forestalling the Senate on this thing, or the Congress, but the whole story has been told. You can have the same thing explained by the engineers, if anybody wants to. You will get more on metacentric height!

CORRESPONDENT: What the heck is that metacentric height?

THE PRESIDENT: I don't know: I frankly don't know, except they always tell me in the Navy it is different from the center of gravity. Apparently they don't know either!

[1] Burton K. Wheeler, Democratic Senator from Montana.

ROYAL SUBSCRIPTION

4 April 1941

Journalist Herbert Bayard Swope wrote a letter to Roosevelt in which he affected the English form of a handwritten salutation and subscription "to give a personalized touch to the typewritten part." In his reply FDR followed his example, subscribing his letter "Royally yours" in longhand.[1]

THE PRESIDENT: Your new form of salutation and subscription is truly regal. You must have inherited it from the Chevalier Bayard who was, as I remember it, the left-handed offspring of the Calif Haroun al Raschid. Whenever I get a letter from present Emperors, Kings, Grand Dukes, etc., that is just what they do. The salutation and the subscription are also written in longhand.

You might pass this on to Emily Post.

[1] Herbert Bayard Swope to the President, 31 March 1941; the President to Swope, 4 April 1941, FDRL.

THE KNIGHT

19 August 1941

At the press conference in Washington after the President's return from the Atlantic Ocean conference with Churchill:

THE PRESIDENT: Well, what's been happening here in the last couple of weeks?

CORRESPONDENT: Surmises.

THE PRESIDENT: Sir who?

MORE GOBBLEDYGOOK

20 March 1942

THE PRESIDENT: Then we have all got a question, I mean here in Washington, as to ... how we are going to blackout Federal buildings in case of an air-raid. So the Director of Civilian Defense wrote a letter, for me to send to the Federal Works Agency which is in charge of public buildings, and to the Director of Civilian Defense. ... It reads as follows:

> Such preparation shall be made as will completely obscure all Federal buildings and non-Federal buildings occupied by the

Federal Government during an air-raid for any period of time from visibility by reason of internal or external illumination. Such——

... Sounds almost like some people I see before me!

Such obscuration may be obtained either by blackout construction or by terminating the illumination.

CORRESPONDENT: Does that mean turning off the lights?
CORRESPONDENT: ... That isn't the one you said Steve wrote, is it?
THE PRESIDENT: No. Steve did not write that. The Dean of the Harvard Law School[1] wrote this. [Continuing to read]

This will of course require that in building areas in which production must continue during a blackout, construction must be provided that internal illumination may continue.——

I have known lots of people that have had internal illumination!

Other areas whether or not occupied by personnel may be obscured by terminating the illumination.

Steve!
STEVE EARLY: Yes, sir.
THE PRESIDENT: Rewrite that for me, will you? Tell them the buildings will have to keep their work going—put something across the windows. In buildings that can afford it, so that work can be stopped for a while, turn out the lights—and stop there!

[1] James M. Landis, Dean of the Harvard Law School.

STEVE AND THE SAMURAI SWORD

19 May 1942

FDR was about to open the press conference. As Steve Early sat on the edge of a side table a big sword fell on the floor with a clang. It had been presented to the President by Francis B. Sayre, US High Commissioner in the Philippines, and it reportedly had belonged to a Japanese general.
STEVE EARLY: Just the Mikado, sir!
THE PRESIDENT: Oh, yes.
CORRESPONDENT: Hara-kiri. ...
THE PRESIDENT: Is the blood still on it?
(Steve Early struggled hard to pull the sword out of the scabbard, making little progress.)

CORRESPONDENT: No wonder he [the Japanese general] got killed.

THE PRESIDENT: [To Steve] . . . Don't monkey with it. You're not old enough!

A GIFT FROM FRED ALLEN

28 December 1942

Comedian Fred Allen sent the President an elaborately wrapped Christmas gift. It was found to be a jewel box and in it was found a single coffee bean.

THE PRESIDENT: You and your wife, more than all others, must be held responsible for my continuance in the White House. During the past anguished months, with their coffeeless breakfasts, I had decided to resign as Commander-in-Chief and had been offered an appointment as Sergeant Major in the Army with the promise that I would be stationed at one of the bases in Brazil where I could have coffee six times a day.

Today all is changed. Your coffee bean has made the sun come out. Under my new patented process I find that I can grind it and percolate it twice a day for at least three months. If you really want to accomplish the heart's objective of some of your fellow radio commentators, you can force me out of the White House by not sending me another coffee bean! On the other hand, if you do not think I am as big a bad wolf as they paint me, send me another bean the end of March.[1]

[1] The President to Fred Allen, 28 December 1942, FDRL.

MAJOR ISSUES BEFORE THE COUNTRY

6 November 1942

THE PRESIDENT: I see my friend, the little Mayor [Fiorello La-Guardia of New York City], . . . has stirred up a hornet's nest in respect to how to prepare coffee.

We will have a lot of grave issues like that during the coming year.

What I am a little afraid of is that somebody will raise the issue that was paramount in this country a few years ago, as to whether one should "crumble" or "dunk" [the doughnut].

Now those are very important things in our national life. And it's part of the grand sense of humor of the American people—and it's all to the good!

FDR OFFERS AMAZING COPHA RECIPE TO ALL HOUSEWIVES—MALE AND FEMALE

16 March 1943

THE PRESIDENT: I have got a special story for you girls today.

CORRESPONDENT: Cooking? Is it cooking?

THE PRESIDENT: Coffee! . . . I have got a story for you housewives—male and female!

You know, sometime ago the Mayor of New York said something about how to make coffee, and in general we were in agreement—my recipe was a little bit different from his, but the same idea.

And he came in today, and he said, "We are justified. We are proved right. We have found up there an old copy of Epicurus translated from the Greek in 1656, which is good authority on account of its age." [FDR held up an old book]

And in the back of the book is written in longhand the following which I had translated. . . . [He reads]

HOW TO USE COPHA

C-O-P-H-A. And of course, you see, at that time in Europe it was one of the new things.

> Take a pint & 4 spoonfulls of water & sett itt bye the fier. . . & boyle itt a little. . . , then take itt from the fier & putt in halfe an ounce of Copha, then sett itt to the fier & keepe itt boyling now a quarter of an hower, sometymes stirring itt to prevent burning; when itt is setled Drink itt hott. The next day—

Now here is the crux of it—

> The next day the same quantetie of water put to the same Copha that was left the day before and next boyle itt, then add to that a quarter of an ounce of fresh Copha & order itt as the first. This do for four dayes & the 5th day beginn anew.

So there we have the most ancient authority on how to prepare coffee in all the world.[1] . . . .

[1] FDR looked for the amusing aspects of the quaint, the outlandish, and the bizarre. He was happy to receive from his friends items of interest belonging to such categories. He read happily an old English butler's recipe book belonging to William Hassett and "got a great kick" out of formulas for "Snayle Water," "Elixir of Long Life," and "Oyle of Charity." William D. Hassett, *Off the Record with F.D.R.* (New Brunswick, 1958), p. 213. In May, 1944, Treasury Secretary Morgenthau sent Roosevelt a full page advertisement from the *Washington Star* entitled "Here

CORRESPONDENT: That's better than any *I* get.
CORRESPONDENT: Is that what the Mayor came in to see you about?
THE PRESIDENT: It was! He came all the way from New York to talk to me about that!

---

is how Safeway Prices of Today Compare with a Year Ago." After perusing the document FDR wrote to Morgenthau, ". . . I am glad to know that a 'Clabber Girl' can be got for 8c and in a larger size for 19c. I also notice that the cost of Toilet Bowl Brushes remains constant!" The President to Henry Morgenthau, Jr., 13 May 1944, FDRL.

FDR'S FAVORITE BARBERSHOP READING
19 October 1943

CORRESPONDENT EARL GODWIN: . . . they are trying to stop "Esquire" from going through the mails. . . .
THE PRESIDENT: Well!! Did you ever write for the Police Gazette? If not, why not?
GODWIN: Never had the opportunity.
THE PRESIDENT: I quit getting shaved in a barber shop when they cracked down on the Police Gazette. They were good. It was wonderful!
GODWIN: I loved the old Police Gazette.
THE PRESIDENT: Yes, yes. Especially the old ones. Remember the pictures on the outside?

WHY MEN'S IDEAS DIFFER
9 November 1943

THE PRESIDENT: We all have different ideas, depending somewhat on our wives, our stomachs, and our place of abode. Those are very important factors in making up one's opinion: wives, stomachs, and places of abode.

A GERMAN PLOT
5 April 1944

While on a brief visit to Curaçao in the Dutch West Indies, Eleanor Roosevelt received a letter from one Charles L. Maduro requesting her to accept a medallion as a souvenir. The writer also stated: "In the early part of this century your husband, then lieutenant on an American warship, visited our Island and at his request we gave him a small live goat to serve as a mascot on the ship." Eleanor playfully wrote a memorandum to FDR: "What have you been holding out on me all these years?"

THE PRESIDENT: I have an alibi. The only time I was ever in Curaçao in my life was in 1904 when I went through the West Indies on a Hamburg-American Line "yacht." I was accompanied by and thoroughly chaperoned by my maternal parent.

I was never given a goat—neither did any one get my goat!

This looks to me like a German plot![1]

[1] Charles L. Maduro to Eleanor Roosevelt, 20 March 1944; Eleanor Roosevelt to the President, 4 April 1944; the President to Eleanor Roosevelt, 5 April 1944, FDRL.

NOT ON MEMORIAL DAY!

30 May 1944

It was Memorial Day.

Reporters had asked FDR whether he regarded certain persons as "wilful."

THE PRESIDENT: I have known some awful fools in my life, and I have been sorry for some people in my life, but I don't hate.

And that is an interesting thing to some of you people. It's rather . . . interesting how many people in—some of them in this room, I think, have talked about how I hate this person, or hate that person, or a feud, or an awful row between so-and-so and me. It just isn't true.

. . . I don't hate people—especially on Memorial Day.

I AM STILL ALIVE

12 June 1944

Allied forces had landed in Normandy a few days earlier and the great invasion of Europe was under way. But FDR could still find time for laughter. The Librarian of Congress, Archibald MacLeish, asked the President whether he could arrange for the loan to his institution of certain naval prints from the "Franklin D. Roosevelt Memorial Library."

THE PRESIDENT: You have been grossly deceived. I am still alive!

Why the "Franklin D. Roosevelt Memorial Library" at Hyde Park? I realize that I have not seen you for a century or two and, at that time, you were intending to be a blacksmith while I was about to join up as an able-bodied seaman with Captain Cook. It is wonderful on a joint return (not income tax) to find you making a naval collection in a Library I have never heard of, while I am writing prayers.

I am sorry that your Library does not "possess anything on earth." I was acquainted with a lending library once but it is a wonderful idea that you have started a borrowing library.

My Library is in that business. I am trying to find those damn prints.[1]

[1] The President to Archibald MacLeish, 12 June 1944, FDRL. FDR's reference to his "writing prayers" probably relates to his D-Day prayer broadcast to the nation on 6 June 1944.

BETTING ON THE ARMY-NAVY GAME

27 November 1944

THE PRESIDENT: I am the only person in the country who cannot bet on the Army and Navy game.

CORRESPONDENT: Why is that? . . . .

THE PRESIDENT: I have to be absolutely impartial.

CORRESPONDENT: Not quietly, between you and "Pa"?

THE PRESIDENT: No, no.

CORRESPONDENT: Have to sit on both sides of the field at once.

THE PRESIDENT: Yes, that I have to do. . . . First half on one side, and the second half on the other side, so I'm all right. That doesn't mean that "Pa" can't bet.

MAJOR GENERAL EDWIN M. "PA" WATSON: No sir. I'm taking anybody's even money that I can get.

FDR'S LAST CHRISTMAS GREETING

22 December 1944

The President: Before we have the rush for the door, . . . it is better for me now to wish you a very Happy Christmas.

Maybe you will all be here a year from now. That is not meant as a prognostication, but a simple statement of fact between gentlemen and ladies.

THE TEN COMMANDMENTS

2 January 1945

THE PRESIDENT: Well, I—I want to wish you all a very Happy New Year. And as I said to Steve, all of you except a very small minority—which is fair enough.

... we were talking to Steve, just before you came in, about the Ten Commandments——

EARL GODWIN: All of them?

STEVE EARLY: Just one of them!

THE PRESIDENT: All of them. All Ten.

MAY CRAIG: Steve!

THE PRESIDENT: And they are pretty good principles, but they are very often interpreted differently in individual cases. And that is the practical problem about peoples of the world, as well as individuals. ... You do the best you can.

JIM WRIGHT OF THE *Buffalo News*: Do it feebly or do it well? ...

THE PRESIDENT: Yes, yes.

WRIGHT: On all Ten?

THE PRESIDENT: All Ten. ... I think you had better not pursue it any further.

GODWIN: The business that Jim is talking about does worry lots of folks. ... As you get older, some of them are easier to keep!

THE PRESIDENT: Yes, It's a New Year, and I like to rub it in at the beginning of a new year.

FDR'S REFLECTIONS ON THE EVE OF THE FOURTH TERM

19 January 1945

CORRESPONDENT JIM REYNOLDS: Mr. President, this being the last full day of your Third Term, it might be proper to ask if you have any general reflections on what was done in the last four years and where do we go from here.

THE PRESIDENT: I will tell you what I will do. I will tell you a great secret, what happened at the Cabinet meeting last week. ... I was asked that same question at the last Cabinet meeting ... and I say that there were three of us there that had probably been thinking along the same lines, cogitating I think is the word. And one of them was Mr. Ickes, and the other was Miss Perkins,[1] and I was the third.

[1] Secretary of the Interior Harold Ickes and Secretary of Labor Frances Perkins had been Cabinet members ever since FDR's assumption

And I . . . sort of guessed that all of us had come to the same conclusion, and that was that the first twelve years were the hardest!

Now—now you are all buffaloed. You will all try to interpret that,
and you will all guess wrong.

CORRESPONDENT: Can you help us avoid that error, Mr. President?

THE PRESIDENT: No, I cannot. I am supposed to give out facts. I am
not supposed to interpret!

CORRESPONDENT: We could use a few facts.

THE PRESIDENT: Well, now, *there's* a fact: The first twelve years
were the hardest. That is good, you know. That is real news.

STEVE EARLY: You hope.

MAY CRAIG: Well, I am wondering, Mr. President, about the significance of the word: *first*.

THE PRESIDENT: You are worse than Tom.

JIM WRIGHT: Tom Reynolds spoke about the last four years. Is this
the last last four years?

THE PRESIDENT: [Laughing] Jim, You're just as bad as the rest.

---

of the Presidency in 1933. The episode recounted by Roosevelt is not
mentioned by Perkins in her memoirs. Of the cabinet meeting held a day
before the Inauguration, Perkins writes: "When he [FDR] came in I
thought he looked badly, and this was the first time that I had ever
thought so. I had never been alarmed by the whispering campaign that
he wasn't well, and I still think that he had been well until that time.
His clothes looked much too big for him. His face looked thin, his color
was gray, and his eyes were dull. I think everyone in the room privately
had a feeling that we must not tire him, that we must end the meeting
quickly, if possible, for he still had so much to do. He was, however, gay
and happy." Frances Perkins, *The Roosevelt I Knew* (New York, 1946),
p. 391.

HE WON'T STARVE!

19 January 1945

Reporters wanted to find out whether FDR intended to offer any post
to Henry A. Wallace, the retiring Vice-President.

CORRESPONDENT: Anything new on Henry Wallace, Mr. President? ...

THE PRESIDENT: What about him?

CORRESPONDENT: That's what we want to know. . . . .

CORRESPONDENT: What's he going to do for a living after tomorrow?

THE PRESIDENT: I don't think he'll starve! Now that's a real tip.

MAY CRAIG: You mean Agriculture?

THE PRESIDENT: What?

CRAIG: You mean Department of Agriculture? Oh, Oh! . . . .

THE PRESIDENT: I don't think he'll starve. That's all I said. Now, don't try to interpret it.

CORRESPONDENT JIM WRIGHT: Well, Mr. President, will he have to live on hybrid corn?[1]

THE PRESIDENT: Jim, pretty good idea. Good corn!

[1] Wallace, a former Secretary of Agriculture, was an authority on hybrid corn.

HAPPINESS

2 March 1945

FDR had made his last address to Congress on the Yalta Conference on 1 March 1945. For the first time since he came to Washington as President in 1933 he remained seated as he addressed the joint session. ". . . I know that you will realize that it makes it a lot easier for me not to have to carry about ten pounds of steel around on the bottom of my legs; and also because of the fact that I have just completed a fourteen-thousand mile trip," he told Congress.

The years of toil and strain had taken their toll. The shadows had begun to close on the great American.

His gaiety and laughter remained undiminished.

The President met reporters on 2 March 1945. With him were the three representatives of the wire services who were the only newsmen to accompany him on his trip.

THE PRESIDENT: I have had a good report from the three gentlemen who went for a nice fishing trip with me. They find that everybody is all right on their return.

They seem to be happy, and I hope everybody else is—like *I* am. That's about the only news I have got.

WHY NOT IN ARABIC?

29 March 1945

During his homeward journey from Yalta, FDR had met the exotic King of Arabia, Ibn Saud.

A few days after his return, George T. Bye, who was FDR's adviser on matters relating to his published works, informed him that an Italian publisher wanted to bring out an Italian language edition of a volume of the President's speeches entitled *Rendezvous with Destiny*.

77

Asking whether permission for publication could be given, Bye wrote: "I now bow low, extend my arms in the best Arabic fashion to which you have become accustomed and exit backwards. But more worshipfully than ever!" FDR responded in his usual whimsical fashion.[1]

THE PRESIDENT: I have no objection to the publication of something I once said in a moment of exultation—even though I do not remember the occasion. This is conditioned, however, on a supervision of the translation of one George T. Bye. I know what an excellent Italian scholar you are. I should prefer that the translation be made in the etruscan [sic] version of the Italian language. I think this antedates the earlier hog Latin. In view of what you say about the Arabic, I think we both could make some profit by getting out at the same time an Arabic version. I may be a candidate for King of Arabia in case anything should happen to that great leader, Ibn Saud.

[1] George T. Bye to the President, 26 March 1945; the President to Bye, 29 March 1945, FDRL.

"IT WOULD REALLY BE FUN"

5 April 1945. Little White House, Warm Springs, Georgia.

It was FDR's 998th press conference since his inauguration as President of the United States of America twelve years earlier. It was to be his last. There was little of the usual banter at this meeting since Roosevelt had a guest, Sergio Osmena, President of the Philippines.

CORRESPONDENT: Mr. President, you mentioned the collapse of the Japanese cabinet. Do you think there is any connection between that and the Russian renunciation of the non-aggression pact with Japan?[1]

THE PRESIDENT: I wouldn't know. I would get into what you boys call the speculative field if I tried to answer. . . . I would have prognosticated if I were a prognosticator. . . . .

CORRESPONDENT: Mr. President, do you think we will have a chance to talk with you again on other subjects before you go [to the San Francisco Conference of the United Nations]? . . . .

THE PRESIDENT: I think you will see me several times before you go. Some of the boys cannot get their facts straight. It would really be fun if I went on the air and simply read the things that I have read in the paper!

[1] With defeat staring him in the face, the Japanese Emperor replaced General Hideki Tojo with Admiral Suzuki as Premier. On 5 April 1945 the Soviet Union announced that it would not renew its treaty of neutrality with Japan.

THE SUNNY OPTIMIST

On 11 April 1945 the gay laughter of Franklin Delano Roosevelt was stilled.

At his press conference on the eve of Christmas, 1944, FDR had jocularly voiced the hope of a reunion with the gentlemen and ladies present at a similar function a year later. It was to be a hope unfulfilled.

In the same press conference Franklin Roosevelt made some informal comments with which the present work may appropriately be concluded:

> The world goes a little bit by peaks and valleys, but on the whole the curve is upward; on the whole the—over these thousands of years human life is on a great deal better scale than it was then. And we have got a long ways to go.
>
> But things are better and things are going to be better, if we work for it. There are some people who don't like to work for it— some people in this room—who are—what will I say—congenitally "agin" that sort of thing. Well, that is part of the peaks and valleys!